MAMMALS *of* ALBERTA

Don Pattie & Chris Fisher

LONE
PINE

The Publisher: Lone Pine Publishing

10145 – 81 Ave.
Edmonton, AB   T6E 1W9
Canada

1901 Raymond Ave. SW, Suite C
Renton, WA 98055
USA

Website: http://www.lonepinepublishing.com

Canadian Cataloguing in Publication Data
Pattie, Donald L., 1933–
   Mammals of Alberta

   Includes index.
   ISBN 1-55105-209-1

   1. Mammals—Alberta—Identification. I. Fisher,
Chris C. (Christopher Charles), 1970– II. Title.
QL721.5.A3P37 1999   599′.097123   C99-911064-0

Editorial Director: Nancy Foulds
Project Editor: Roland Lines
Production Manager: Jody Reekie
Book Design: Heather Markham
Cover Design: Rob Weidemann
Production: Heather Markham, Rob Weidemann, Elliot Engley
Cover Photograph: Terry Parker (White-tailed Deer fawn)
Separations & Film: Elite Lithographers Company

The photographs in this book are reproduced with the generous permission of their
copyright holders.

Photograph and Illustration Credits
All the photographs are by Terry Parker, except as follows: Leslie Degner, p. 83; Mark
Degner, pp. 80, 97 & 101; Wayne Lynch, pp. 94, 102, 105, 126, 129, 134 & 137.

All the animal illustrations are by Gary Ross, except for the ones on pages 147, 151,
158, 162, 165, 230, 232 & 235, which are by Kindrie Grove. All the track illustrations
are by Ian Sheldon.

*We acknowledge the financial support of the Government of Canada through the Book Publishing
Industry Development Program (BPIDP) for our publishing activities.*

PC: P4

Canadä

CONTENTS

HOOFED MAMMALS

American Bison
p. 26

Mountain Goat
p. 30

Bighorn Sheep
p. 34

Pronghorn
p. 38

Elk
p. 42

Mule Deer
p. 46

White-tailed Deer
p. 50

Moose
p. 54

Caribou
p. 58

CARNIVORES

Mountain Lion
p. 64

Canada Lynx
p. 68

Bobcat
p. 72

Striped Skunk
p. 76

American Marten	Fisher	Short-tailed Weasel	Least Weasel
p. 78	p. 80	p. 84	p. 86

Long-tailed Weasel	American Mink	Black-footed Ferret
p. 88	p. 90	p. 92

Wolverine	American Badger	Northern River	Common Raccoon
p. 94	p. 98	Otter, p. 102	p. 106

Black Bear	Grizzly Bear	Coyote
p. 110	p. 114	p. 118

CARNIVORES

Grey Wolf
p. 122

Arctic Fox
p. 126

Red Fox
p. 130

Swift Fox
p. 134

RODENTS

Common
Porcupine, p. 140

Meadow Jumping
Mouse, p. 144

Western Jumping
Mouse, p. 145

Western Harvest
Mouse, p. 146

Deer Mouse
p. 148

Northern Grasshopper
Mouse, p. 150

Bushy-tailed
Woodrat, p. 152

Norway Rat
p. 154

House Mouse
p. 156

Southern Red-backed
Vole, p. 158

Western Heather
Vole, p. 159

Water Vole
p. 160

| Meadow Vole p. 161 | Long-tailed Vole p. 162 | Yellow-cheeked Vole, p. 163 | Prairie Vole p. 164 |

| Sagebrush Vole p. 165 | Common Muskrat p. 166 | Brown Lemming p. 168 | Northern Bog Lemming, p. 169 |

| American Beaver p. 170 | Olive-backed Pocket Mouse, p. 174 | Ord's Kangaroo Rat p. 176 | Northern Pocket Gopher, p. 178 |

| Least Chipmunk p. 180 | Yellow-pine Chipmunk, p. 182 | Red-tailed Chipmunk, p. 183 | Woodchuck p. 184 |

RODENTS

Yellow-bellied Marmot, p. 186

Hoary Marmot p. 188

Columbian Ground Squirrel, p. 190

Richardson's Ground Squirrel, p. 192

Thirteen-lined Ground Squirrel, p. 194

Franklin's Ground Squirrel p. 196

Golden-mantled Ground Squirrel, p. 198

Eastern Grey Squirrel p. 200

Red Squirrel p. 202

Northern Flying Squirrel p. 204

PIKAS & HARES

American Pika p. 207

Mountain Cottontail, p. 210

Snowshoe Hare p. 212

White-tailed Jackrabbit, p. 214

BATS

Long-eared Bat
p. 217

Northern Bat
p. 218

Western Small-
footed Bat, p. 219

Little Brown Bat
p. 220

Long-legged
Bat, p. 222

Eastern Red
Bat, p. 223

Hoary Bat
p. 224

Silver-haired
Bat, p. 226

Big Brown Bat
p. 227

INSECTIVORES

Pygmy Shrew
p. 229

Masked Shrew
p. 230

Hayden's Shrew
p. 231

Vagrant Shrew
p. 232

Dusky Shrew
p. 233

Common Water Shrew
p. 234

Arctic Shrew
p. 236

9

INTRODUCTION

American
Bison

Few things characterize wilderness as well as wild animals, and few animals are better distinguished than our fellow mammals. In fact, many people use the term "animal" when they really mean "mammal"—they forget that birds, reptiles, amphibians, fish and all the many kinds of invertebrates are animals, too.

Mammals come in a wide variety of colours, shapes and sizes, but they all share two characteristics that distinguish them from the other vertebrates: only mammals have real hair, and only mammals nurse their young from mammary glands (the feature that gives this group its name). Other, less well-known features that are unique to mammals include a muscular diaphragm, which separates the lower abdominal cavity from the cavity that contains the heart and lungs, and a lower jaw that is composed of a single bone on each side. Additionally, a mammal's skull joins with the first vertebra at two points of contact—a bird's or reptile's skull only has one point of contact, which is what allows birds to turn their heads so far around. As well as setting mammals apart from all other kinds of life, these characteristics also solidify the presence of humans as part of the mammalian group.

In Alberta, we are fortunate to have some of the best mammal-watching opportunities remaining anywhere, whether it is walking among ground squirrels in a prairie field, watching deer feed in the soft evening light or experiencing the phenomenon of a "bear jam" in the mountains. Much has changed in Alberta since the last of the great bison herds roamed freely some 150 years ago, but our province remains an internationally recognized destination for visitors who are interested in rewarding natural experiences. To honour this undervalued treasure is to celebrate Alberta's intrinsic virtues, and this book is intended to provide readers with the knowledge upon which to build an appreciation of the rich assortment of mammals in our province. Whether you are an amateur naturalist, a photographer, a wildlife enthusiast or all three, you will find terrific opportunities in Alberta to satisfy your greatest wilderness expectations.

The Alberta Region

Alberta is one of the most biologically diverse provinces in Canada. Encompassing an area of more than 660,000 km² (255,000 mi²), Alberta is Canada's fourth-largest province, and throughout it there are dramatic differences in the characteristics of the landscape. Snow-capped mountains, rugged backcountry, vast expanses of arid grasslands, clear-blue lakes amidst dense boreal forests and the diverse areas of aspen parkland all contribute to our province's scenic beauty and ecological uniqueness.

The wildlife and wildlife associations that occur in Alberta are linked to the geological, climatic and biological influences of our different landscapes. Some regions, such as the mountains, have been well protected, and the value of that foresight is easily seen in the wealth of wildlife encounters granted to all visitors. Even elsewhere, Alberta remains perched near the frontier, and wildlife is never far. Coyotes, deer, foxes and the occasionally Moose or Black Bear are seen in our largest cities, while, in more remote areas, some Albertans nightly drift to sleep to distant wolf howls.

Alberta is commonly divided into six natural regions—Rocky Mountains, Foothills, Boreal Forest, Parkland, Grassland and Canadian Shield. Looking at these natural regions in detail can lead to a better understanding of Alberta's mammals and how they live and interact with each other.

Rocky Mountains

Unsurpassed in their magnificence, the Rocky Mountains make up the most rugged natural region in Alberta: major glaciation events recently carved the Rockies into deep, U-shaped valleys and jagged, steep slopes. Sinuous rivers line the valley bottoms, and sapphire lakes dot the gullies between the rugged peaks.

The Rockies, which occupy about 8 percent of the province, are the babes of the world's mountains; they were thrust upward about 140 to 145 million years ago. Two major mountain series occur in the province: the easterly Front Ranges and the westerly Main Ranges (shared with British Columbia). Both ranges are composed of thrust-faulted sedimentary rock underlain by folded bedrock.

The Rocky Mountains region is divided into three subregions—Montane, Subalpine and Alpine—whose boundaries primarily reflect differences in climate that are linked to changes in elevation. At the low elevations of the Montane, winters have heavy snowfalls but fairly mild temperatures, and summers are very warm.

The thick forests in these areas give way to thinner forests in the Subalpine and eventually to tundra in the Alpine, which starts at about 2000–2300 m (6600–7500 ft).

The ubiquitous mammals of the Rockies, such as the Elk, the Golden-mantled Ground Squirrel and the Bighorn Sheep, can easily be met in Alberta's mountainous areas. The charismatic carnivores, however, such as the Mountain Lion, the Grizzly Bear and the Grey Wolf, are elusive creatures—many hopeful wildlife watchers must be content in the knowledge that these great mammals still survive tucked into the mountain wilderness.

Foothills

It is a common misconception that the foothills are part of the mountains. The upthrusting event that formed the Rocky Mountains also created the foothills to the east by causing buckles or ripples in the bedrock, but this rippled land is geologically and biologically distinct. In Alberta, the Foothills region is an area of transition, generally from the Rocky Mountains to the Boreal Forest natural regions. In a few small areas in southwestern Alberta, however, the Foothills region links the Rocky Mountains to the Parkland.

In this landscape of rolling hills and long ridges, small streams meander through valley bottoms of dwarf birch, willow and grasses, and the hills are cloaked in mixedwood forests. Fens and bogs occur in some parts of the region. The climate of the Foothills is quite mild, being generally cooler than the Boreal Forest in summer and warmer in winter.

The characteristic mammals that occur in the Foothills region are numerous: the American Mink, the Grey Wolf, the Black Bear, the Mountain Lion, the White-tailed Deer and the Mule Deer. You may also encounter the Elk and the Moose, or even the endangered Woodland Caribou.

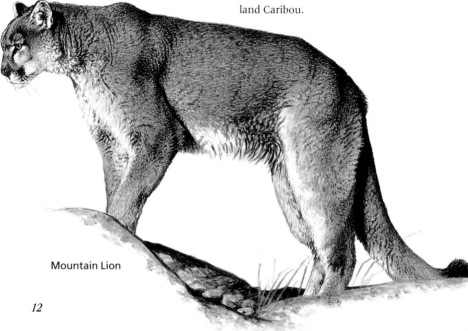

Mountain Lion

Boreal Forest

The great Boreal Forest, the largest natural region in Alberta, covers almost half of the province and dominates the north. Its underlying geology is very similar to that of the prairies—a rolling landscape covered in glacial till—but the Boreal Forest has more rainfall, longer winters and less intense summer heat. As a result, the land is covered in thick forests and muskegs, bogs and fens. Great rivers, such as the Peace and the Athabasca, have carved routes through this land carrying water from the Rocky Mountains to the Arctic Ocean.

Common Water Shrew

From afar, the Boreal Forest all looks the same, but on the ground it is quite diverse, changing gradually from one locality to the next. Because of its predominance in our province, this natural region is important both climatically and biologically; the nutrient cycling and gas exchange of the Boreal Forest have far-reaching effects.

No other natural region defines Canada as well as the Boreal Forest, and many of its most recognizable mammals have inspired our country's defining images. The Boreal Forest is home to the Northern Flying Squirrel, the Wolverine, the Canada Lynx, the Grey Wolf, the Red Squirrel, the Black Bear and the Moose.

Parkland

Alberta's aspen parkland is a patchy mosaic of deciduous forests, ponds, marshes, prairies and brushy grasslands. Comprising about 12 percent of Alberta, the Parkland region is primarily a transition between the colder coniferous forests of the northern and upland regions and the drier grasslands of the plains. Geologically, the rolling terrain and hummocky landscape is a result of post-glacial deposits. The Parkland's mild, moist climate and its extremely rich, black soil support deciduous forests and extensive wetlands with bounteous vegetation and high biological diversity.

Only isolated pockets of natural Parkland vegetation remain; humans have altered the rest into a patchwork of croplands and pastures. The wildlife of this region has, in some cases, adapted to the human alterations. Common mammals of the Parkland include the Woodchuck, the Northern Pocket Gopher, the Least Weasel, the Common Porcupine, the Franklin's Ground Squirrel and the Red Fox.

Grassland

No one who has walked Alberta's grasslands would describe them as flat; rather, the landscape is a series of gently rolling, shallow hills set in a sea of grass. A few major rivers, destined for either the Hudson Bay or the Gulf of Mexico, cut through the Grassland region, sometimes carving deep valleys and creating the haunting beauty of the badlands.

The Grassland Natural Region is well suited for field crops, and more than 80 percent of the native grasslands have been converted to agriculture. Many of the high-profile mammals that historically roamed this landscape, such as the Grey Wolf, the Grizzly Bear and, of course, the American Bison, no longer occur on Alberta's grasslands, but you can still experience awe-inspiring wildness in the lives of the Coyote, the American Badger, the Pronghorn and the Ord's Kangaroo Rat.

Canadian Shield

One of the harshest environments in Alberta, the Canadian Shield is a spectacular landscape of granite cliffs, great sand dunes and pristine waters. The rocky outcroppings of the underlying bedrock produce a terrain of dry, soil-impoverished highlands and wet, sparsely forested lowlands. Although it is a dominant region in much of Canada, the Canadian Shield covers just a sliver of the far northeastern corner of Alberta.

The strange, wind-blown pines and sand dunes of this remote region create mysterious feelings of true wilderness. It is home to many mammals, such as the Moose, the Black Bear, the Fisher and the American Mink. In winter, this corner of Alberta may also attract typically Arctic animals, such as the Arctic Fox and the Woodland Caribou.

Neighbouring Regions

Like all their human counterparts, Alberta's mammals have come from elsewhere. The province was almost completely ice-covered just 10,000 to 20,000 years ago, and all the different types of animals now found here have immigrated since that time.

All points of the compass are recognised in Alberta's current wildlife assemblage: the Caribou is an example of the Arctic influences from the north; the Hoary Marmot is part of the western, cordilleran element; the Pronghorn is one of the southern immigrants from the Great Plains; and the White-tailed Deer, for example, moved into Alberta from the east.

Ord's Kangaroo Rat

Seasonality

The extreme nature of seasons in Alberta has considerable influences upon the lives of the mammals in this province. With the exception of bats, Alberta's mammals are confined to relatively slow forms of terrestrial travel. As a result, individuals are restricted to limited geographic ranges, and they must cope in various ways with the changing seasons.

With the receding of winter snows and the greening of Alberta's natural areas, spring signals renewal. It is at this time of year that many mammals have their young. The lushness of new growth provides ample food for herbivores, and with the arrival of new herbivore young, the predatory mammals enjoy good times as well. While some small mammals, particularly the shrews and rodents, mature within weeks, the off-spring of the larger mammals are dependent on their parents for much longer periods.

During the warmest time of the year, the animals' bodies have recovered from the strains of the previous winter's food scarcity and spring's reproductive efforts, but summer is not a time of relaxation. To prepare yet again for the upcoming fall and winter, some mammals must eat vast quantities of food to build up fat reserves, while others work furiously to stockpile food caches in safe places. Some mammals, such as the Richardson's Ground Squirrel, start hibernation as early as late July, which signals to the keen naturalist that the inevitable slope to winter has already begun.

For some of Alberta's most charismatic species, fall is the time for mating. At this time of the year bull Elk become bugling, testosterone-driven maniacs that demonstrate extremes in aggression and vigilance. Some small mammals, however, such as voles and mice, mate every few months, and the last of the year's litters are often just starting out on their own as the first snows begin to dust the land.

Winter is the most difficult time for many of Alberta's mammals. For many herbivores, high-energy foods are difficult to find, often requiring more energy to locate than they provide in return. This negative energy budget gradually weakens most mammals through winter, and the ones that were not fit enough at the start of winter end up feeding the equally needy carnivores, which ironically find an ally in winter's severity. Voles and mice live out this season under an insulating layer of snow that buffers their elaborate trails from the worst of winter's cold. Food, shelter and warmth are all found in this thin layer, and the months devoted to food storage now pay off.

Winter eventually wanes, and while death is an omni-present associate, this season sets the foundation for another springing of life.

Richardson's Ground Squirrel

Watching Mammals

Many types of mammals are most active at night, so the best times for viewing mammals are during the "wildlife hours" at dawn and dusk. At these times of day, mammals are out from their daytime hideouts and on the move. During winter, hunger may force certain mammals to be more active during midday; conversely, when the conditions are more favourable during spring and summer, mammals may become less active.

With Alberta's abundance of large protected areas, many of the larger mammals, in particular, can be easily viewed from the safety of a vehicle along the many roadways that cut through our parks. If you walk the backcountry trails or hike across the prairies, you can find yourself in the very homes of some mammals, although the residents often demonstrate their sensory superiority by remaining hidden.

While many of the mammals that are encountered in Alberta often appear easy to approach, it is important to respect your own safety as much as the safety of the animal being viewed. This advice seems obvious for the larger species (although it is ignorantly dismissed in some areas), but small mammals should also be treated with respect. Honour both the encounter and the animal by demonstrating a respect that is owed to the special occasion.

Alberta's Top Mammal-Watching Spots

Writing-on-Stone Provincial Park

The finest example of native grasslands remaining in Alberta can be found near Writing-on-Stone Provincial Park. The Milk River has cut an emerald valley that hosts many different types of mammals. Watch for Mule Deer, Bushy-tailed Woodrats, Mountain Cottontails, Striped Skunks, Pronghorns, Coyotes, Yellow-bellied Marmots and Western Small-footed Bats.

NATIONAL PARKS
1. Banff NP
2. Elk Island NP
3. Jasper NP
4. Waterton Lakes NP
5. Wood Buffalo NP

PROVINCIAL PARKS
6. Chain Lakes PP
7. Cold Lake PP
8. Cypress Hills PP
9. Dinosaur PP
10. Dry Island Buffalo Jump PP
11. Fish Creek PP
12. Gooseberry Lake PP
13. Kinbrook Island PP
14. Lakeland PP
15. Lesser Slave Lake PP
16. Miquelon Lakes PP
17. Peter Lougheed PP
18. Rochon Sands PP
19. Saskatoon Island PP
20. Sir Winston Churchill PP
21. Whitney Lakes PP
22. William A. Switzer PP
23. Willow Creek PP
24. Writing-on-Stone PP

OTHER VIEWING AREAS
25. Brûlé Lake
26. Castle Wilderness
27. Caw Ridge
28. Gold Springs Park
29. Head-Smashed-In Buffalo Jump
30. Kananaskis Country
31. Lake Athabasca
32. Pine Lake
33. Sheep River Wildlife Sanctuary
34. Willmore Wilderness
35. White Goat Wilderness

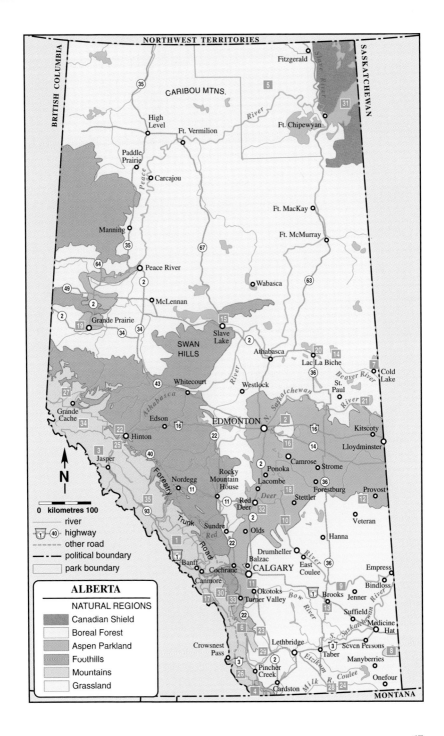

NORTHWEST TERRITORIES

BRITISH COLUMBIA

SASKATCHEWAN

CARIBOU MTNS.

Fitzgerald

High
Level
Ft. Vermilion

Ft. Chipewyan

Paddle
Prairie

Carcajou

Ft. MacKay

Manning

Ft. McMurray

Peace River

Wabasca

McLennan

Grande Prairie

Slave
Lake

SWAN
HILLS

Athabasca

Lac La Biche

St.
Paul

Cold
Lake

Grande
Cache

Whitecourt

Westlock

Edson

EDMONTON

Kitscoty

Hinton

Jasper

Lloydminster

Nordegg

Rocky
Mountain
House

Ponoka

Camrose

Strome

Lacombe

Forestburg

Provost

Red
Deer

Stettler

Sundre

Olds

Veteran

Banff

Drumheller
Balzac

Hanna

Cochrane

CALGARY

East
Coulee

Empress

Canmore

Okotoks

Bindloss

Turner Valley

Brooks

Jenner

Suffield

Medicine
Hat

Crowsnest
Pass

Lethbridge

Seven Persons

Manyberries

Pincher
Creek

Taber

Onefour

Cardston

MONTANA

0   kilometres 100

N

—— river
—(40)— highway
—— other road
— · — · — political boundary
⌐ ¬ park boundary

ALBERTA

NATURAL REGIONS

Canadian Shield
Boreal Forest
Aspen Parkland
Foothills
Mountains
Grassland

Peace River

Athabasca River

Slave River

Beaver River

N. Saskatchewan River

Red Deer River

Bow River

S. Saskatchewan River

Milk River

Forestry
Trunk
Road

17

Cypress Hills Provincial Park

Tucked into the southeastern corner of our province, far from its closest forest neighbour, rise the tree-clad Cypress Hills. This area hosts many animals that are found more typically to the north and west. Mule Deer, White-tailed Deer, Moose, Elk, Coyotes and Thirteen-lined Ground Squirrels are all commonly encountered.

Dinosaur Provincial Park

The wildlife of the Triassic Period is what is most celebrated at this World Heritage Site, but the badlands' modern-day wildlife is equally fascinating. Mule Deer, Mountain Cottontails, Pronghorns, Western Small-footed Bats, Coyotes, Common Porcupines and White-tailed Jackrabbits are all common in the area.

Edmonton River Valley

Whether you are driving or walking through Edmonton's ribbon of green, be on the lookout for mammals. White-tailed Deer, Red Squirrels, Northern Flying Squirrels, Common Porcupines, Red-backed Voles, Snowshoe Hares, Common Muskrats, American Beavers, Red Foxes and Woodchucks all live in the capital city.

Calgary River Parks

Beautifully protected and enhanced parks line the Bow River as it winds through Calgary. A lunchtime or after-dinner walk may yield encounters with White-tailed Deer, Mule Deer, Eastern Grey Squirrels, Coyotes, Common Muskrats, American Beavers, Red Foxes, weasels and American Badgers.

Mule Deer

Waterton Lakes National Park

From rolling grasslands to alpine peaks, this small national park has it all. View Bighorn Sheep, Black Bears, Grizzly Bears, Elk, Mule Deer, Columbian Ground Squirrels, Golden-mantled Ground Squirrels, American Bison, Coyotes, Mountain Lions, American Minks and Red-tailed Chipmunks on your next visit.

Kananaskis Country

The internationally recognized trail system of this provincial recreation area gives you easy entry into the world of Elk, Moose, Black Bears, Grizzly Bears, Mountain Lions, Coyotes, American Pikas, Bighorn Sheep, Columbian Ground Squirrels, Golden-mantled Ground Squirrels and American Beavers.

Banff National Park

Alberta's premier tourist destination continues to be a naturalist's paradise. Elk, Moose, Black Bears, Grizzly Bears, Mountain Lions, Coyotes, American Pikas, Bighorn Sheep, Columbian Ground Squirrels, Golden-mantled Ground Squirrels, American Beavers, Bushy-tailed Woodrats, Grey Wolves and Pine Martens are just some of the mammals you may encounter during backcountry explorations.

Jasper National Park

Many mammals complement the rugged beauty of this large mountain park, including Elk, Moose, Black Bears, Grizzly Bears, Coyotes, American Pikas, Bighorn Sheep, Mountain Goats, Columbian Ground Squirrels, Golden-mantled Ground Squirrels, American Beavers, Grey Wolves, Caribou, Hoary Marmots and Pine Martens.

Elk Island National Park

A very high concentration of hoofed mammals is a unique feature of this park. Expect to encounter American Bison, Moose, White-tailed Deer, Elk, American Beavers, Common Muskrats, Long-tailed Weasels, Richardson's Ground Squirrels and Red Squirrels on most visits.

Lakeland Country to Fort McMurray

This northern frontier of lake-dotted forests remains wild enough to support populations of Black Bears, Moose, White-tailed Deer, Red Foxes, Franklin's Ground Squirrels, River Otters, Short-tailed Weasels, American Minks, American Beavers, Common Muskrats, Snowshoe Hares and Grey Wolves.

Wood Buffalo National Park

Nature continues to rule in this massive northern park, which extends into the Northwest Territories and includes the impressive Peace-Athabasca Delta. Herds of American Bison and Caribou continue their ancient dances with the Grey Wolves, while Canada Lynx, Moose, American Beavers, Black Bears and Pine Martens play their own roles in the boreal food web.

About This Book

Organization of the Species Accounts

Biologists divide mammals into a number of subgroups, called orders, which form the basis for the organization of this book. Six mammalian orders have wild representatives in Alberta: hoofed mammals (Artiodactyla), carnivores (Carnivora), rodents (Rodentia), pikas and hares (Lagomorpha), bats (Chiroptera) and insectivores (Insectivora). In turn, each order is subdivided into families, which group together the more closely related species. For example, within the hoofed mammals, the White-tailed Deer and the Moose, which are both in the deer family, are more closely related to each other than either is to the Pronghorn, which is in its own family.

This guide describes 91 species of "wild" mammals that have been reported from Alberta. Feral populations of some domestic species, such as horses and pigs, have occurred in parts of Alberta, but they are not described here. Two species, the Black-footed Ferret and the Chestnut-cheeked Vole, are not thought to be part of Alberta's current fauna, but there is strong evidence that they once were, and they have been included in the accounts. Also included, although with much reduced descriptions, are the Common Grey Fox (there is just one questionable record from Alberta) and the Black Rat (it is known primarily from transport containers and warehouses in Edmonton and Calgary). Humans, a member of the order Primates, have lived in Alberta at least since the end of the last Pleistocene glaciation, but the relationship between our species and the natural world is well beyond the scope of this book, and in terms of identifying features, all you really need is a mirror.

Mammal Names

Although the international zoological community closely monitors the use of scientific names for animals, common names, which change with time, local language and usage, are more difficult to standardize. In the case of birds, the American Ornithologists' Union has been very effective at standardizing the common names used by professionals and recreational naturalists alike, but there is, as yet, no similar organization to oversee and approve the common names of mammals in North America, which can lead to some confusion.

True moles do not occur in our province, for example, but many Albertans apply that name to the Northern Pocket Gopher, a burrowing mammal that leaves loose cores of dirt in

Black-footed Ferret

fields. These piles reminded early settlers of the moles they knew from Eastern Canada and Europe. To add to the confusion, most Albertans use the name "gopher" to refer not to the Northern Pocket Gopher, but to the ubiquitous Richardson's Ground Squirrel. If you were to venture out of Alberta to Minnesota, it would get even worse. There, a "gopher" is neither the Richardson's Ground Squirrel nor even the Northern Pocket Gopher, but rather that state's most commonly encountered rodent, the Thirteen-lined Ground Squirrel.

You may think that such confusion is relegated to the less charismatic species of mammals, but even some of our best-known animals are victims of human inconsistencies. Every Albertan clearly knows the identity of both the Moose and the Elk, but these names can cause great confusion for Europeans visitors. The species that we know as the Elk, *Cervus elaphus*, is called the Red Deer in Europe, where "Elk" is the named used for *Alces alces* ("elk" and *alces* come from the same root), which is known as the Moose in North America. We don't have to take the blame for this confusion, however, because early European settlers were the ones who misapplied the name "Elk" to our populations of *Cervus elaphus*—inconsistently, by the way, because some of them were astute enough to call one of their towns Red Deer. In an as-yet-unsuccessful attempt to resolve the confusion, many naturalists use of the name "wapiti" for the species *Cervus elaphus* in North America. There is a small amount of hometown pride involved, as well: "wapiti" derives from the Shawnee name for that animal,

just as "moose" is from Algonquian and "caribou" is from Micmac.

Despite the absence of an "official" list of mammal names, there are some widely accepted standards, such as the "Revised checklist of North American mammals north of Mexico, 1997" (Jones et al. 1997, Occasional Papers, Museum of Texas Tech University, No. 173), which this book follows for both the scientific and common names of the mammals (except in regard to the common names of the *Myotis* bats).

Range Maps

Mapping the range of a species is a problematic endeavour: mammal populations are continually expanding and reducing their distributions, and dispersing individuals are occasionally encountered in unexpected areas. The range maps included in this book are intended to show the distribution of breeding/sustaining populations in Alberta, and not the extent of individual specimen records. Full colour intensity on the map indicates a species' presence; pale areas indicate its absence.

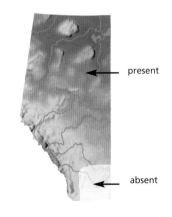

present

absent

Similar Species

Before you finalize your decision on the species of a mammal, check the "Similar Species" section of the account; it briefly describes other mammals that could be mistakenly identified as the species you are considering. By concentrating on the most relevant field marks, the subtle differences between species can be reduced to easily identifiable traits. As you become more experienced at identifying mammals, you might find you can immediately shortlist an animal to a few possible species. By consulting this section you can quickly glean the most relevant field marks to distinguish between those species, thereby short-cutting the identification process.

Best Sites

If you are looking for a particular mammal in Alberta, you will have more luck in some places than in others, even within the range shown on the map. Under the "Best Sites" heading, we have listed places that provide a good chance of seeing a species and are easily accessible, which is why so many parks are mentioned. All of these "best sites" appear on the province map on page 17.

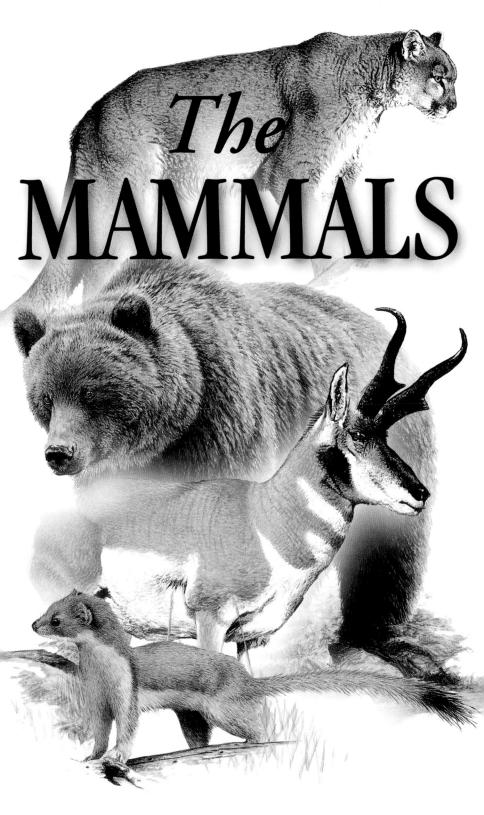

The
MAMMALS

HOOFED MAMMALS

All Alberta's native hoofed mammals almost exclusively eat plant material, and they are sometimes referred to as "megaherbivores" because of their diet and generally large size. They always have an even number of toes—either two or four—on each limb. If there are four toes, the outer two, which are called dewclaws, are always smaller and higher on the leg, touching the ground only in soft mud or snow. The ankle bones of all hoofed mammals are grooved on both their upper and lower surfaces, which enables these animals to rise from a reclining position with their hindquarters first. This ability means that the large hindleg muscles that facilitate escape are available for action more quickly than in horses, which must rise front first. Additionally, all our hoofed mammals have incisors only on the lower jaw; they have a cartilaginous pad at the front of the upper jaw instead of teeth.

American Bison

Cattle Family (Bovidae)

Alberta's three native bovids are the American Bison, the Mountain Goat and the Bighorn Sheep, but this family is best known for its contributions to our domestic fauna, including cattle, sheep and goats. Both sexes of all bovids have true horns that are never shed and grow throughout the animal's life. The horns consist of a keratinous sheath (keratin is the main type of protein in our fingernails and hair) over a bony core that grows from the frontal bones of the skull. Bovids are cud chewers, and they have complex, four-chambered stomachs.

Pronghorn

Pronghorn Family (Antilocapridae)

This exclusively North American family contains just the one species. The Pronghorn has only two toes (no dewclaws), and it lacks canine teeth (as well as upper incisors). Both sexes have true horns, but unlike bovids, the Pronghorn sheds and regrows the keratinous sheath each year (the bony core is not shed).

Moose

Deer Family (Cervidae)

All adult male cervids (and female Caribou) have antlers, which are bony outgrowths of the frontal skull bones that are shed and regrown annually. In males with an adequate diet, the antlers generally get larger each year. New antlers are soft and tender, and they are covered with "velvet," a layer of skin with short, fine hairs and a network of blood vessels to nourish the growing antlers. The antlers stop growing in late summer, and the velvet dries up and is rubbed off. Cervids are also distinguished by the presence of scent glands in pits just in front of the eyes and by the absence of upper canine teeth. Their lower canine teeth look like incisors, so there appear to be four pairs of lower incisors.

American Bison
Buffalo
Bos bison

Historically, few areas of Alberta were left unoccupied by the American Bison. From the northern woods to the western foothills to the southern grasslands, bison roamed our province and left their impressive marks on the landscape. Evidence of their once-great presence can still be found, particularly in southern Alberta. Large boulders isolated on the plains are often smoothly polished and set in shallow pits—stark evidence of thousands of years of itchy bison rubbing their hides for relief. More eerie still are the bones that spill out of prairie riverbanks, a testament to nature's cyclic order and a reminder that the American Bison, for the most part, is no longer a significant participant. Still, in places like Wood Buffalo National Park, wolves and bison continue their long-standing predator-prey relationship, and in smaller areas, such as Elk Island and Waterton Lakes national parks, the impressive physique of the American Bison is apparent to all visitors.

While almost everyone knows of the disastrous plight that saw the great American Bison herds plunge from millions of individuals to only a few hundred, few people realize the role Alberta has played in this animal's recovery. Little more than a century ago, most of the world's remaining bison were found on one man's ranch in northern Montana. From 1907 to 1924, Don Michel Pablo sold 709 of his bison to the Canadian government, which first kept them at Elk Island National Park, and then at the newly established Wainwright Buffalo Park. There, the herd soon increased to over 10,000 animals. To prevent overcrowding, several thousand bison were shipped north by rail and barge to Wood Buffalo National Park, which had been established in 1922 to protect one of the few remaining wild populations of American Bison. The Wainwright park was closed as a bison range in 1939; its remaining residents went to either Elk Island or Wood Buffalo national parks.

Intensive management and manipulation of the American Bison has been the rule since European colonization, and it continues today amid much debate. Some people question the ethics of "farming" one of the world's great terrestrial roamers, while others envision a future with bison herds in massive common areas. In Wood Buffalo

---

BEST SITES: Elk Island NP; Wood Buffalo NP; Waterton Lakes NP.

RANGE: The historical range extended from the southeastern Yukon south to northern Mexico and east to the Appalachian Mountains. Free-ranging herds are now almost exclusively restricted to protected areas. Many small herds are raised in fenced game ranches.

Total length: 2.4–3.9 m (8–13 ft)

Shoulder Height: 1.3–1.8 m (4–6 ft)

Tail length: 28–39 cm (11–15 in)

Weight: 360–1090 kg (790–2400 lb)

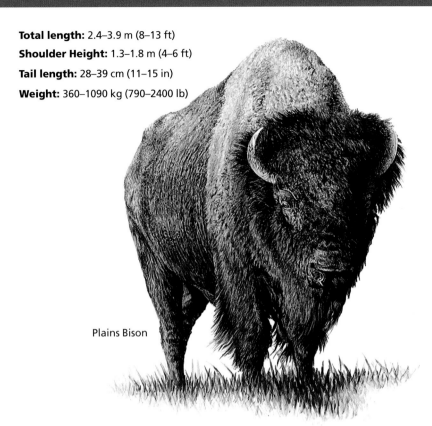

Plains Bison

National Park, the "Wood Bison" form that originally occurred there has hybridized with the "Plains Bison" from Wainwright to such an extent that some biologists worry there are no pure Wood Bison left in the park. Additionally, the Wainwright bison brought with them tuberculosis and bucellosis infections, which are now represented throughout the bison of Wood Buffalo.

DESCRIPTION: The head and forequarters is covered with long, shaggy, woolly, dark brown hair that abruptly becomes shorter and lighter brown behind the shoulders. The head is massive and appears to be carried low because of the high shoulder hump and massive forequarters. Both sexes have short, round, curved, black horns that grow upward. The legs are short and clothed in shaggy hair. The tail is long and has a tuft of hair

at the tip. The calf is reddish at birth but becomes darker by its first fall.

HABITAT: Although the American Bison originally was most abundant in the prairies, it also historically inhabited alpine tundra and areas of boreal forest and aspen parkland with abundant short vegetation.

FOOD: Most of the diet is made up of grasses, sedges and forbs. In winter, the American Bison sometimes browses on shrubs, cattails and lichens, but grasses are still the primary food. A bison will paw away the snow or push it to the side with its head if the snow is not too crusted.

DEN: Historically, the American Bison was nomadic, so it did not have a permanent den. It typically beds down at night and during the hottest part of the day. After a herd has been in an area for a while, it will leave behind wallows— dusty, saucer-like depressions where the bison rolled and rubbed repeatedly.

YOUNG: After a gestation of 9 to 10 months, a cow bison typically gives birth to a single, 18-kg (40-lb) calf in May. The calf is able to follow the cow within hours of birth. It begins to graze at about one week, but it is not weaned until about seven months. A cow typically mates for the first time at two to three years old. A bull is sexually mature then, too, but competition from older males customarily prevents him from breeding until he is seven to eight years old.

hoofprint

Wood Bison

walking trail

Moose

SIMILAR SPECIES: No other native Albertan mammal resembles an American Bison. The Moose (p. 54) has a similarly coloured coat, but it is taller and has long, thin legs and a much longer and leaner body overall. A bull Moose has broad antlers, not horns.

Mountain Goat
Oreamnos americanus

Acrophobia—the fear of heights—is a mystery to the Mountain Goat. This mammal is Alberta's foremost natural mountaineer, and the very heights that instil fear in so many beings are of comfort and assurance to it. As a consequence of its habitat preference, the Mountain Goat has the added bonus of living its entire life surrounded by the sweeping scenery of the Rocky Mountains.

The steep aspect of its rocky home offers many protective qualities for a Mountain Goat, but the ever-present risk of avalanches is an expensive trade-off. Snowslides are likely the main cause of death among Mountain Goats, particularly during late winter and spring. These tragic incidents are not universally cursed, however, because recently awakened, winter-starved bears forage along avalanche slides for the snow's victims.

The Mountain Goat has several physical characteristics that help it live in such precarious situations. The hard outer ring of its hooves surrounds a softer, spongy, central area that provides good grip on rocky surfaces. The dewclaws are long enough to touch the ground on soft surfaces, and they provide greater "flotation" on weaker snow crusts. To keep it relatively comfortable in the subzero temperatures and strong winter winds that sweep along mountain faces, the Mountain Goat's winter coat consists of a thick, fleecy undercoat and guard hairs that are more than 17 cm (6¾ in) long. By May, the goats begin to shed "blankets" of thick hair, often in their dusting pits dug high on the sides of mountains. The fur falls off in pieces, and during early summer, when many tourists visit the mountain parks, Mountain Goats are not in their picturesque prime. Their

Total Length: 1.2–1.6 m (4–5 ft)
Shoulder Height: 0.9–1.2 m (3–4 ft)
Tail Length: 9–14 cm (3½–5½ in)
Weight: 45–136 kg (99–300 lb)

short, neat, white summer coat comes in by July, and it continues to grow to form the thick winter coat.

DESCRIPTION: The coat of this stocky, hump-shouldered animal is white and usually shaggy, with a longer series of guard hairs surmounting the fleecy undercoat. The lips, nose, eyes and hooves are black. Both sexes may sport a noticeable beard, which is longer in winter. The short legs often look like they are clothed in breeches in winter, because the hair of the lower leg is much shorter than that of the upper leg. The tail is short. The ears are relatively long. Both sexes have narrow, black horns. The billy's horns are thicker and curve backward along a constant arc. The nanny's horns are narrower and tend to rise straight from the skull and then bend sharply to the rear near their

DID YOU KNOW?

The Mountain Goat's skeleton is arranged so that all four hooves can fit on a ledge as small as 15 cm (6 in) long and 5 cm (2 in) wide. A goat can even rear up and turn around on such a tiny foothold.

BEST SITES: Disaster Point and south of Athabasca Falls, Jasper NP; Parker Ridge, Mt. Coleman and Mt. Wilson, Banff NP.

RANGE: The natural range extends from southeastern Alaska south through the Coast Mountains into the Washington Cascades and southeast through the Rockies into Idaho and Montana. It has been successfully introduced to several locations in the western states and three islands in Alaska.

tips. The kid has a grey-brown stripe along its back.

HABITAT: The Mountain Goat generally occupies steep slopes and rocky cliffs in alpine or subalpine areas, where low temperatures and deep snow are common. Although it typically inhabits treeless areas, the Mountain Goat may travel through dense subalpine or montane forests going to and from mineral licks. In summer, it tends to be seen more frequently at lower elevations, moving to the highest windswept ledges in winter to find vegetation that is free of snowcover.

FOOD: This adaptable herbivore varies its diet according to its environment: in a Montana study, it ate shrubs almost exclusively, with the balance of the diet coming from mosses, lichens and forbs; in Alberta, only one-quarter of the diet was shrubs and three-quarters was grasses, sedges and rushes. The Mountain Goat's winter feeding areas are generally separate from the summer areas.

DEN: A Mountain Goat beds down in a shallow depression scraped out in shale or dirt at the base of a cliff. Clumps of the goat's white hair are often scattered in the vicinity of the scrape.

YOUNG: After a gestation of five to six months, a nanny bears a single kid (75 percent of the time) or twins, weighing 2.9–3.8 kg (6½–8½ lb), in May. A kid can follow its mother within hours. After a few days, the kid starts eating grasses and forbs, but it is not weaned until it is about six weeks old. Both sexes become sexually mature after about 2½ years. Nannies mate every other year.

hoofprint

SIMILAR SPECIES: The Bighorn Sheep (p. 34) has brown upperparts and a whitish rump patch. Its brown horns are either massive and thick at the base (in the ram) or flattened (in the ewe), but never round, thin, stiletto-like or black like a Mountain Goat's horns.

Bighorn Sheep

Bighorn Sheep
Ovis canadensis

No matter where you travel in North America, Alberta simply cannot be beat for its diversity of hoofed mammals. It seems fitting, therefore, that one of the world's most recognizable and revered species, the Bighorn Sheep, is Alberta's provincial mammal. It is also not surprising that our province has produced many of the naturalists who pioneered a celebration of the esthetic appeal of these large mammals. Andy Russell, one of Alberta's foremost storytellers, was among the first people who traded in guns for cameras to observe wild animals on their own terms and study their behaviours. Before it was widely known, Russell dutifully noted in one of his many books that, "offered friendly treatment and respect, [Bighorn Sheep] will respond in a most extraordinary manner." Russell's observations, which occurred at a time when Bighorn Sheep were shy of humans, owing to hunting, foresaw sheep behaviour that is now experienced daily in our mountain parks.

Although Bighorn Sheep can routinely be seen along roadsides in parks and preserves, it is along steep slopes and rocky ledges that they truly seem to be at home. The youngest animals, which have not yet learned the sanctuary of cliffs, are particularly vulnerable to Coyotes, Grey Wolves and occasionally Mountain Lions. Provided they survive their first year, however, most Bighorns live long lives; few of their natural predators have the ability to match the Bighorn Sheep's sure-footedness and vertical agility.

The magnificent courtship battles between ram Bighorns have made these animals darlings of TV wildlife specials and corporate advertising. During October and November, adult rams establish a breeding hierarchy that is based on the relative sizes of their horns and the outcomes of their impressive head-to-head combats. In combat, opposing rams rise on their hindlegs, step towards one another and smash together with glorious fervour. Once the breeding hierarchy has been settled, mating takes place, after which the rams and ewes tend to split into separate herds. For the most part, the rams abandon their head blows until the next fall, but broken horns and ribs are reminders of their hormone-induced clashes.

DID YOU KNOW?

The Bighorn Sheep is a popular species for re-establishing into areas from which it has long been absent. In particular, many states in the western U.S. have re-established herds, often using Bighorn Sheep originally from Alberta.

BEST SITES: Disaster Point, Medicine Lake and Wilcox Pass, Jasper NP; Highwood Pass, Kananaskis Country; Mt. Norquay and south end of Hwy 1A, Banff NP; Red Rock Canyon and Waterton townsite, Waterton Lakes NP.

RANGE: From the mountains of Alberta and west-central British Columbia, the Bighorn Sheep's range extends east through Montana and south through California and New Mexico into northern Mexico.

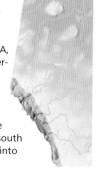

Total Length: 1.2–1.9 m (4–6 ft)
Shoulder Height: 75–105 cm (30–41 in)
Tail Length: 8–15 cm (3¼–6 in)
Weight: 53–156 kg (120–340 lb)

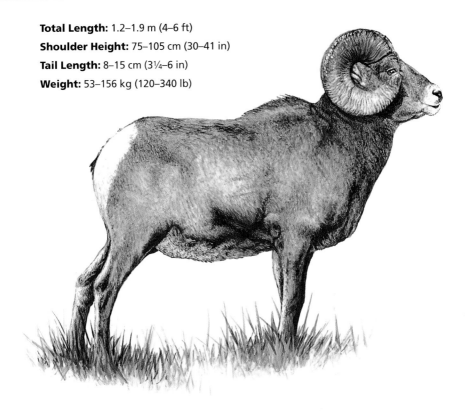

DESCRIPTION: This robust, brownish sheep has a bobbed tail and a large white rump patch. The belly, the backs of the legs and the end of the muzzle are also white. The brown coat is darkest in fall, gradually fading with winter wear. It looks motley in June and July while the new coat grows in. "Bighorn" is a well-deserved name, because the circumference of a ram's horn can be as much as 45 cm (18 in) at the base. The curled horns can be 110 cm (43 in) long and spread 65 cm (26 in) from tip to tip. Heavy ridges, the pattern of which is unique to each individual, run transversely across the horn. A deep groove forms each winter, which makes it possible to determine a sheep's age from its horns. The ewe's horns are shorter and noticeably more flattened from side to side than the ram's. Also, the ewe's horns never curl around to form even a half circle, whereas an older ram's horns sometimes form a full curl or more.

HABITAT: Although it is most common in non-forested, mountainous areas where cliffs provide easy escape routes, the Bighorn Sheep can thrive outside the mountains as long as precipitous slopes are present in the vicinity of appropriate food and water.

FOOD: The diet consists primarily of broad-leafed, non-woody plants and grasses. Exposed, dry grasses on windswept slopes provide much of the winter food. The Bighorn Sheep exhibits an incredible appetite for salt—to fulfil this need, herds may travel kilometres, even through dense forests, to reach natural mineral licks. They often eat debris alongside highways to get the road salt that is applied during winter, which unfortunately increases the number of collisions with vehicles.

DEN: The Bighorn Sheep typically beds down for the night in a depression that is about 1.2 m (4 ft) wide and up to 30 cm (1 ft) deep. The depression usually smells of urine and is almost always edged with the sheep's tiny droppings.

YOUNG: Typically, a ewe gives birth to a single lamb in seclusion on a remote rocky ledge in late May or early June, after a gestation period of about six months. The ewe and her lamb rejoin the herd within a few days. Initially, the lamb nurses every half hour; as it matures, it nurses less frequently, until it is weaned at about six months old. Lambs are extremely agile and playful: they jump and run about, scale small cliffs, engage in mock fights and even jump completely over one another, which are all activities that prepare them for escaping predators later in life.

hoofprint

trotting trail

SIMILAR SPECIES: The Mule Deer (p. 46) also has a large, whitish rump patch and an overall brown colour, but bucks typically have branched antlers (rather than unbranched, curled horns), and does have no head protrusions (other than their ears). The Mountain Goat (p. 30), which sometimes shares habitat with the Bighorn Sheep, is white, not brown, and its horns are black and cylindrical.

Mule Deer

Pronghorn
American Antelope
Antilocapra americana

Through the blurred, heat-shimmered light of a grassland afternoon, the shape of a Pronghorn emerges from the rolling landscape to stand and stare. Just as suddenly, it turns and retreats into the open prairie.

The Pronghorn superficially resembles a deer, and it is often called an antelope, but it has no close living relatives—it is the sole member of an ancient family of hoofed mammals that dates back a third of the way to the dinosaurs. This animal's unique, pronged horns are not antlers, and only the outer keratin sheath of males is shed each year, not the bony core.

In the treeless landscape of the southern Alberta prairies, the Pronghorn's phenomenal eyesight serves it well in detecting predators. The Pronghorn's large eyes protrude so far out from the sides of its head that it has stereoscopic vision to the rear as well as in front. A Pronghorn is rarely seen first.

Should danger press, a Pronghorn will erect the hairs of its white rump patch to produce a mirror-like flash that is visible at a great distance. Speed, which comes easily and quickly to the Pronghorn—three-day-old fawns are quite capable of outrunning a human— is this animal's chief defence. The Pronghorn is the swiftest of North America's land mammals, and among the fastest in the world. With its efficient metabolism, powered by an extremely large heart and lungs for its body size, the Pronghorn can run at about 90 km/h (55 mph) for several minutes at a time. Its lack of dewclaws is yet another adaptation for speed.

For all its speed, the Pronghorn is a poor jumper, and its numbers declined rapidly with the fencing of rangelands throughout the West. In the 1920s, the Canadian Government established two reserves in Alberta to protect the dwindling Pronghorn populations: Wawaskey National Park (from the Cree name for the Pronghorn) along the South Saskatchewan River, and Nemiskan National Park near Foremost. Near Brooks, rancher Charlie Blazier established a private reserve on his homestead. By the late 1940s, the Pronghorn population seemed to have stabilized

Total Length: 1.7–2.5 m (5½–8 ft)
Shoulder Height: 88–103 cm (35–41 in)
Tail Length: 6–17 cm (2¼–6¾ in)
Weight: 32–63 kg (71–139 lb)

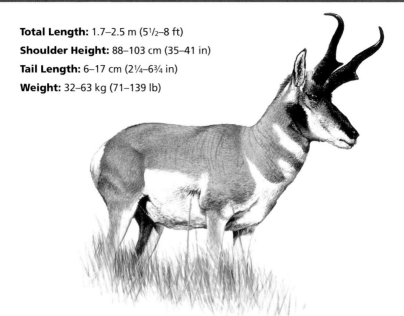

sufficiently, and the Canadian Government permanently closed the reserves.

The fences still remain on Alberta's prairies, but now they are constructed to leave enough room for a Pronghorn to fit underneath. Running Pronghorns surprise many a passing motorist when, one after another, they hardly break stride to deftly dip beneath the lowest strand of barbed wire in a fence.

DESCRIPTION: The upperparts, legs and tail are generally tan. The belly, lower sides and lower jaw are white, and there are two broad white bands across the throat and a large white rump patch. Both sexes may have horns, but those of the doe are never as long as her ears, and they do not have the ivory-coloured tips seen on the buck's. The buck's horns are straight near the base, and then bear a short branch or "prong" before they usually curve backward or inward to sharp tips. The muzzle is black, and on the buck the black extends over the face to the horn bases. The buck also has a broad black stripe running from the ear base

BEST SITES: Hwy 36 between Taber and Hanna; Hwy 1 from Brooks to Medicine Hat; native grasslands in the Suffield area; Manyberries region.

RANGE: The Pronghorn is found through much of western North America, from southern Alberta and Saskatchewan southwest into Oregon and south through California and western Texas into northern Mexico.

to behind the lower jaw. There is a short, black-tipped mane on the nape of the neck. There are no dewclaws on the legs.

HABITAT: The Pronghorn is a staunch resident of treeless areas. It inhabits open, often arid grasslands, grassy brushlands and semi-deserts and avoids woodlands.

FOOD: The winter diet is composed almost exclusively of sagebrush and other woody shrubs. In one study, the spring diet switched to snowbrush, snowberry, rabbitbrush and sagebrush for 67 percent of the intake; forbs make up 17 percent, alfalfa and crops about 15 percent and grasses only 1 percent.

DEN: Because it is a roaming animal that remains active day and night—it alternates short naps with watchful feeding—the Pronghorn does not maintain a home bed.

YOUNG: Forty percent of does bear a single fawn with their first pregnancies, but 60 percent of first pregnancies and nearly all subsequent pregnancies result in the birth of twins. A doe finds a

secluded spot on the prairie to give birth in June, following a gestation period of 7½ to 8 months. Fawns lie hidden in the grass at first, and their mothers return to nurse them about every 1½ hours. The does gradually reduce the frequency of the nursings, and when a fawn is about two weeks old and capable of outrunning most potential predators, mother and young rejoin the herd. Some does may breed during the short, mid- to late September breeding season of their first year, but most do not breed until their second year.

hoofprint

SIMILAR SPECIES: The Mule Deer (p. 46) also has a white rump, but it is larger, and the buck has antlers, not black horns. The White-tailed Deer (p. 50) does not have a white rump. Neither deer has the white throat bands or white lower sides of the Pronghorn.

Mule Deer

Elk
Wapiti
Cervus elaphus

The pitched bugle of the bull Elk is, across much of Alberta, as much a feature of fall as the first killing frost, golden leaves and the honk of migrating geese. The Elk has likely always held some form of fascination for humans, as evidenced by etchings of this great deer in the sandstone at Writing-on-Stone Provincial Park. That the Elk does not commonly occur in that park, or elsewhere throughout much of the province, is a testament to the near-eradication of this species by humans. More recent efforts by humans, however, are among the reasons that both the range and provincial population of Elk are now expanding.

By 1903, only 75 Elk remained in the Beaver Hills east of Edmonton. Historically, there had been thousands of Elk there, and their depletion during the fierce winters of 1880 to 1890 prompted the Canadian Government to create Elk Island National Park in 1907. Even the great numbers of Elk currently seen in Alberta's mountain parks owe their presence to mitigative human efforts: Alberta's mountain populations of Elk were so depleted that animals from Yellowstone National Park in Wyoming were used to develop herds in Banff from 1917 to 1920. Today Elk are common throughout these areas, and they have spread naturally or have been transplanted with varying degrees of success to much of the forested regions of Alberta. They are even becoming more common along prairie rivers.

Elk form breeding harems to a much greater degree than the other members of the deer family in Alberta. A bull Elk expends a considerable amount of energy during the fall rut—his fierce battles with rival bulls and the upkeep of cows in his harem demand more work than time permits—and, as a result, he starts winter in a weakened state. A cow, on the other hand, usually sees the first snows while she is fat and healthy. This disparity is ecologically sound: many cows will enter winter pregnant with the future of the Elk population, whereas, once winter arrives, the bulls' major contributions are past.

Fortunately for the Elk, modern-day Alberta provides nutritious grazing opportunities, even during winter. Artificially lush golf courses and agricultural fields supply high-quality forage throughout the year, while roads, townsites and human activity discourage major predators.

DID YOU KNOW?

The alternate name "wapiti" is from a Shawnee word meaning "white deer," which is probably a reference to the Elk's large white rump. Many people prefer this name because "elk" refers to the Moose in Europe.

BEST SITES: Banff townsite and area; Whistler campground, Jasper NP; Elk Island NP; other mountain parks.

RANGE: In North America, this holarctic species occurs from northeastern British Columbia southeast to southern Manitoba, south to southern Arizona and New Mexico and along the Pacific Coast from Vancouver Island to northern California. It has been introduced as game species and as ranch livestock in many areas.

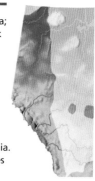

Total Length: 1.8–2.8 m (6–9 ft)
Shoulder Height: 1.2–1.5 m (4–5 ft)
Tail Length: 12–18 cm (4³/₄–7 in)
Weight: 180–500 kg (400–1100 lb)

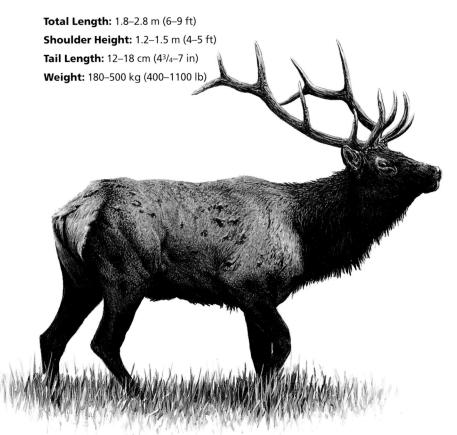

DESCRIPTION: The summer coat is generally golden brown. The winter coat is longer and greyish brown. Year-round, the head, neck and legs are darker brown and there is a large yellowish to orangish rump patch that is bordered by black or dark brown fur. The bull has a dark brown throat mane, and he starts growing antlers in his second year. By his fourth year, the bull's antlers typically bear six "points" to a side, but there is considerable variation both in the number of points a bull will have and the age when he acquires the full compliment of six. A bull will rarely have seven or eight points. The antlers are usually shed in March. New ones begin to grow in late April, becoming mature in August. The oval metatarsal glands on the outside of the hocks are outlined by stiff yellowish hairs.

HABITAT: Although the Elk prefers upland forests and prairies, it sometimes ranges into alpine tundra, coniferous forests or brushlands. In the Rockies, the Elk tends to move to higher elevations in spring and lower elevations in fall.

FOOD: The Elk is probably Alberta's most adaptable browser or grazer: woody plants and fallen leaves frequently form much of its winter and fall diet; sedges and grasses frequently make up 80 to 90 percent of the diet in spring and summer. Salt is a necessary dietary component for all animals that chew their cud, and Elk may travel vast distances to devour mineral-rich soil.

DEN: The Elk does not keep a permanent den, but it often leaves flattened areas of grass or snow where it has bedded down during the day.

YOUNG: The cow gives birth to a single calf between late May and early June, following an 8½-month gestation. The young stand and nurse within an hour, and within two to four weeks the cow and calf rejoin the herd. The calf is weaned in fall.

gallop print   walking trail

Moose

SIMILAR SPECIES: The Moose (p. 54) is darker and taller and has lighter-coloured lower hindlegs. The Bighorn Sheep (p. 34) and the Mule Deer (p. 46) have whitish, rather than yellowish, rump patches and are generally smaller, and the Bighorn Sheep has curled horns, not antlers.

Mule Deer
Odocoileus hemionus

If you have a desire to see large deer, there may be no better candidate to initiate contact than the Mule Deer. This animal is exceedingly gentle, it is approachable in many protected areas, and it is widespread throughout the southern half of the province. Campgrounds in Dinosaur, Writing-on-Stone and Cypress Hills provincial parks and the townsites in Jasper and Waterton national parks afford tremendous opportunities to begin collecting wildlife memories.

The Mule Deer has been around since prehistoric times, and it continues to do well in the mountains and in broken and fragmented landscapes. Province-wide, the Mule Deer is probably outnumbered by the White-tailed Deer, but the Mule Deer often seems to be more numerous because it tends to frequent open areas, and in parks and other protected areas it can be very bold and conspicuous.

One of the Mule Deer's best-known characteristics is its bouncing gait, known as "stotting" or "pronking." When it stots, a Mule Deer bounds and lands with all four legs simultaneously, so that it looks like it's using a pogo stick. This fascinating gait allows the deer to move safely and rapidly across the many obstructions it encounters in the complex habitats of brush and hillsides it typically inhabits. Although stotting is very characteristic of the Mule Deer, this animal also walks, trots and gallops on occasion. A Mule Deer will often stop for a last look at whatever disturbed it before it disappears completely from view.

DESCRIPTION: As its name suggests, the Mule Deer has large ears. The large, whitish rump patch is divided by the

Total Length: 1.3–1.9 m (4¹/₂–6 ft)
Shoulder Height: 90–105 cm (35–41 in)
Tail Length: 11–22 cm (4¹/₄–8³/₄ in)
Weight: 31–215 kg (68–474 lb)

short, black-tipped tail. The dark forehead contrasts with both the face and upperparts, which are tan in summer and dark grey in winter. There is a dark spot on either side of the nose. The throat and insides of the legs are white year-round. The buck has fairly heavy, up-swept antlers that are equally branched into forked tines. The meta-tarsal glands on the outside of the lower hindlegs are 10–15 cm (4–6 in) long.

HABITAT: The summer habitats vary from lowland coulees and dry brushland to alpine tundra. The bucks tend to move to higher altitudes and form small bands, while the does and fawns remain at lower altitudes. In drier regions, both

DID YOU KNOW?

Although the Mule Deer is usually silent, it can snort, grunt, cough, roar or whistle, and a fawn will sometimes bleat. Even people who have observed deer extensively may be surprised to encounter one vocalizing.

BEST SITES: Edmonton and Calgary parks; Dinosaur PP; Writing-on-Stone PP; Oldman River valley; Waterton Lakes NP; Cypress Hills PP.

RANGE: Widely distributed through western North America, this deer ranges from the southern Yukon southeast to Minnesota and south through California and western Texas into northern Mexico.

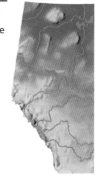

sexes are often found in streamside situations. The Mule Deer thrives in the early successional stages of forests, so it is often found where fire or logging removed the canopy a few years before.

FOOD: Grasses and forbs form most of the summer diet. In fall, the Mule Deer consumes both the foliage and twigs of shrubs. The winter diet makes increasing use of twigs and woody vegetation, and grazing occurs in hayfields adjacent to cover.

DEN: The Mule Deer leaves oval depressions in grass, moss, leaves or snow where it lays down to rest or chew its cud. It typically urinates upon rising; a doe typically steps to one side first, but a buck will urinate in the middle of the bed.

YOUNG: Following a gestation period of 6½ to 7 months, a doe gives birth to one to three (usually two) fawns in May or June. The birth weight is 3.5–3.8 kg (7¾–8½ lb). A fawn is born with light dorsal spots, which it carries until the fall

moult in August. The fawn is weaned when it is four to five months old; it becomes sexually mature at 1½ years.

stotting group

SIMILAR SPECIES: The White-tailed Deer (p. 50) has shorter ears and a much smaller rump patch that is usually hidden by the brownish upper surface of the tail. It shows the white undersurface of its tail when it runs. A buck White-tail's antlers consist of a main beam with typically unbranched tines. The Elk (p. 42) is larger, has a dark mane on the throat and has a yellowish or orangish rump patch. The Pronghorn (p. 38) has black horns and white throat bands, and the lower half of its sides are white.

White-tailed Deer

White-tailed Deer
Odocoileus virginianus

Given the current status of the White-tailed Deer in Alberta, it is hard to imagine that prior to the arrival of Europeans, these graceful animals were only found in the Cypress Hills and in isolated pockets in the foothills. With the spread of agricultural development and forest fragmentation, however, the White-tailed Deer has become much more widespread.

The White-tailed Deer is a master at avoiding detection, and it can be frustratingly difficult to observe. It is very secretive during daylight hours, when it tends to remain concealed in thick shrubs or forest patches. Once the sun begins to set, however, the White-tailed Deer leaves its daytime resting spot to move to a foraging site. Driving through rural Alberta would simply not be as exciting without seeing a small group of White-tailed Deer mingling together to feed in agricultural fields at dusk. Within the parks and other protected areas of Alberta, the White-tailed Deer only occasionally becomes as habituated to people as the Mule Deer.

For such a large animal, the White-tailed Deer moves gracefully through dense shrubs and over fallen trees, weaving a path that is nearly impossible for a predator to follow. A White-tailed Deer in prime form seems to be uncatchable within the confines of its habitat, but the animal itself clearly does not share this view—its nose and ears continually twitch, aware that any shadow could conceal a predator.

These defences are effective against most of the White-tail's predators, but all deer are vulnerable to the Alberta

Total Length: 1.3–2.2 m (4¹/₂–7 ft)

Shoulder Height: 68–114 cm (27–45 in)

Tail Length: 21–36 cm (8¹/₄–14 in)

Weight: 50–200 kg (110–440 lb)

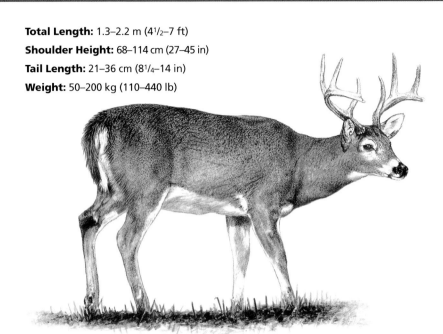

winter. Deep snows and a scarcity of high-energy foods leaves the deer with a negative energy budget from the time of the first deep snowfalls until green vegetation re-emerges in spring. In spite of their slowed metabolic rates during winter, many deer starve before spring arrives; in doing so, they cushion the remainder of the winter for scavengers.

DESCRIPTION: The upperparts are generally reddish brown in summer and greyish brown in winter. The belly, throat, chin and underside of the tail are white. There is also a narrow white ring around the eye and a band around the muzzle. The buck starts growing antlers in his second year. The antlers first appear as unbranched "spikehorns"; later, generally unbranched tines grow off the main beam. The main beams, when viewed from above, usually take the shape of a Valentine heart, with their origin a short distance above the notch of the heart and the terminal tines ending just before the apex. The metatarsal

DID YOU KNOW?

The White-tailed Deer is named for the bright white undersides of its tail. A deer raises, or "flags," its tail when it is alarmed. The white flash of the tail communicates "danger" to nearby deer and provides a guiding signal for following individuals.

BEST SITES: Agricultural lands within the aspen parkland; Elk Island NP; Edmonton river valley; Lakeland area; Police Point Park, Medicine Hat.

RANGE: From the southern third of Canada the White-tailed Deer ranges south into the northern quarter of South America. It is largely absent from Nevada, Utah and California. It has been introduced to New Zealand, Finland, Prince Edward Island and Anticosti Island.

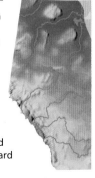

gland on the outside of the lower hind-leg is about 2.5 cm (1 in) long.

HABITAT: The optimum habitat is rolling country with a mixture of open areas near cover. This deer frequents riparian forests, woodlands and abandoned farmsteads with tangled shelter-belts. Areas cleared for roads, parking lots, summer homes, logging and mines support much of the vegetation on which the White-tailed Deer thrives.

FOOD: During winter, the leaves and twigs of evergreens, deciduous trees and brush make up most of the diet. In early spring and summer, the diet shifts to forbs, grasses and even mushrooms. On average, a White-tailed Deer eats 2–5 kg (4½–11 lb) of food a day.

DEN: A deer's bed is simply a shallow, oval, body-sized depression in leaves or snow. Favoured bedding areas, often in secluded spots where a deer can remain safe while it is inactive, will have an accumulation of new and old beds.

YOUNG: A doe gives birth to one to three fawns in late May or June, after a gestation of 6½ to 7 months. At birth, a fawn weighs about 3 kg (6½ lb), and its coat is tan with white spots. The fawn can stand and suckle shortly after birth, but it spends most of the first month lying quietly under the cover of vegetation. It is weaned at about four months old. A few well-nourished females may mate as fall fawns, but most wait until their second year.

gallop group

SIMILAR SPECIES: The Mule Deer (p. 46) looks very similar, but it has a whitish rump patch and much longer ears, and a buck's antlers usually have forked tines. The Pronghorn (p. 38) has black horns, a large white rump patch and white throat bands, and the lower half of its sides are white.

Mule Deer

Moose
Alces alces

The monarch of Alberta's north, the Moose is supremely adapted to its environment. People who know it only from TV cartoons may not have such feelings for the Moose, but those who have followed its trails through waist-deep snow and mosquito-choked bogs respect its abilities. The great Alberta mammologist, J. Dewey Soper, a man of the woods and admirer of Moose, wrote: "The peculiar, hoarse bellowing of the bull moose in the mating season is a memorable, far-reaching sound fraught with tingling qualities of the primordial. While deep-throated and raucous to the human ear, it doubtless broadcasts haunting and seductive overtones to the patiently waiting [cow moose] in the woods."

The Moose's long legs, short neck, humped shoulders and big, bulbous nose may lend it an awkward appearance, but they all serve the Moose well in its natural habitat. With its long legs, the Moose can easily step over downed logs and forest debris and cross streams. Metre-deep snow, which seriously impedes the progress of wolves, is no obstacle for the Moose, which lifts its legs straight up and down to create very little snowdrag. The short neck holds the head, with its huge battery of upper and lower cheek teeth, in a perfect position for the Moose to nip off the twigs that make up most of its winter diet. The big bulbous nose and lips hold the twigs in place so they can be ripped off by the lower incisors.

Winter ticks are often a problem for the Moose. A single badly infected Moose can carry more than 200,000 ticks, and their irritation causes the Moose to rub against trees for relief. With excessive rubbing, a Moose will lose much of its guard hair, resulting in a pale grey or "ghost" Moose, which is sometimes seen in late winter. Winter Moose deaths are usually the result of blood loss to the ticks, rather than starvation—the twigs, buds and bark of deciduous trees and shrubs that form the bulk of its winter diet, although low in energy, are rarely in short supply. The Moose's common name can also be traced to this feeding habit: the Algonquin called it *moz*, which means "twig eater." The summer diet of aquatic vegetation and other greenery seems quite palatable and varied, but even then more than half the intake is wood.

DID YOU KNOW?

The Moose is an impressive athlete: individuals have been known to run as fast as 55 km/h (34 mph), swim continuously for several hours, dive to depths of 6 m (20 ft) and remain submerged for up to a minute.

BEST SITES: Elk Island NP; Kananaskis Country; any backroad in the boreal forest.

RANGE: This holarctic species ranges through most of Canada and Alaska. It has southward extensions through the Rocky Mountains, into New England and the northern Appalachians and into the northern Midwest states. Its range is expanding into the farmlands of the Dakotas, Alberta and Saskatchewan, from which it has been absent for decades.

Total Length: 2.1–2.8 m (7–9 ft)
Shoulder Height: 1.9–2.2 m (6–7 ft)
Tail Length: 10–19 cm (4–7½ in)
Weight: 227–535 kg (500–1180 lb)

DESCRIPTION: The Moose is the largest living deer in the world. The dark, rich brown to black upperparts fade to lighter, often greyish tones on the lower legs. The head is long and almost horse-like. It has a humped nose, and the upper lip markedly overhangs the lower lip. In winter, a mane of hair as long as 16 cm (6¼ in) develops along the spine over the humped shoulders and along the nape of the neck. In summer, the mane is much shorter. There is usually a large dewlap, or "bell," from the throat. The cow has a distinct light patch around the vulva. The calf is brownish to greyish red during its first summer. Only the bull has antlers. Unlike the antlers of other deer, the Moose's antlers emerge laterally, and many of the tines are merged through much of their length, giving the antler a shovel-like appearance. Elk-like antlers are common in young bulls (and they are the only type seen in Eurasian specimens today).

HABITAT: Typically associated with the northern coniferous forest, the Moose is most numerous in the early successional stages of willows, balsam poplars and aspens. In less-forested foothills and lowlands, it frequents streamside or brushy areas with abundant deciduous woody plants. In summer, it may range well up into the subalpine or tundra areas of the mountains. Today, it is re-invading riverine environments far out into the prairies, and it is now not unusual to see the Moose along the lower Red Deer River and its tributaries.

FOOD: About 80 percent of the Moose's diet is wood, mostly twigs and branches. In summer, it also feeds on submerged vegetation, sometimes sinking completely below the surface of a lake to acquire the succulent aquatics, but they never make up a large part of the diet. It prefers deciduous trees and shrubs over conifers.

DEN: The Moose makes daytime beds in sheltered areas, much like other cervids, leaving areas of flattened grass from its weight. Other signs around the bed include tracks, droppings and browsed vegetation.

YOUNG: In May or June, after a gestation of about eight months, a cow bears one to three (usually two) unspotted calves, each weighing 10–16 kg (22–35 lb). The calves begin to follow their mother on her daily routine at about two weeks old. A few cows breed in their second year, but most wait until their third year.

trotting trail

SIMILAR SPECIES: With its large size and long head, the Moose resembles a bay or black horse more than any native mammal. The Elk (p. 42) and the Caribou (p. 58) are both lighter in colour, and the males do not have the lateral, palmate antlers of the bull Moose.

Elk

Caribou
Rangifer tarandus

The Caribou carves out a living in the deep snows and black fly fens where most other species of deer do not venture. The Caribou is a northern specialist, and it appears to do best in areas of expansive wilderness that allow it to undergo seasonal migrations between its summer and winter feeding grounds. Lichens, the Caribou's favourite winter food, grow very slowly and are frequently restricted to older spruce and fir forests, but a herd's movements typically prevent it from overgrazing one particular area. The Caribou's broad hooves are a great help in securing a tasty meal, whether an animal has to dig through the snowpack to expose ground-dwelling cladonia lichens or walk high upon snow to reach the old man's beard hanging from the spruce trees.

Unlike all other North American cervids, both sexes of the Caribou grow antlers. A mature bull sheds his large sweeping rack in December, a younger bull retains his antlers until February, and a cow keeps hers until April—within a month she is growing a new set.

Antlers are but one of many characteristics that make this graceful wildland trotter distinctive and special. The delicate Alberta population of the Caribou is of continuous concern to resource managers, biologists and naturalists. There are few places in Alberta where you can be assured of seeing this threatened animal, but the Grande Cache region is probably your best bet for Caribou viewing. There, the Caribou spends its summers at high elevations, avoiding the heat and the flies, and, in spring and fall, several hundred animals migrate

Total Length: 1.7–2.5 m (5½–8 ft)
Shoulder Height: 0.7–1.4 m (2½–4½ ft)
Tail Length: 13–23 cm (5–9 in)
Weight: 90–250 kg (200–550 lb)

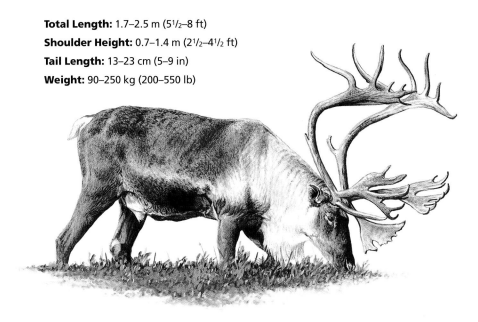

between the mountains and the foothills forests.

That population's seasonal migrations are more pronounced than the movements of the Caribou in Alberta's northern boreal forest, but it does nothing to approach the incredible movements of the Arctic's Caribou, which occasionally move into the northeastern-most corner of Alberta during the depths of winter.

There was a time when Alberta's Caribou were separated into three groups—the Mountain Caribou, the Woodland Caribou and the Barren Ground Caribou—but now all the North American Caribou and the Reindeer of Eurasia are generally considered to be one species.

DESCRIPTION: In summer, the coat is brown or greyish brown above and lighter below, with white along the lower side of the tail and the hoof edges. The winter coat is much lighter, with dark brown or greyish-brown areas on the upper part of the head, the back and

DID YOU KNOW?

The word "caribou" comes from eastern Canada, from the Micmac name halibu, *which means "pawer" or "scratcher." It is a reference to this animal's foraging strategy in deep snows.*

BEST SITES: Hwy 40 between William Switzer PP and Grande Cache; Beauty Creek and Tonquin Valley, Jasper NP; Caribou Mountains.

RANGE: Another holarctic animal, in North America the Caribou occurs across most of Alaska and northern Canada, from the Arctic Islands south into the boreal forest, with a southward extension through the Canadian Rockies.

the front of the limbs. Both the bull and the cow have antlers, but the bull's are much larger. Two tines come off the front of each main antler beam; one lower "brow" tine is palmate near the tip and is used to push snow to the side as the Caribou feeds. All the other tines come off the back of the main beam, which is a condition unique to the Caribou.

HABITAT: Most of Alberta's Caribou remain in forests of spruce, fir, pine and aspen for much of the year, but mountain populations move into alpine meadows and the adjacent subalpine forests in summer.

FOOD: Grasses, sedges, mosses, forbs, mushrooms and terrestrial and arboreal lichens make up the summer diet. In winter, the Caribou eats the buds, leaves and bark of both deciduous and evergreen shrubs, together with primarily arboreal lichens. This restless feeder takes only a few mouthfuls before walking ahead, pausing for a few more bites and then walking on again.

DEN: Like other cervids, the Caribou's bed is a simple, shallow, body-sized depression, often in a snowbank in summer.

YOUNG: Calving occurs in late May or June after a gestation of about 7½ months. The unspotted calf, usually born singly (rarely as twins), weighs about 5 kg (11 lb) at birth. It often follows its mother within hours of birth, and it begins grazing when it's two weeks old. A calf may be weaned after a month, but some continue to nurse into winter. A cow usually first mates when she is 1½ years old; most males do not get a chance to mate until they are at least three to four years old.

hoofprint

SIMILAR SPECIES: The heavy body and rectangular head of the Caribou serve to distinguish it from other species of deer, which have more triangular-shaped heads and less massive bodies. Both males and females bear antlers, and even calves may have spikes, which is a feature that distinguishes them from other female or young deer. Of all the deer, only the feet of the Caribou produce clicking sounds when the animal is moving.

White-tailed Deer

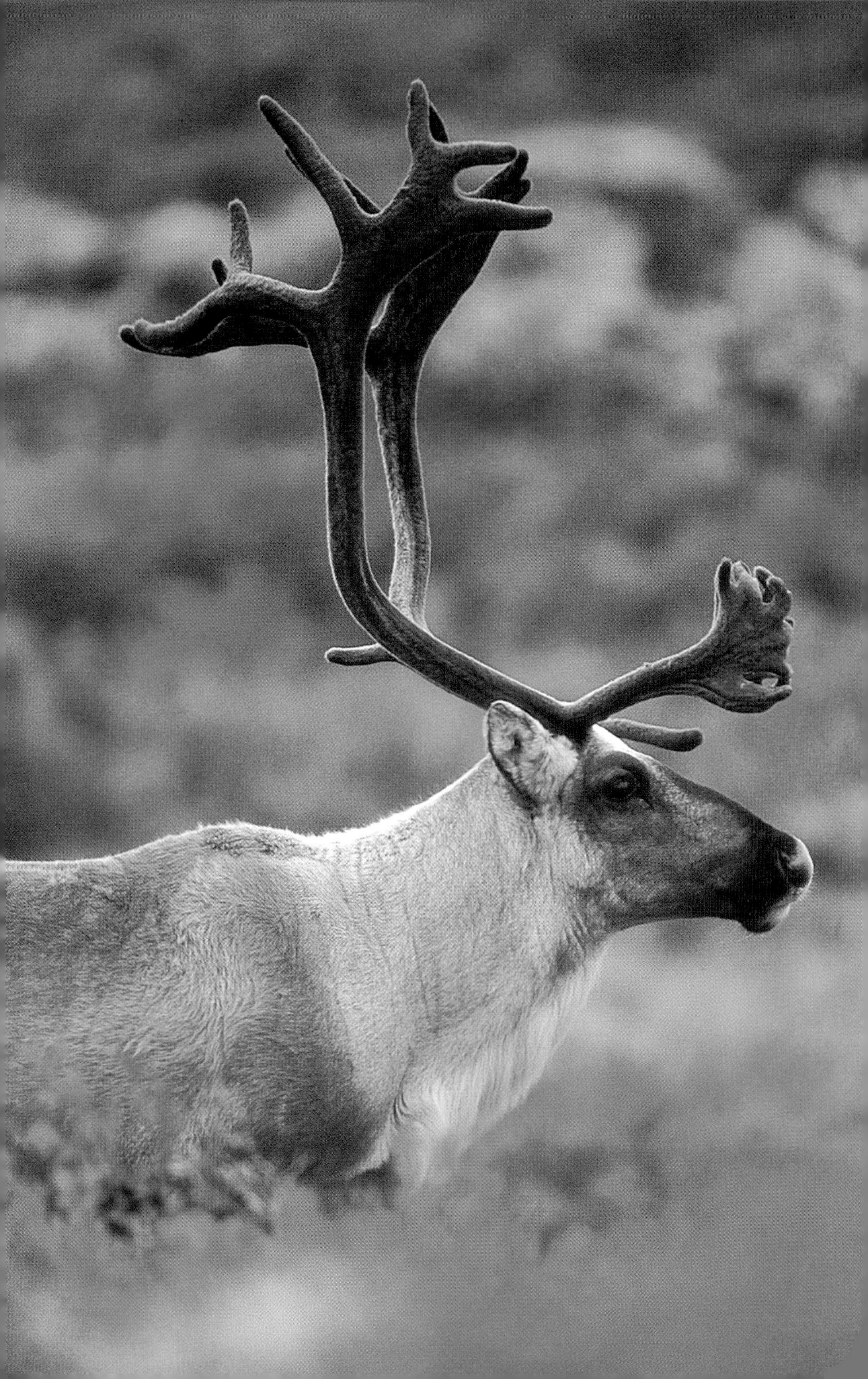

CARNIVORES

T he name of this group of animals, which means "meat-eating," is appropriate, because while some of its members are actually omnivorous (and eat a great deal of plant material), most of them prey on other vertebrates. Alberta's carnivores vary greatly in size, however, from the tiny Least Weasel to the Grizzly Bear.

Cat Family (Felidae)

Solitary hunters, all our cats have long, curved, sharp, retractile claws. Like dogs, cats walk on their toes—they have five toes on each forefoot and four toes on each hindfoot—and their feet have naked pads and furry soles. As anyone who has a house cat knows, the top of a cat's tongue is rough with spiny, hard, backward-pointing papillae, which the cat uses in grooming its fur. Together with weasels, cats are among the most carnivorous mammals, and they are usually at the top of the food chain.

Mountain Lion

Skunk Family (Mephitidae)

Biologists previously placed skunks in the weasel family, but recent investigations, including examinations of genetic sequences, have led taxonomists to group the North American skunks (and the stink badgers of Asia) in their own family. Unlike most weasels, skunks are usually boldly marked, and when threatened they can spray a foul-smelling musk from their anal glands.

Striped Skunk

Weasel Family (Mustelidae)

All weasels are committed predators with short legs and elongated bodies. They have anal scent glands that produce an unpleasant-smelling musk, but, unlike skunks, they use it to mark territories rather than in defence. Most species have been trapped by humans for their valuable, long-wearing fur.

Fisher

Raccoon Family (Procyonidae)

Raccoons are small to mid-sized carnivores that, like bears (and humans), walk on their heels. They are good climbers. Their teeth are adapted to eating vegetation as well as meat. They are best known for their face masks and long bushy tails, which have dark and light banding.

Common Raccoon

Bear Family (Ursidae)

The three North American members of this family (two of which occur in Alberta) are the world's largest terrestrial carnivores. All bears are plantigrade—they walk on their heels—and they have powerfully built forelegs and a short tail. Although most bears sleep through the harshest part of winter, they do not truly hibernate—their sleep is not deep and their body temperature only drops a couple of degrees.

Grizzly Bear

Dog Family (Canidae)

This family of dogs, wolves, coyotes and foxes is one of the most widespread terrestrial, non-flying mammalian families. The snout, which is typically long, is made up of a complex series of bones housing the sense of smell, which plays a major role in finding prey and in intraspecific communications. Members of this family walk on their toes, and their claws are blunt and non-retractile.

Coyote

Mountain Lion
Cougar
Puma concolor

A pug-mark in the snow or a heavily clawed tree trunk are two powerful reminders that some places in Alberta are still wild enough for the Mountain Lion. Alberta's largest cat was once found throughout the province, but conflicts with settlers and their stock animals have fated it to a shrunken range. With less than 700 breeding adults in all of Alberta, and less than 100 of those in national parks, the provincial status of this North American "lion" is stable, but far from its historic highs.

The Mountain Lion is generally a solitary hunter—except when a mother is accompanied by her young—that waits in ambush in a tree or on a ledge until prey approaches. By leaping onto the shoulders of its prey, biting deeply into the back of the neck while attempting to knock the prey off balance, the Mountain Lion can subdue an animal as large as an adult Elk. A Mountain Lion needs the equivalent of about one deer a week to survive, and Mountain Lion densities in Alberta seem to correlate to deer numbers.

The Sheep River area on the eastern edge of Kananaskis Country has some of the most productive Mountain Lion habitat remaining in the province, but the expansion of the human population southwest of Calgary towards Bragg Creek and Turner Valley has influenced that population. Mountain Lions are occasionally seen near human settlements, particularly in late winter when a lack of food in the high country drives them to lower elevations. In these situations, they occasionally prey on house pets—to a Mountain Lion, dogs and cats are easily managed, dim-witted versions of their wild relatives. When humans hunt these "problem" Mountain Lions,

Total Length: 1.5–2.7 m (5–9 ft)
Shoulder Height: 66–81 cm (26–32 in)
Tail Length: 50–90 cm (20–35 in)
Weight: 41–73 kg (90–161 lb)

they typically tree the cats with hounds and then shoot them from this lofty retreat with relative ease.

DESCRIPTION: This extremely large cat has dull, dirty white underparts and buffy-grey to tawny or cinnamon upperparts. The chest, throat, tip of the muzzle and backs of the ears are black. The tail is more than half the length of the head and body.

HABITAT: Remote, wooded, rocky places, usually with a plentiful supply of deer, are where the Mountain Lion is most frequently found. In Alberta, such places are most abundant in the foothills.

DID YOU KNOW?

During an extremely cold winter, a Mountain Lion can starve if the carcasses of its prey freeze solid before it can get more than one meal. This cat's jaws are designed for slicing, and it has trouble chewing frozen meat.

BEST SITES: Sheep River Sanctuary, Kananaskis Country; Waterton Lakes NP; Castle Wilderness; Sundre to Nordegg; Grande Cache area.

RANGE: This cat formerly ranged from northern British Columbia to the Maritimes and south to Patagonia, but in North America it has been extirpated from most areas except the western mountains. A tiny population remains in the Everglades, and there are occasional reports from the Northeast.

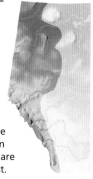

FOOD: The Mountain Lion primarily eats deer, but it sometimes preys on Bighorn Sheep, Mountain Goats, Elk, Moose, American Beavers and Common Porcupines. In rare instances, it might eat mice, rabbits, birds, domestic dogs and even other cats.

DEN: A cave or crevice between rocks usually serves as a den, but this cat may den under an overhanging bank, beneath the roots of a windthrown tree or in a hollow tree.

YOUNG: A female Mountain Lion may give birth to a litter of one to six (usually two or three) kittens at any time of the year after a gestation of just over three months. The tan, black-spotted kittens are blind and helpless at birth, but their eyes open at two weeks. They are weaned at about six weeks, when they weigh about 3 kg (6½ lb). A young Mountain Lion may stay with its mother for up to two years.

foreprint

walking trail

SIMILAR SPECIES: Alberta's two other native cats, the Canada Lynx (p. 68) and the Bobcat (p. 72), are smaller (the Bobcat very much so) and have mottled coats and bobbed tails.

Canada Lynx

Canada Lynx
Lynx canadensis

Meat is on the nightly menu for the Canada Lynx, and the meal of choice is the Snowshoe Hare. The classic predator-prey relationship of these two species is now well known to all students of zoology, but what generally is not known is that this association was first studied in Alberta. Periodic fluctuations in the numbers of Canada Lynx had been observed previously, but it took a study near Athabasca to corroborate that the cycles were primarily due to the rise and fall of Snowshoe Hare populations. When hares are abundant, lynx kittens are more likely to survive to reproduce; when hares are scarce, many kittens starve and the lynx population declines, sometimes rapidly and usually one to two years after the decline in hares.

The Canada Lynx is primarily a solitary hunter of remote forests. During peaks in its population, however, young cats may disperse into less hospitable environs. In recent memory, the Canada Lynx has been reported within the city limits of both Edmonton and Calgary. These incidents are unusual, however, and the Canada Lynx typically refrains from contact with humans. With each rare observation of a wild lynx, there undoubtedly comes surprise to people who are well accustomed to the appearance of a house cat—the stilt-legged lynx is more than twice the size and gangly in appearance.

This resolute carnivore copes well with the difficult conditions of its north-woods home; its well-furred feet allow it almost silent progress and serve as snowshoes in deep winter snows. The

Total Length: 78–101 cm (31–40 in)
Shoulder Height: 46–58 cm (18–23 in)
Tail Length: 9–12 cm (3½–4¾ in)
Weight: 6.8–18 kg (15–40 lb)

Canada Lynx is not an all-out speed-ster—it generally ambushes or silently stalks its prey—but the ultimate capture of an animal relies on a sudden over-whelming rush. With its long legs, it can travel rapidly when trailing evasive prey in the tight confines of a deep forest. It can also climb trees quickly to escape enemies or to find an ambush site.

DESCRIPTION: This medium-sized, short-tailed, long-legged cat has huge feet and protruding ears tipped with 5-cm (2-in) black hairs. The long, lax, silvery-grey to buffy fur bears darker suggestions of stripes on the sides and chest and dark spots on the belly and insides of the forelegs. There are black stripes on the forehead and the long facial ruff. The

DID YOU KNOW?

Some taxonomists consider the Canada Lynx to be the same species as the European Lynx, which occupies the northern for-ests of Europe and Asia.

BEST SITES: Wood Buffalo NP; Fort McMurray; Lesser Slave Lake PP; Jasper NP; Banff NP.

RANGE: Primarily an inhabitant of the boreal forest, the Canada Lynx occurs across much of Canada and Alaska and south into the western mountains and the northern parts of Wisconsin, Michigan, New York and New England.

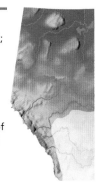

entire tip of the stubby tail is black. The long buffy fur of the hindlegs makes it look like the cat is wearing baggy trousers.

HABITAT: The Canada Lynx is closely tied to the northern coniferous forests. Numerous fallen trees and occasional dense thickets are desired habitat components. It is rarely found in streamside forests and brushy badlands on the prairies.

FOOD: The Snowshoe Hare typically makes up the bulk of the diet, but the Canada Lynx will also sustain itself on squirrels, grouse, other rodents or even domestic animals. In northern Alberta, the Red Squirrel is often the main prey species.

DEN: The den is typically an unimproved space beneath a fallen log, among rocks or even in a cave.

YOUNG: Lynx breed in March or April, and the female gives birth to one to five (usually two or three) kittens in May or June. The kittens are grey with indistinct longitudinal stripes and dark grey barring on the limbs. Their eyes open in about 12 days, and they are weaned at

two months. They stay with their mother through the first winter and acquire their adult coats at 8 to 10 months. A female usually bears her first litter near her first birthday.

walking trail

SIMILAR SPECIES: The only other native cat that resembles the Canada Lynx is the smaller, shorter-legged Bobcat (p. 72). The Bobcat also has shorter ear tufts, and the tip of its tail is black above and white below.

Bobcat

Bobcat
Lynx rufus

While wild canids, most notably the Coyote and the Red Fox, are frequent sights in parts of rural Alberta, many years can pass without even a sign of a native Alberta cat. Among this select group of three species, the Bobcat is likely the least numerous, but in comparison to the Canada Lynx and the Mountain Lion, the chances of seeing one may be just as (un)reasonable.

Bobcats have a fondness for sandstone ledges, brushy valley bottoms and thickets that afford cover for their ambush style of hunting. Most of their hunting takes place between sundown and sunrise, and Bobcats remain immobile in any handy shelter during the day—most sightings are from chance encounters or along headlight-illuminated roads. Night drives along the rims of Alberta's southern river valleys offer the best opportunity for seeing a Bobcat, although, at best, the experience is a mere glimpse of a cat bobbing along in the lights, hopefully leaving the momentary experience forever retained within the viewer's mind.

Bobcat tracks in soft ground may be the easiest way to determine the presence of this small cat in areas of the province. Unlike Coyote and Red Fox prints, Bobcat prints rarely show any claw marks, and there is one cleft on the front part of the main foot pad and two on the rear. A Bobcat print is quite like a large version of domestic cat track (except that it tends to be found far from human structures). Like all cats, Bobcats bury their scat, and these scratches and scrapings can help confirm their presence.

DESCRIPTION: The coat is generally tawny or yellowish brown. The sides are spotted with dark brown and there are

Total Length: 75–125 cm (30–49 in)
Shoulder Height: 43–50 cm (17–20 in)
Tail Length: 13–17 cm (5–6¾ in)
Weight: 4.1–18 kg (9–40 lb)

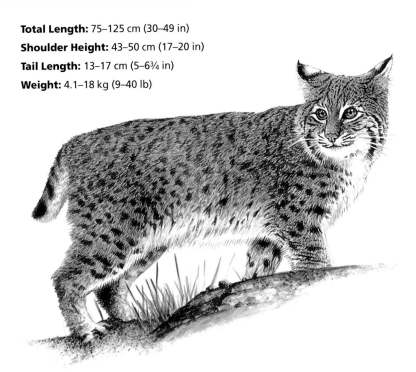

dark horizontal stripes on the breast and the outsides of the limbs. There are two black bars across each cheek and a brown forehead stripe. The ear tufts are less than 2.5 cm (1 in) long. The chin and throat are whitish. The tip of the short tail is black above and light below.

HABITAT: The Bobcat occupies coniferous and deciduous forests and brushy areas in southern coulees. Where the Canada Lynx is absent, it may range well up into mountain forests.

FOOD: The preferred food seems to be Mountain Cottontail, but the Bobcat will catch and eat squirrels, rats, mice, voles, beavers, skunks and ground-nesting birds. It even captures and kills deer and Pronghorns on occasion.

DID YOU KNOW?

Most cats have long tails, which they lash out to the side to help corner more rapidly in pursuit of prey. The Bobcat and the Canada Lynx, however, which typically hunt in brushy areas, have short, or "bobbed," tails that won't get caught in branches.

BEST SITES: Milk River valley; lower Red Deer River valley east of Dinosaur PP; foothills forests in Kananaskis Country.

RANGE: The Bobcat occurs across southern Canada and south to southern Mexico.

DEN: During the day, Bobcats use any available shelter—they do not keep a permanent den. Female Bobcats prefer rocky crevices for the natal den, but they may use hollow logs. They do not attempt to provide a lining for the kittens.

YOUNG: Bobcats typically breed in February or March and give birth to one to seven (usually three) hairy, grey kittens in April or May. The kittens' eyes open after nine days. They are weaned at two months, but they remain with the mother for three to five months. Female Bobcats become sexually mature at one year old; males at two.

foreprint

transition from trotting
to loping trail

SIMILAR SPECIES: The Canada Lynx (p. 68) is the only other native, bob-tailed cat in North America, and it is larger and taller and has much longer ear tufts. Also, if you get a good enough look, the tip of its tail is entirely black.

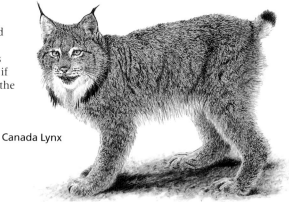

Canada Lynx

Striped Skunk
Mephitis mephitis

The famed warning colours of skunks are so effective that they communicate their message to people who know little or nothing else about wildlife. This recognition is enhanced by the tendency of skunks to be involved in collisions on Alberta highways—slow-moving skunks, led by their noses, find foraging in roadside ditches dangerously tempting.

Butylmercaptan is the reason behind all the stink. Seven different sulphide-containing "active ingredients" have been identified in the musk, which not only smells, but irritates. A distressed skunk twists its body into a "U" prior to spraying, so that both its head and tail face the threat. If a skunk successfully targets the eyes, there is intense burning, copious tearing and sometimes a short period of blindness. The musk is also known to stimulate nausea in humans.

Despite all these good reasons to avoid close contact with the Striped Skunk, it is surprisingly tolerant of observation from a discreet distance, and watching a skunk can be very rewarding—it goes against the hyperactive norm of its weasel cousins. The Striped Skunk's activity begins at sundown, when it emerges from its daytime hiding-place. It usually forages among shrubs, but it often enters open areas where it can be spotted with relative ease. The Striped Skunk is a clumsy predator that frequently digs shallow pits in search of food. During winter its activity is much reduced, and skunks spend the coldest periods in communal dens.

The only regular predator of the Striped Skunk is the Great Horned Owl. Lacking a highly developed sense of smell, this owl does not seem to mind the skunk's odour—nor do other birds that commonly scavenge roadkills.

DESCRIPTION: This cat-sized, black-and-white skunk is familiar to most people. Its basic colour is glossy black. A narrow white stripe extends up the snout to above the eyes, and two white stripes begin at the nape of the neck, run back on either side of the midline and meet again at the base of the tail. The tail often has a continuation of the white bands ending in a white tip, but there is much variation in the amount and distribution of the white markings. The front claws are long and are used for digging; the rear claws are short. A

DID YOU KNOW?

Fully armed, the Striped Skunk's scent glands have about 30 ml (1 oz) of noxious, smelly stink. The spray has a maximum range of almost 6 m (20 ft), and the skunk is relatively accurate for half that distance.

BEST SITES: Agricultural areas in the aspen parkland; Writing-on-Stone PP; Calgary, Lethbridge and Medicine Hat river valley parks.

RANGE: The Striped Skunk is found across most of North America, from Nova Scotia to Florida in the East and from the southwestern Northwest Territories to northern Baja California in the West. It is absent from parts of the deserts of southern Nevada and Utah and eastern California.

Total Length: 54–79 cm (21–31 in)
Tail Length: 15–24 cm (6–9½ in)
Weight: 1.9–4.2 kg (4¼–9¼ lb)

pair of perineal musk glands on either side of the anus discharge the foul-smelling, yellowish liquid for which skunks are famous.

HABITAT: In the wild, the Striped Skunk seems to prefer streamside woodlands, groves of hardwood trees, semi-open areas, brushy grasslands and valleys. It also regularly occurs in cultivated areas, around farmsteads and even in the hearts of cities, where it eats garbage and raids gardens.

FOOD: All skunks are omnivorous. Insects, including bees, grasshoppers, June bugs and various larvae, make up the largest portion, about 40 percent, of the spring and summer diet. To get at bees, skunks will scratch at a hive entrance until the bees emerge, and then chew up and spit out great gobs of mashed bees, thus incurring the bee-keeper's wrath. The rest of the diet is composed of fruits and berries, small mammals, bird eggs and nestlings, amphibians, reptiles, grains and green vegetation. Along roads, carrion is often an important component of a skunk's diet. By fall, small mammals,

fruits and berries become more important in the diet.

DEN: In most instances, the Striped Skunk builds a bulky nest of dried leaves and grasses in an underground burrow or beneath a building.

YOUNG: A female skunk gives birth to 2 to 10 (usually 5 or 6) blind, helpless young in April or May, after a gestation of just over two months. The typical black-and-white pattern of a skunk is present on the skin at birth. The eyes and ears open at three to four weeks. At five to six weeks, the musk glands are functional. Weaning follows at six to seven weeks. The mother and her young will forage together into the fall, and they often share a wintertime den.

SIMILAR SPECIES: Being the only skunk in Alberta, the Striped Skunk's striking black-and-white coat makes it hard to confuse it with any other species. The American Badger (p. 98) has the white stripe running up its snout, but it is larger and squatter and has a grizzled, yellowish-grey body.

American Marten
Martes americana

Ferocity and playfulness are perfectly blended in the form of the American Marten. This quick, active, agile weasel is equally at home on the forest floor or along branches and tree trunks. The fluidity of its motions and its attractive appearance are not the least bit marred by its carnivorous and often vicious hunting tactics. A predator to the core, the American Marten sniffs out voles, steals birds' eggs and young and becomes involved in acrobatic pursuits of Red Squirrels.

This animal's insatiable curiosity is not easily observed, however, because it tends to occur in the wilder areas of the province. The American Marten has been known to occupy human structures for short periods of time, should a food source be near, but more typical marten sightings are restricted to flashes across roadways or trails. The pursuit of an animal rarely leads to satisfying encounters; this weasel's mastery of forests is ably demonstrated in its ability to hide.

Outside Alberta's deep spruce forests, the American Marten, which is closely related to the Eurasian Sable, is most widely known for its soft, lustrous fur—it is still targeted along traplines in remote parts of the province. As with so many species of boreal mammals, marked fluctuations seem to occur every few years, and the experiences of trappers reinforce the notion that populations of the American Marten tend to be cyclical. Scientists generally attribute these cycles to changes in prey abundance; northern trappers often suggest that marten populations migrate from one area to another. Whatever the case, the provincial status of this animal currently appears to be stable, which is a good sign—because of its dependence upon mature coniferous forests, the American Marten is an indicator of environmental conditions. The effects of long-term logging in coniferous forests remain unknown, but it is to be hoped that modern methods of forest management will maintain marten populations and not result in the widespread extirpation that occurred elsewhere.

DESCRIPTION: This slender-bodied, fox-faced weasel has a beautiful, pale yellow to dark brown coat and a long, bushy tail. The feet are well furred and equipped with strong, non-retractable claws. The prominent ears are 3.5–4.5 cm

---

DID YOU KNOW?

Although the American Marten, like most weasels, is very carnivorous, it has been known to consume an entire apple pie left cooling outside a window.

BEST SITES: Cave and Basin Hot Springs and Lake Edith Tea House, Banff NP; Malign road, Jasper NP; Fort McMurray area.

RANGE: The range of the American Marten coincides almost exactly with the distribution of boreal and montane coniferous forests across North America. It is re-establishing where mature forests have returned to areas that were formerly cut or burned.

Total Length: 49–65 cm (19–26 in)
Tail Length: 14–20 cm (5½–7¾ in)
Weight: 0.6–1.3 kg (1¼–2¾ lb)

(1⅛–1¾ in) long. The eyes are dark and beady. The breast spot, when present, is usually orange but sometimes whitish or cream, and it varies in size from a small dot to a large patch that occupies the entire region from the chin to the belly. The male is about 15 percent larger than the female. There is a well-defined scent gland, about 7.5 cm (3 in) long and 2.5 cm (1 in) wide, on the centre of the abdomen.

HABITAT: Mature, particularly coniferous forests that contain numerous dead trunks, branches and leaves, which provide cover for its rodent prey, are the American Marten's preferred haunts. It does not tend to occupy recently burned or cut-over areas.

FOOD: Although voles make up most of the diet, the American Marten is an opportunistic feeder that will eat squirrels, Snowshoe Hares, birds' eggs and chicks, insects, carrion, pikas and occasionally berries and other vegetation. This active predator hunts both day and night.

DEN: The preferred denning site is a hollow tree or log that the female lines with dry grass and leaves.

YOUNG: Breeding occurs in July or August, but with delayed implantation of the embryo, the litter of one to six (usually three or four) young isn't born until March or April. The young are blind and almost naked at birth and weigh just 28 g (1 oz). The eyes open at six to seven weeks, at which time the young are weaned from a diet of milk to one of mostly meat. The mother must quickly teach her young to hunt, because when they are only about three months old she will re-enter estrus, and, with mating activity, the family group disbands. Young female martens have their first litter at about the time of their second or third birthdays.

SIMILAR SPECIES: The Fisher (p. 80) is twice as long, seldom has an orange chest patch, has a long black tail and often has frosted or grizzled-grey to black fur. The American Mink (p. 90) has the white chin and irregular white spots on the chest, but it has shorter ears, shorter legs (it does not climb trees well) and a much less bushy, cylindrical tail.

Fisher

Martes pennanti

For the lucky Alberta naturalist, meeting a wild Fisher is a once-in-a-lifetime opportunity. For the rest of us, we must content ourselves with the realization that this reclusive animal remains a top predator in the province's conifer wildlands. Historically, the Fisher was more numerous—over-trapping and the alteration of its habitat through forestry and exploration operations resulted in its decline or extirpation over much of its range. The Alberta population has not been large enough to make it an expected part of a trapper's harvest for many decades.

The Fisher is among the most formidable of predators in the province, and it could probably be considered the most athletic of Alberta's carnivores. According to Ernest Thompson Seton, a legendary naturalist of the 19th century, as fast as a squirrel can run through the treetops, a marten can catch it, and as fast as the marten can run, a Fisher can catch and kill it. Making full use of its athleticism during foraging, the Fisher incorporates all manner of ecological communities into its extensive home range, which can reach 120 km (75 mi) across. As a result of its wide-ranging ways, it is often absent from parts of its range for two to three weeks at a time. The Fisher is a good swimmer, but, despite its name, it rarely eats fish.

Few of the animals on which the Fisher preys can be considered easy picking; the most notable example is the Fisher's famed ability to hunt the Common Porcupine. What the porcupine lacks in mobility it more than makes up for in defensive armoury, and it requires all the Fisher's speed and strength to yield

Total Length: 79–102 cm (31–40 in)
Tail Length: 30–40 cm (12–16 in)
Weight: 1.3–5.9 kg (2¾–13 lb)

a successful hunt. The Fisher targets its attack on the porcupine's unquilled head. Much has been made of this hunting skill, but Fishers are by no means porcupine specialists; rather, they opportunistically hunt whatever trail they cross.

DESCRIPTION: The face is fox-like, with noticeable, protruding ears. The tail is dark and more than half as long as the body. The upperparts are typically frosted grey to black. The underparts, tail and legs are dark brown. There may be a white chest spot. The male has a longer, coarser coat than the female and is typically 20 percent larger.

HABITAT: The preferred habitat is the dense coniferous forests of the north and the Rocky Mountains. It is generally not found in young forests or where logging or fire has thinned the trees.

DID YOU KNOW?

The scientific name pennanti *honours Englishman Thomas Pennant. In the late 1700s he predicted the decline of the American Bison and postulated that Native Americans entered North America via a Bering land bridge.*

BEST SITES: Forested wilderness areas; Fort McMurray area.

RANGE: At one time the Fisher ranged throughout the northern boreal forest, the northeastern hardwood forests and the forests of the Rocky Mountains and the Pacific ranges. There has been a gradual recovery of some of its former range over the past two decades.

FOOD: Like other members of the weasel family, the Fisher is an opportunistic hunter, killing squirrels, Snowshoe Hares, mice, muskrats, grouse and other birds. More than any other carnivore, however, the Fisher hunts the Common Porcupine, which it kills by repeatedly attacking the head. It also eats berries and nuts, and carrion can be an important part of its diet.

left foreprint

DEN: Hollow trees and logs, rock crevices, brush piles and cavities beneath boulders all serve as den sites. Fishers may excavate winter dens in the snow.

YOUNG: A litter of one to four (usually two or three) young is born in March or April. The mother will breed again about a week after the litter is born, but implantation of the embryo is delayed until January. The helpless young nurse and remain in the den for at least seven weeks, after which time their eyes open. When they are three months old they begin to hunt with their mother, and by fall they are independent. The female is generally sexually mature when she is two years old.

running trail

SIMILAR SPECIES: The American Marten (p. 78) is generally smaller and lighter in colour, and it usually has a buff or orange chest spot. The American Mink (p. 90) is smaller and has shorter ears, shorter legs and a much less bushy, cylindrical tail.

American Marten

Short-tailed Weasel
Mustela erminea

Weasels have an image problem: they are often described as pointy-nosed villains and are frequently used to characterize dishonest cheats. These representations are unjust, because weasels are not manipulators but rather earnest little predators with a flair for killing.

The Short-tailed Weasel is Alberta's most common weasel and may be the most abundant land carnivore in the province, as well. Despite its abundance, the Short-tailed Weasel is not commonly seen, because, like all weasels, it tends to be active at night and inhabits areas with heavy cover.

As Short-tailed Weasels roam about their ranges, they explore every hole, burrow, hollow log or brush pile for potential prey. In winter, they travel both above and below the snow while searching for prey. Once it is located, the prey is typically overwhelmed with a rush; then the weasel wraps its body around the animal and drives its needle-sharp canines into the back of the skull or neck. If the weasel catches an animal larger than itself, it seizes the prey by the neck and strangles it.

The Short-tailed Weasel's dramatic change between its winter and summer coats led Europeans to give it two different names: an animal wearing the dark summer coat is called a "stoat"; in the white winter pelage it is known as an "ermine." In Alberta, three weasel species alternate between white in winter and brown in summer, so the common name "Short-tailed Weasel" has been widely accepted to prevent confusion.

DESCRIPTION: The short summer coat has brown upperparts and creamy white underparts, often suffused with lemon yellow. The last third of the tail is black. The short, oval ears extend noticeably above the elongated head. The eyes are black and beady. The long neck and narrow thorax make it appear as if the forelegs are positioned farther back than on most mammals and give the weasel a snake-like appearance. Starting in October and November, Alberta animals become completely white, except for the black tail tip. The lower belly and inner hindlegs often retain the lemon yellow wash. In late March or April, the weasel moults back to its summer coat.

DID YOU KNOW?

These weasels typically mate in late summer, but after little more than a week the embryos stop developing. In early spring, up to eight months later, the embryos implant in the uterus and the young are born about one month later.

BEST SITES: Elk Island NP; rockslides in mountain parks.

RANGE: In North America, this weasel occurs throughout most of Alaska and Canada and south to northern California and northern New Mexico in the West and northern Iowa and Pennsylvania in the East.

HABITAT: The Short-tailed Weasel is most abundant in coniferous or mixed forests and streamside woodlands. In summer it may often be found in the alpine tundra, where it hunts in rockslides and talus slopes.

FOOD: The diet appears to consist almost entirely of animals, including mice, voles, shrews, chipmunks, pocket gophers, pikas, rabbits, birds' eggs and nestlings, insects and even amphibians. These weasels are quick, lithe and unrelenting in their pursuit of anything they can overpower. They often eat every part of a mouse except the filled stomach, which may be excised with surgical precision and left on a rock.

DEN: Short-tailed Weasels commonly take over the burrows and nests of mice, ground squirrels, chipmunks, pocket gophers or lemmings and modify them for weasel occupancy. They line the nest with the pelts and feathers of prey, dried grasses and shredded leaves. Sometimes a weasel accumulates the pelts of so many small mammals that the nest grows to 20 cm (8 in) in diameter. Some nests are located in hollow logs, under buildings or in an abandoned cabin that once supported a sizeable mouse population.

YOUNG: In April or May, the female gives birth to 4 to 12 (usually 6 to 9) blind, helpless young that weigh just 2 g ($\frac{1}{16}$ oz) each. Their eyes open at five weeks, and soon thereafter they accompany the adults on hunts. At about this time, a male has typically joined the family; in addition to training the young to hunt, he

Total Length: 22–32 cm (8¾–13 in)

Tail Length: 4–9 cm (1⅝–3½ in)

Weight: 45–106 g (1⅝–3¾ oz)

impregnates the female and all the young females, which become sexually mature at two to three months. Young males do not mature until the next February or March; they take part in reproduction during their second summer.

SIMILAR SPECIES: The Least Weasel (p. 86) is generally smaller, and, although there may be a few black hairs at the end of the short tail, the entire tip is not black. The Long-tailed Weasel (p. 88) is generally larger and has orangish underparts, generally lighter upperparts and brown feet in summer.

summer
colours

Least Weasel
Mustela nivalis

If mice could talk, they would no doubt say that they live in constant fear of the Least Weasel. This pint-sized marauder is small enough to squeeze into the burrows of mice and voles, and vicious enough to kill an entire population within minutes. Prey that is not consumed immediately is stored to be eaten later.

This species is the smallest weasel (in fact, the smallest member of the carnivore order) in the world. On average, it consumes about 1 g ($\frac{1}{32}$ oz) of meat an hour, which means that it may eat almost its own weight in food in a day.

Least Weasels can be active at any time, but they concentrate most of their roamings at night. As a result, few people ever see these animals in action. Most human encounters with a Least Weasel result from lifting plywood, sheet metal or hay bales. These encounters are understandably brief—the weasel wastes little time in finding the nearest escape route, and any hole the diameter of a "loonie" or greater is fair to enter, much to the dismay of its current resident. Because the Least Weasel changes colour with the seasons, a snowless fall or an early melt in spring can help make a weasel stand out against its environs. In spite of even this visual disadvantage, Least Weasels possess an uncanny ability to find shelter where there seems to be none.

DESCRIPTION: In summer, this small weasel is walnut brown above and white below. The short tail may have few black hairs at the end, but never an entirely black tip. The ears are short, scarcely extending above the fur. In winter, the entire coat is white, including the furred soles of the feet. Only a few black hairs may remain at the tip of the tail.

HABITAT: The presence of abundant prey seems more important than a particular habitat type, and the Least Weasel occurs in shortgrass prairies, tundra, coniferous forests and marshes. It sometimes occupies abandoned buildings and rock piles.

FOOD: Voles, mice and insects are the usual prey, but amphibians, birds and eggs are opportunistically taken.

DEN: The burrow and nest of a vole that fell prey to the weasel is the usual den.

DID YOU KNOW?

Weasel signs are not uncommon if you know what to look for: the tracks typically follow a paired pattern; the droppings are about the size of your pinkie finger, are twisted and full of hair, and are often left atop a rock pile.

BEST SITES: Abandoned farmsteads in the aspen parkland.

RANGE: In North America, the Least Weasel's range extends from western Alaska southeast through most of Canada to Nebraska and east to Tennessee. It is largely absent from southern Ontario, New York, New England and the Maritimes.

Total Length: 15–22 cm (6–8¾ in)
Tail Length: 2.2–4.2 cm (⅞–1⅝ in)
Weight: 25–73 g (⅞–2⅝ oz)

summer
colours

The nest is usually lined with rodent fur and fine grass, which may become matted like felt and reach a thickness of 2.5 cm (1 in). In winter, frozen, stored mice may be dragged into the nest to thaw prior to consumption.

left foreprint

YOUNG: The Least Weasel does not exhibit delayed implantation of the embryos, and a female may give birth in any month of the year after a gestation of 35 days. A litter contains 1 to 10 (usually 4 or 5) wrinkled, pink, hairless young. At three weeks they begin to eat meat. After their eyes open at 26 to 30 days, their mother begins to take them hunting. They disperse at about seven weeks old, living solitary existences except for brief mating encounters.

SIMILAR SPECIES: The Short-tailed Weasel (p. 84) is generally larger, has a longer tail with an entirely black tip and usually has a lemon yellow wash on the belly. The Long-tailed Weasel (p. 88) is larger, has a much longer tail and has orangish underparts, generally lighter upperparts and brown feet in summer.

bounding trail

Long-tailed Weasel
Mustela frenata

There may be no more fun an animal to track on a sunny winter day than a Long-tailed Weasel. This curious animal zig-zags as though it can never make up its mind which way to go, and every little thing it crosses seems to offer a momentary distraction. The Long-tailed Weasel seems continually excited, and this bountiful emotion is easily read in its tracks as it leaps, bounds, walks and circles through its territory.

Long-tailed Weasels hunt wherever they can find prey: on and beneath the snow, along wetland edges, in burrows and even occasionally in trees. They can overpower smaller prey, such as mice, large insects and snakes, and kill them instantly. Larger prey species, up to the size of a rabbit, they grab by the throat and neck and wrestle to the ground. As the weasel wraps its snake-like body around its prey in an attempt to throw it off balance, it tries to kill the animal with bites to the back of the neck and head.

Unlike the Short-tailed Weasel and the Least Weasel, the Long-tailed Weasel only occurs in North America. With the conversion of native prairies to farmland, the Long-tailed Weasel has declined to a point where it is now regarded as a species of concern in Alberta. Still, in some native pastures that teem with ground squirrels, the Long-tailed Weasel can be found bounding about during the daytime, continually hunting throughout its waking hours.

DESCRIPTION: The summer coat is a rich cinnamon brown on the upperparts and usually orangish or buffy on the underparts. The feet are brown in summer. The tail is half as long as the body, and the terminal quarter is black. The winter coat is entirely white, except for the black tail tip and sometimes an orangish wash on the belly. As in all weasels, the body is long and slender—the forelegs appear to be positioned well back on the body—and the head is hardly wider than the neck.

HABITAT: The Long-tailed is a weasel of open country: it may be found in agricultural areas, on grassy slopes and in the alpine tundra. Sometimes, in places where the Short-tailed Weasel is rare or absent, it forages in aspen parklands, intermontane valleys and open forests.

DID YOU KNOW?

During the fall moult, the white fur first appears on the animal's belly and spreads towards the back. The reverse occurs in spring: the brown coat begins to form on the weasel's back and moves towards its belly.

BEST SITES: Elk Island NP; native pastures and grazing reserves around ground squirrel colonies.

RANGE: From a northern limit in central British Columbia and Alberta, the range extends south through most of the U.S. (except the southwestern deserts) and Mexico into northern South America.

Total Length: 34–49 cm (13–19 in)
Tail Length: 12–19 cm (4¾–7½ in)
Weight: 85–400 g (3–14 oz)

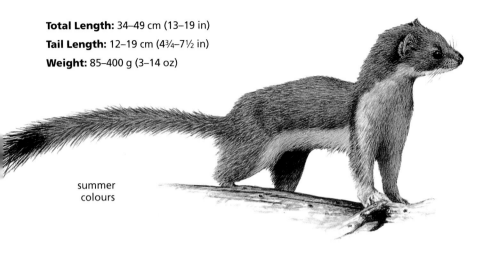

summer
colours

FOOD: Although the Long-tailed Weasel can successfully subdue larger prey than its smaller relatives, voles and mice still make up the majority of its diet. It also preys on ground squirrels, wood-rats, red squirrels, rabbits and shrews, and it takes the eggs and young of ground-nesting birds when it encounters them.

DEN: The female usually makes her nest in the burrow of a ground squirrel or mouse that she has eaten. She often lines the nest with the fur or feathers of prey.

YOUNG: Long-tailed Weasels typically mate in midsummer, but, through delayed implantation of the embryos, the young aren't born until April or May. The litter contains four to nine (usually six to eight) blind, helpless young. They are born with sparse white hair, which becomes a fuzzy coat by one week and a sleek coat in two weeks. At 3½ weeks the young begin to supplement their milk diet with meat; they are weaned when their eyes open, just after seven weeks. By six weeks, there is a pronounced difference in size, with young males weighing about 100 g (3½ oz) and

females 80 g (2⅞ oz). At this time a male weasel typically joins the group to breed with the mother and the young females as they become sexually mature. The group travels together and the male and female teach the young to hunt. The group disperses when the young are 2½ to 3 months old.

SIMILAR SPECIES: The Short-tailed Weasel (p. 84) is typically smaller, has a relatively shorter tail and has a lemon yellow (not orangish) belly and white feet in summer. The Least Weasel (p. 86) is much smaller and may have a few black hairs on the tip of its very short tail, but never an entirely black tip.

left foreprint

American Mink

Mustela vison

The liquid undulations of a loping mink's travels exceeds its much-prized fur in value to those people who appreciate nature and all its virtues. It is a smooth-travelling weasel that was described by famed Alberta naturalist Andy Russel as "moving ... like a brown silk ribbon." Indeed, the American Mink, like most Alberta weasels, seems to move with the luxuriant flexibility of a toy slinky in a child's hands.

Minks are tenacious hunters, following scent trails left by potential prey over all kinds of obstacles and terrain. Almost as aquatic as otters, these opportunistic feeders routinely dive for fish to depths of several metres. Their fishing activity tends to coincide with breeding aggregations of fish in spring and fall, and also during winter, when low oxygen levels force fish to congregate in oxygenated areas. It is along watercourses, therefore, that minks are most frequently observed, and their home ranges often stretch out in linear fashion, following rivers for up to 5 km (3 mi).

The American Mink is active throughout the year, and it is often easiest to follow it by trailing its winter tracks in snow.

The paired prints left by its bounding gait traces the inquisitive animal's adventures as it comes within sniffing distance of every burrow, hollow log and bush pile. This active forager always seems to be on the hunt; scarcely any feeding opportunities are passed up, and surplus kills are stored for later use. A mink's food caches are often tucked away in its overnight dens, which are often dug into riverbanks, beneath rock piles or in permanently evicted muskrat mounds.

DESCRIPTION: The sleek coat is generally dark brown to black, usually with white spots on the chin, chest and sometimes belly. The legs are short. The tail is cylindrical and only somewhat bushy. The male is nearly twice as large as the female. The anal scent glands produce a rank, almost skunk-like odour.

HABITAT: The American Mink is almost never found far from water: it frequents wet zones in coniferous or hardwood forest, bushlands and streamside vegetation in the foothills.

FOOD: Minks are fierce predators of muskrats, but in their desire for nearly

---

DID YOU KNOW?

"Mink" is from a Swedish word that means "stinky animal." Although not as bad as skunks, minks are among the smelliest of the weasels. The anal musk glands can release the stinky liquid, but not aim the spray, when the mink is threatened.

BEST SITES: Whitney Lakes PP; Lakeland area; Lesser Slave Lake PP; William Switzer PP; Elk Island NP; Waterton Lakes NP; upper Bow River.

RANGE: This wide-ranging weasel occurs across most of Canada and the U.S., except for the high Arctic tundra and the deserts and dry regions from southern California to western Texas.

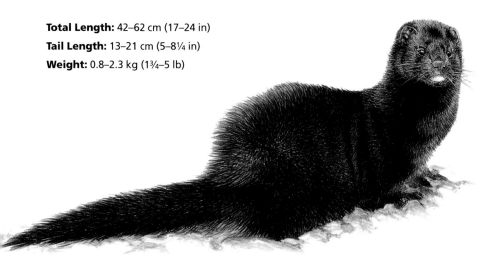

Total Length: 42–62 cm (17–24 in)
Tail Length: 13–21 cm (5–8¼ in)
Weight: 0.8–2.3 kg (1¾–5 lb)

any meat they also take frogs, fish, waterfowl and their eggs, mice, voles, rabbits, snakes and aquatic invertebrates.

DEN: Usually the den is in a burrow close to water. A mink may dig its own burrow, but more frequently it takes over a muskrat or beaver burrow and lines the nest with grass, feathers and other soft materials.

YOUNG: Minks breed any time between late January and early April, but because the period of delayed implantation is variable in length (from one week to 1½ months), the female almost always gives birth in late April or early May. The actual gestation period is about one month. There are 2 to 10 (usually 4 or 5) helpless, blind, pink, wrinkled young in a litter. The eyes open at 24 to 31 days. Weaning begins at five weeks. The mother teaches the young to hunt for two to three weeks, after which they fend for themselves.

SIMILAR SPECIES: The American Marten (p. 78) has a bushier tail, longer legs and an orange or buff throat patch, and it is not as sleek looking. The Northern River Otter (p. 102) is much larger and has a tapered tail and webbed feet.

left foreprint

left hindprint

Black-footed Ferret
Mustela nigripes

Once thought to have become extinct, the Black-footed Ferret seemed to rise from the dead in the U.S. in 1981 when a rancher's dog laid a limp corpse in a farmyard. Since that time, small populations of North America's only ferret have been discovered, and others re-established, near prairie-dog colonies in several places on the U.S. prairies. The Black-footed Ferret, which once occurred throughout the Great Plains, preys on prairie-dogs almost exclusively, and the attempts to exterminate that animal led to the collapse of ferret populations.

While it seems that prairie-dogs have never occurred in Alberta, several sources have made convincing arguments that our province may have fostered a small population of ferrets that were dependent on ground squirrels and other small rodents. Several specimens of Black-footed Ferrets, all of dubious origin, are known from Alberta, with perhaps the most famous one on display at the Belmore's Altamont Museum near the Coutts border crossing.

There have also been sight records of the Black-footed Ferret in Alberta, including a convincing observation near the western edge of Pakowki Lake in extreme southern Alberta. Not all observations submitted to wildlife authorities have passed the grade. In the late 1980s, in Alberta's best-known case of wildlife fakery, photographs supposedly taken of Black-footed Ferrets in Waterton Lakes National Park were determined to be cut-out portraits propped up in convincing locations and poses.

It is quite possible that Black-footed Ferrets once occurred, at least sporadically, in Alberta, but it seems doubtful that this species, which has already surprised conservationists, still holds an unknown population in our province. That this statement is qualified, however, continues to inspire naturalists to search the native prairies of southeastern Alberta in the hopes of perhaps encountering this enigmatic weasel.

DESCRIPTION: The body is heavier than that of other weasels, but it still has the typically long, thin shape, with an elongated head, broadly oval, furred ears, short legs and a fairly cylindrical tail. The short, glossy hairs of the upperparts are creamy white or sometimes yellowish, often with a brownish or

---

BEST SITES: No longer thought to occur in Alberta; try southeast of Manyberries to Eastend, Saskatchewan, for nostalgic reasons alone.

RANGE: The Black-footed Ferret formerly inhabited most of the Great Plains, from southern Alberta and Saskatchewan to northern Texas. A few ferret populations may still exist is isolated prairie regions. The last reports were from Wyoming and the Dakotas.

hypothetical former range

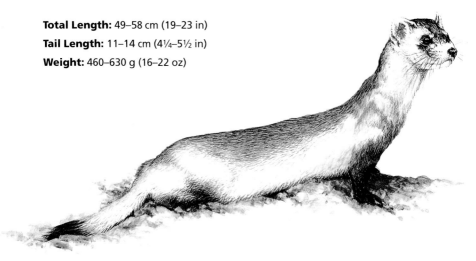

Total Length: 49–58 cm (19–23 in)
Tail Length: 11–14 cm (4¼–5½ in)
Weight: 460–630 g (16–22 oz)

charcoal wash down the back. The snout, forehead, ears and underparts are white. A dark brown mask extends across the cheeks and eyes, and the legs, feet and end of the tail are also brown.

HABITAT: Open, arid grasslands, mostly in the vicinity of prairie-dog "towns."

FOOD: Prairie-dogs are the primary food source. When prairie-dogs are scarce, the Black-footed Ferret will eat other rodents, including ground squirrels, mice and pocket gophers, as well as small birds, eggs and even reptiles.

DEN: A ferret typically makes its den in a prairie-dog burrow, after having eaten the inhabitant. The ferret may enlarge the burrow and add new chambers. Unlike prairie-dogs, ferrets do not tamp down the excavated dirt, but they may drag away loose dirt, leaving two parallel lines of dirt from the burrow entrance. If you find a prairie-dog burrow with loose dirt around it, it could be the home of this endangered mammal.

YOUNG: Ferrets mate in March or April, and the litter is born after a gestation of about 1½ months. The female ferret bears one to five young, although three or four is the most common litter size. The young are born helpless, and, like other weasels, they grow rapidly. The details of their development are unknown.

SIMILAR SPECIES: The Long-tailed Weasel (p. 88) lacks the black mask and black legs, is somewhat smaller and tends to have orangish underparts.

right foreprint

right hindprint

Wolverine

Gulo gulo

Like a magnet to iron, the Wolverine is drawn to wilderness—it lives almost exclusively in unpopulated areas. Its strict avoidance of human settlements has limited this animal's provincial distribution to the Rockies and areas north of Edson and Cold Lake. Even within this range it is thinly distributed, and only a select few of these northwood legends are seen each year.

Wolverines range widely, often covering tens of kilometres in a single day and up to 2000 km^2 (770 mi^2) in the course of a year. Of the fewer than 1000 breeding individuals thought to occur within our province, only a small proportion lives within protected areas. Even in the wilderness of Alberta's mountain parks, Wolverine sightings are extremely rare. It is somewhat ironic that trappers have the greatest insight into the lives of Wolverines. These large weasels are greatly valued for their fur, but their low densities prevent any significant efforts directed exclusively at acquiring them.

One of the most isolated and rare of North American mammals, the Wolverine marks its large territory with feces, urine and scent from its anal glands. The abundant stinky scent produced by the glands was the inspiration for the local name "skunk bear."

The Wolverine's habitat preferences seem to vary as its diet shifts with seasons. In summer it eats mostly ground squirrels, other small mammals, birds and berries; in winter the Wolverine lives off hoofed mammals, the majority of which it scavenges from wolves or roadkills—it has a keen ability to detect dead animals by scent. The Wolverine has one of the most powerful of jaws of

Total Length: 87–107 cm (34–42 in)
Tail Length: 19–26 cm (7½–10 in)
Weight: 6.6–16 kg (15–35 lb)

all Alberta mammals, which allows it to break the large bones of big game species it finds dead or kills.

DESCRIPTION: Although the head is small and weasel-like, the long legs and long fur look like they belong on a small bear. Unlike a bear, however, the back is arched and the tail is long and bushy. The coat is mostly a shiny, dark cinnamon brown to nearly black. There may be yellowish-white spots on the throat and chest. A buffy or pale brownish stripe runs down each side from the shoulder to the flank, where it becomes wider. The two stripes meet just before the base of the tail, leaving a dark saddle.

DID YOU KNOW?

The Wolverine's lower jaw is more tightly bound to its skull than most mammals' jaws. The articulating hinge that connects the upper and lower jaws is wrapped by bone, and in order for the jaws to dislocate, this bone must break.

BEST SITES: Jasper NP; remote alpine areas in other mountain parks; wilderness areas in extreme northwestern Alberta.

RANGE: In North America, the Wolverine is a species of the coniferous forests and tundra of Alaska and northern Canada. It follows the montane coniferous forests as far south as California and Colorado.

HABITAT: The Wolverine prefers large areas of remote wilderness, where it frequently occupies wooded foothills and mountains. In summer it forages into the alpine tundra and hunts along slopes. In winter it drops to lower elevations and may move far away from the mountains.

FOOD: Wolverines prey on mice, ground squirrels, birds, beavers and fish. Deer, Caribou, Mountain Goats and even Moose have been attacked, often successfully. In winter Wolverines often scavenge winter kills or the remains left by other predators. To a limited extent, they also eat berries, fungi and nuts.

DEN: The den may be among the roots of a fallen tree, in a hollow tree, in a rocky crevice or even in a semi-permanent snowbank.

YOUNG: Wolverines breed between late April and early September, but the embryos do not implant in the uterus wall until January. Between late February and mid-April the female gives birth to a litter of one to five (generally two or three) cubs. The stubby-tailed cubs are born with their eyes and ears closed and with a fuzzy white coat that sets off the darker paws and face mask. They are suckled for eight to nine weeks; then they leave the den and their mother teaches them to hunt. The mother and her young typically stay together through the first winter. The young disperse when they become sexually mature in spring.

right foreprint

right hindprint

SIMILAR SPECIES: The American Badger (p. 98) is squatter, has light patches on its head and does not have the lighter side stripes of a Wolverine. The Black Bear (p. 110) and the Grizzly Bear (p. 114) are larger, have shorter tails and lack the light buffy stripe along the sides.

American Badger

American Badger
Taxidea taxus

American Badgers are nature's answer to rototillers and backhoes. While animal life is concentrated in trees in many other ecoregions, on the Alberta prairies, much of life occurs on or below the ground. Badgers, with their flair for remodelling, create much of the required architecture in the open grasslands. The large holes left by badgers are of critical importance as den sites for dozens of species, from Coyotes and Burrowing Owls to Black-widow Spiders. When the population of badgers is eliminated from an area, numbers of these burrow-dependent animals often slowly disappear.

The American Badger enjoys a reputation for fierceness and boldness that was acquired in part from a not very closely related mammal bearing the same name in Europe. While it is true that a cornered badger will put up an impressive show of attitude, like most animals it prefers to avoid a fight.

Pigeon-toed and short-legged, the American Badger is not much of a sprinter, but its heavy front claws enable it to move large quantities of earth in short order. Although its predatory nature is of benefit to landowners, the badger's natural digging skills have sealed many a death warrant—cattle and horses have been known (rarely) to break their legs when stepping carelessly into badger workings. Interestingly, this crippling misfortune does not seem to be in evidence among Alberta's wild hoofed mammals.

Badgers tend to spend a great part of winter sleeping in their burrows, but they do not enter a full state of hibernation like their European relatives, or like so many of their rodent prey. Instead, badgers emerge from their slumber to hunt when winter temperatures become more moderate.

In spite of low population densities, almost all sexually mature female badgers are impregnated during the nearly three months that they are sexually receptive. As with most members of the weasel family, once the egg is fertilized further embryonic development is put off until the embryos implant, usually in January, which would coincide with a spring birth.

DESCRIPTION: Long, yellowish-grey, grizzled hair covers these short-legged

---

DID YOU KNOW?

Badgers make an incredible variety of sounds: adults hiss, bark, scream and snarl; in play, young badgers grunt, squeal, bark, meow, chirr and snuffle.

BEST SITES: Fish Creek PP; Dry Island Buffalo Jump PP; Hwy 1 between Brooks and Medicine Hat; Waterton Lakes NP.

RANGE: From north-central Alberta and Saskatchewan, the American Badger ranges to the southeast throughout the Great Plains and prairies and southwest to Baja California and the central Mexican highlands.

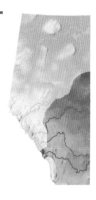

Total Length: 78–85 cm (31–33 in)
Tail Length: 13–16 cm (5–6¼ in)
Weight: 5–11 kg (11–24 lb)

muscular members of the weasel family. The hair is longer on the sides than on the back or belly, which adds to the flattened appearance of the body. A white stripe originates on the nose and runs back onto the shoulders or sometimes slightly beyond. The top of the head is otherwise dark. A dark vertical crescent, like a badge, runs between the short, rounded, furred ears and the eyes. The sides of the face are whitish or very pale buff. The short, bottle brush tail is more yellowish than the body. The lower legs and feet are very dark brown, becoming blackish at the extremities. The three central claws on each forefoot are greatly elongated for digging.

HABITAT: Essentially an animal of open places, the badger shuns forests. It is usually found in association with ground squirrels, typically in the open grasslands of the parkland and prairies. In the mountains it forages on treeless slopes or in riparian meadows.

FOOD: Burrowing mammals fulfil most of the badger's dietary needs, but it also eats eggs, young ground-nesting birds, mice and sometimes carrion and insects.

DEN: A badger may dig its own den or take over a ground squirrel's burrow. The den may approach 10 m (33 ft) in length and have a diameter of about 30 cm (12 in). It builds a bulky grass nest in an expanded chamber near or at the end of the burrow. A large pile of excavated earth is generally found to one side of the burrow entrance.

YOUNG: One to five (usually four) naked, helpless young are born between late April and mid-June. Their eyes open after a month, and at two months their mother teaches them to hunt. The young disperse in autumn, when they are three-quarters grown. The mother and some of the young females may mate in summer, but most badgers do not mature sexually until they are a year old. Delayed implantation of the embryo is characteristic.

left foreprint

left hindprint

walking trail

SIMILAR SPECIES:
The Wolverine (p. 94) is the only species that you might confuse with a badger, but the badger trots, whereas the Wolverine lopes. Also, the badger's body is much more flattened and the white stripe on its nose is unique.

Wolverine

Northern River Otter
Lontra canadensis

It may seem to be too good to be true, but all those playful characterizations of the Northern River Otter are founded on truth. River otters often amuse themselves by rolling about, sliding, diving or "body surfing," and they may also push and balance floating sticks with their noses or endlessly drop and retrieve pebbles. They seem particularly interested in playing on slippery surfaces—they leap onto the snow or mud with their forelegs folded close to their bodies for a streamlined toboggan ride. Unlike most members of the weasel family, river otters are social animals, and they will frolic together in the water and take turns sliding down banks.

With their streamlined bodies, rudder-like tails, webbed toes and valved ears and nostrils, river otters are well adapted for aquatic habitats. The large amounts of playtime they seem to have results from their efficiency at catching prey. Although otters generally cruise along slowly in the water by paddling with all four feet, they can sprint after prey with the ease of a seal whenever hunger strikes. When an otter swims quickly, it chiefly propels itself with vertical undulations of its body, hindlegs and tail.

Because of all their activity, Northern River Otters leave many signs of their presence when they occupy an area. Their slides are the most obvious and best-known evidence, but be careful not to mistake the slippery beaver trails that are common around beaver ponds for otter slides. Despite their other aquatic tendencies, otters always defecate on land. Their scat is simple to identify: it is almost always full of fish bones and scales.

In the past, the Northern River Otter's thick, beautiful, durable fur led to exces-

Total Length: 1–1.3 m (3½–4½ ft)
Tail Length: 30–51 cm (12–20 in)
Weight: 4.5–11 kg (10–24 lb)

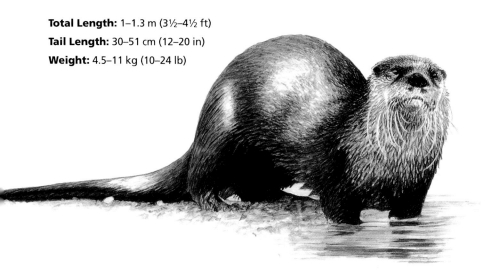

sive trapping that greatly diminished the provincial population. Trapping pressure has since been reduced, and the otter seems to be slowly recolonizing parts of Alberta from which it has been absent for decades. Even in areas where it is known to occur, however, it is infrequently seen, but its marks of playfulness remind us that we are not alone in enjoying the good life.

DESCRIPTION: This large, weasel-like carnivore has dark brown upperparts that look black when wet. It is paler below, and the throat is often silver grey. The head is broad and flattened, and it has small eyes and ears and prominent, whitish whiskers. The feet are webbed. The long tail is thick at the base and gradually tapers to the tip. The male is larger than the female.

HABITAT: Year-round, river otters primarily occur in or along wooded rivers, ponds and lakes, but they sometimes roam far from water. They may be active during day or night, but they tend to be more nocturnal in areas where they are disturbed by human activity.

DID YOU KNOW?

In winter, river otters almost invariably seek out beaver lodges or dams for easy access to the water. In fact, otters are so dependent on beavers that their northern limit coincides with that of beavers, even though their prey ranges further north.

BEST SITES: Beaver River drainage in Lakeland Country; Wood Buffalo NP.

RANGE: The Northern River Otter occurs from near treeline across Alaska and Canada south through forested regions to northern California and northern Utah in the West, and Florida and the Gulf Coast in the East. It is largely absent from the Midwest and Great Plains.

FOOD: Fish and frogs form the bulk of the diet, but otters occasionally depredate bird nests and eat small mammals, such as mice, young muskrats and young beavers, and sometimes even insects and earthworms.

DEN: The permanent den is often in a bank, with both underwater and above-water entrances. During its roamings, an otter rests under roots or overhangs, in hollow logs, in the abandoned burrows of other mammals or in abandoned beaver lodges.

YOUNG: The female bears a litter of one to six blind, fully furred young in March or April. The young are 140 g (5 oz) at birth. They first leave the den at three to four months, and leave their parents at six to seven months. Otters become sexually mature at two years. The mother breeds again soon after her litter is born, but delayed implantation of the embryos puts off the birth until the following spring.

running trail

SIMILAR SPECIES: The American Beaver (p. 170) is stouter and has a wide, flat, hairless, scaly tail. The American Mink (p. 90) is smaller, its feet are not webbed, and its tail is cylindrical, not tapered.

American Beaver

Common Raccoon
Procyon lotor

While most North Americans are intimately familiar with this adaptable and recognizable mammal, Albertans who have never ventured beyond our provincial borders have probably never encountered one. The Common Raccoon is becoming increasingly abundant and widespread in Alberta, but it remains uncommon, even in southern areas, and every sighting is a special circumstance.

When raccoons are seen, which is mostly at night, they quickly shuffle away, effectively evading flashlight beams by slipping into burrows or tree retreats with surprising nimbleness. These agile climbers can ascend almost any tree, and they are among the few animals that can manage the feat of descending a tree trunk headfirst—they can rotate their hindfeet 180 degrees. Should their sanctuaries be found, raccoons remain nervously still at a safe distance, impatient for the experience to end.

Although personal encounters with the Common Raccoon are rare in Alberta, this animal's tendency to frequent muddy environments allows people to find its diagnostic tracks along the edges of wetlands and waterbodies. It methodically circumnavigates wetlands in the hopes of finding duck nests or unwary amphibians upon which to dine, and its varied diet has helped it colonize many environments elsewhere. Long, cold winters, however, are an ecological barrier in the dispersal of this animal. It does not enter a dormant state in the coldest periods of winter, but requires year-round food availability.

Although most of our mothers taught us not to put our hands in places we could not see, raccoons don't share this caution; they typically feel their way through the world. In fact, our word "raccoon" is derived from the Algonquin name for this animal, *aroughcoune*, which means "he scratches with his hands." One of the best-known characteristics of the Common Raccoon is its habit of dunking its food in water before eating it. It had long been thought that the raccoon was washing its food— the scientific name *lotor* is Latin for "washer"—but biologists now believe that a raccoon's sense of touch is enhanced by water, and that it is actually kneading and tearing the food, feeling for inedible bits to discard.

DID YOU KNOW?

Raccoons have many thousand more nerve endings in their "hands" and "fingers" than we do. It is an asset they constantly put to use, probing under rocks and in crevices for food.

BEST SITES: Willow Creek PP; Milk River valley; lower Red Deer River valley.

RANGE: The Common Raccoon occurs from southern Canada south through most of the U.S. and Mexico. It is absent from parts of the Rocky Mountains, central Nevada, Utah and Arizona.

Total Length: 66–96 cm (26–38 in)
Tail Length: 19–29 cm (7½–11 in)
Weight: 5.4–14 kg (12–31 lb)

Common Raccoons are capable of producing a wide variety of vocalizations: they can purr, growl, snarl, scream, hiss, whinny and whimper. Raccoons are typically solitary, and when two raccoons whose ranges overlap meet, they will growl at each other, flatten their ears, lower their heads, raise their hackles and bare their teeth. Although raccoons will ferociously attack predators if cornered, their territorial posturings rarely escalate into an actual fight with another raccoon.

DESCRIPTION: The coat is brownish grey overall, with lighter, greyish-brown underparts. The bushy tail, with its four to six alternating blackish rings on a yellowish-white background, makes the raccoon one of the most recognizable North American carnivores. There is a black "mask" across the eyes, bordered by

the white "eyebrows" and mostly white snout, and a strip of white fur separates the upper lip from the nose. The ears are relatively small.

HABITAT: Raccoons are most often found in treed areas near streams, lakes and ponds.

FOOD: The Common Raccoon fills the role of medium-sized omnivore in the food web. Besides eating fruits, nuts, berries and insects, it avidly seeks out and eats frogs, fish, eggs, young birds and rodents. Just as a bear does, the raccoon consumes vast amounts of food in autumn to build a large fat reserve that will disappear over winter.

DEN: The den is often located in a hollow tree, but sites beneath abandoned buildings or under discarded construction materials are increasingly being used. Dens can sometimes be found in rock crevices, where grasses or leaves carried in by the female may cover the floor.

YOUNG: After about a two-month gestation, the female bears two to seven (typically four) young in late spring. The young weigh just 60 g (2 oz) at birth. Their eyes open at about three weeks, and when they are six to seven weeks old they begin to feed outside the den. At first, the mother carries her young about by the nape of the neck, as a cat carries kittens. About a month later she starts taking them on extended nightly feeding forays. Some young disperse in fall, but others remain until their mother forces them out when she needs room for her new litter.

right foreprint

walking trail

SIMILAR SPECIES: The Common Raccoon is very distinctive. Only the American Badger (p. 98) could possibly be confused with it, but a badger is much squatter, its facial markings are vertically oriented, unlike the horizontal "mask" of a raccoon, and its shorter, thinner tail doesn't have the raccoon's distinctive rings.

American Badger

Black Bear
Ursus americanus

Mocked by bushmen and feared by city dwellers, Alberta's Black Bears never seem to get fair representation. These animals are generally peaceful, in most cases fleeing at the first sign of humans, but memories of rare reported violent encounters are retained by many people.

Alberta's mountain and boreal parks offer excellent opportunities to encounter the Black Bear, particularly while a bear grazes on roadside dandelions in late spring and early summer. Photos are taken, wisely from the safety of vehicles, and memories are created by this overtly docile animal. Accustomed to people, these roadside bears seem to hold no harm for the overly curious, but for people who truly care for their safety and for that of the bear, intimacy is better displaced for distance—all bears are potentially dangerous.

On rare occasions, a particular bear can become well known to people who frequent an area, facilitating a personal relationship with the wild. The "Cinnamon Bear" of the Maligne Valley in Jasper National Park may be Alberta's most notable example. Named for her colour—not all Black Bears are black—the Cinnamon Bear was a frequent sight along the road up to Maligne Lake. She was undoubtedly seen by thousands of people during her long life, and she was even public with both of her litters. Unfortunately, not one of her offspring survived through its first year of life. Although she no longer grazes the roadsides in spring, she is mourned by many people who knew her well. Her memory is surely alive in the many photo albums and wildlife calendars that celebrate all Black Bears through her image.

Recently, the reputed Viagra-like qualities of bear paws and gall bladders have resulted in increased bear poaching in Canada to fill the demand of the aphrodisiac market. Alberta still has a stable population of these engaging animals but careful management must continue to protect their future.

DESCRIPTION: The coat is long and shaggy and ranges from black to brown to honey coloured. The body is short and relatively stout, with short, powerful legs. The large, wide feet have curved, black claws. The head is large and has a straight profile. The eyes are small, and

---

DID YOU KNOW?

During its winter slumber, a Black Bear loses 20 to 40 percent of its body weight. To prepare for winter, the bear eats more than 20,000 calories a day during late summer and fall.

BEST SITES: Maligne Lake Road, Jasper NP; Icefields Parkway, Banff and Jasper NPs; David Thompson Highway west of Nordegg; Hwy 63 to Fort McMurray; Lesser Slave Lake PP; Cold Lake PP; Hwy 35 north of Peace River.

RANGE: The Black Bear occurs nearly everywhere across North America where there are forests, swamps and shrub thickets. It avoids grasslands and deserts.

Total Length: 1.3–1.9 m (4½–6 ft)
Shoulder Height: 91–107 cm (36–42 in)
Tail Length: 8–18 cm (3¼–7 in)
Weight: 40–270 kg (88–595 lb)

the ears short, rounded and erect. The tail is very short. An adult male is about 20 percent larger than a female.

HABITAT: Black Bears are primarily forest animals, and their sharp, curved front claws enable them to easily climb trees, even as adults. In spring they often forage in natural or roadside clearings.

FOOD: Away from human influences, up to 95 percent of the Black Bear's diet is plant material: leaves, buds, flowers, berries, fruits and roots are all consumed. This omnivore also eats animal matter: insects, bees and honey and even young hoofed mammals may be killed and eaten. Carrion and human garbage are eagerly sought out.

DEN: The den, which is only used during winter, may be in a cave or hollow tree, beneath a fallen log or the roots of a windthrown tree, or even in a haystack. The bear usually carries in a few mouthfuls of grass to lie on during its sleep. It will not eat, drink, urinate or defecate during its time in the den.

YOUNG: Black Bears mate in June or July, but the embryos do not implant and begin to develop until the sow enters her den in November. One to five (usually two or three) young are born and nursed while she sleeps. Their eyes open and they become active when they are five to six weeks old. They leave the den with their mother when they weigh 2–3 kg (4½–6½ lb), usually in April. The sow and her cubs generally spend the next winter together in the den, separating the following spring—Black Bears typically bear young in alternate years.

right hindprint

walking trail

SIMILAR SPECIES: The Grizzly Bear (p. 114) is generally larger and has a dished-in face, a noticeable shoulder hump and long, brown to ivory-coloured, blunt claws. The Wolverine (p. 94) looks a little like a small Black Bear, but it has a long tail and an arched back.

Grizzly Bear

Grizzly Bear
Brown Bear
Ursus arctos

The mighty Grizzly Bear, more than any other animal, makes camping and travelling in Alberta's mountains an adventure, not just another picnic. Fuelled by a mix of fear and curiosity, millions of visitors to our national parks scan the roadsides and open meadows in the hopes of catching a glimpse of this wilderness icon. Most people leave the parks without a personal Grizzly experience, but when a bear is sighted, the human melee that ensues is unlike that which surrounds any other Alberta animal. Crowds and "bear jams" result, further contributing to the paradox that surrounds this perplexing animal.

Grizzly Bears are indisputably strong: their massive shoulders and skull anchor muscles that are capable of rolling 100-kg (220-lb) rocks, dragging Elk carcasses and crushing some of the most massive ungulate bones. Ironically, Grizzlies are uncommonly obliged to feed in this manner. Instead, their routinely docile foragings are concentrated on roots, berries and grasses.

An adaptable diner, the Grizzly's diet changes from spring through fall to match the availability of foods. For instance, it eats huge quantities of berries when they are available in late summer. The bear swallows many of the berries whole, and its scat often ends up looking like blueberry pie filling. During this time of feasting, a Grizzly's weight may increase by 1 kg (2¼ lb) a day, preparing it for the long winter ahead. It will remain active through the fall, until the bitter cold of November limits foods and favours sleep.

Recently, many people have questioned the continuation of the annual Grizzly hunt in Alberta. They argue that the reduced range of this species from its historic limits, imprecise population estimates (perhaps between 500 and 800 in the province), increased mortality rates, ethical considerations and the necessity of killing nuisance bears should prohibit a recreational hunt. While the range of the Grizzly in Alberta has changed little in the last 20 years, naturalists with wilderness-envy dream of past times when Grizzlies lumbered over Alberta's grasslands in the company of bison.

DESCRIPTION: The usually brownish to yellowish coat typically has white-

BEST SITES: Cameron Road and Cameron Lake, Waterton Lakes NP; Icefields Parkway, Banff and Jasper NPs; Caw Ridge.

RANGE: In North America, this holarctic bear is largely confined to Alaska and northwestern Canada, with montane populations extending south into Idaho and Wyoming. It formerly ranged much further, but most open-area populations were extirpated, leaving remnants in the remote mountain wilderness.

Total Length: 1.8–2.6 m (6–8½ ft)
Shoulder Height: 0.9–1.2 m (3–4 ft)
Tail Length: 7.5–18 cm (3–7 in)
Weight: 110–530 kg (240–1170 lb)

tipped guard hairs that give it a grizzled appearance (from which the name "grizzly" is derived). Some individuals are completely black; others can be nearly white. The face has a concave profile. The eyes are small and the ears are short and rounded. A large hump at the shoulder means that the forequarters are higher than the rump. The large, flat paws have long claws; at least some of the front claws can be more than 5 cm (2 in) long.

HABITAT: Originally, most Grizzly Bears were animals of the prairies and open areas, where they could use their long claws to dig up roots, bulbs and the occasional burrowing mammal. Although their current range is largely forested, mountain bears often forage on open slopes and in the alpine tundra.

FOOD: Although 70 to 80 percent of the diet is plants—leaves, stems, flowers, roots and fruits are all eaten—the Grizzly Bear eats more animals, including mammals, fish and insects, than its black cousin does. It may dig insects, ground squirrels, marmots and even mice out of the ground; young hoofed mammals are eagerly sought by sow bears with cubs; and even large adult cervids and Bighorn Sheep may be attacked and killed. Particularly after it emerges from its winter sleep, a bear is attracted to carrion, which it can smell from 17 km (11 mi) away. The Grizzly Bear can eat huge meals of meat: a single adult consumed an entire road-killed Elk in four days.

DEN: Most dens are on northeast- or north-facing slopes, in areas where snowmelt does not begin until late April or early May. The den is usually a cave, or it is dug into tree roots. The bear enters its den in late October or November during a heavy snowfall that will cover its tracks. The bear soon falls asleep; it will not eat, drink, urinate or defecate for six months.

YOUNG: A sow has litters in alternate years, typically having her first after her seventh birthday. Grizzlies mate in June or July, but with delayed implantation of the embryo, the cubs are not born until some time between January and early March, when the mother is asleep in the den. The one to four (generally two) cubs are born naked, blind and helpless. They nurse and grow while their mother continues to sleep, and they are ready to follow her when she leaves the den in April or May. A sow and her cubs typically den together the following winter.

walking trail

SIMILAR SPECIES: The Black Bear (p. 110) is generally smaller, is tallest at the rump (it doesn't have a humped shoulder) and has a straight facial profile and shorter, black, curved claws.

Black Bear

Coyote
Canis latrans

Achorus of yaps, whines, barks and howls complements the darkened skies over much of rural Alberta. Although Coyote calls are most intense during late winter and spring, corresponding to courtship, these maniacal sounds can be heard during suitable weather at any time of the year. Often initiated by one animal, many family groups soon join in, and the calls pour from the hillsides, making it obvious to all that these animals relish getting together and making noise. In these vocalizations, you can hear the abundance of Coyotes and their influence on Alberta's landscape.

When Anthony Henday and David Thompson travelled through Alberta little more than 200 years ago, they made frequent references in their journal entries to foxes and wolves, but they seldom mentioned Coyotes. Today, Coyotes occur throughout our province, and they have increased their numbers across North America in the past century. This increase is in response to the expansion of agriculture and forestry and the reduction of wolf populations, and it flouts the widespread human efforts to exterminate Coyotes.

One of the few natural checks on Coyote abundance in Alberta seems to be the presence of Grey Wolves. As the much larger and more powerful canids of the wilderness neighbourhood, wolves typically exclude Coyotes from their territories. The conditions in 18th-century Alberta favoured wolves and foxes, but changes in our province since then have greatly benefited the Coyote. The Coyote is now so widely distributed and common throughout our province that all Albertans live within an hour's drive of this animal.

Because of its relatively small size, the Coyote typically preys on smaller animals, such as mice, voles, ground squirrels and hares, but it has been known to kill Pronghorns, Bighorn Sheep and deer in Alberta, particularly the young. Although it usually hunts alone, the Coyote occasionally forms packs, especially when it hunts hoofed mammals. The Coyotes may split up, with some waiting in ambush while the others chase the prey toward them, or they may run in relays to tire their quarry—the Coyote, which is the best runner among the canids, typically cruises at 40–50 km/h (25–31 mph).

BEST SITES: Banff NP; Waterton Lakes NP; Jasper NP; Kananaskis Country; Elk Island NP; along any stretch of road that passes through semi-open to open areas.

RANGE: Coyotes are not found in the western third of Alaska, the tundra regions of northern Canada and the extreme southeastern United States; their range essentially covers the remainder of North America.

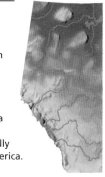

Total Length: 1.1–1.3 m (3½–4½ ft)
Shoulder Height: 58–66 cm (23–26 in)
Tail Length: 30–40 cm (12–16 in)
Weight: 8–34 kg (18–75 lb)

Coyotes owe their modern-day success to their varied diet, early age of first breeding, high reproductive output and flexible life history requirements. They consume carrion throughout the year, but they also feed on such diverse offerings as eggs, mammals, birds and berries. Their generalist diet and habitat choices seem to adapt to just about any conditions in the province, quite unlike species of specialized mammals, which makes them a perfect fit in the rural matrix of modern Alberta.

DESCRIPTION: The Coyote looks like a grey, buffy or reddish-grey, medium-sized dog. The nose is pointed and there is usually a grey patch between the eyes that contrasts with the tawny top of the snout. The tail is bushy and has a black tip. The underparts are light to whitish. When frightened, a Coyote runs with its tail tucked between its hindlegs.

HABITAT: Occurring in all Alberta's terrestrial habitats, the Coyote has greatly expanded its range, in part where humans extirpated the Grey Wolf, and in part because the clearing of forests brought about changes in habitat that made it easier for the Coyote to establish populations in new areas.

FOOD: Although primarily carnivorous, feeding on squirrels, mice, hares, birds, amphibians and reptiles, Coyotes will sometimes eat cactus fruits, berries and vegetation. Most ranchers dislike coyotes because they frequently take sheep, calves and pigs that are left exposed. They may even attack and consume dogs.

DEN: The den is usually a burrow in a slope, frequently an American Badger or Woodchuck hole that has been expanded to 30 cm (12 in) in diameter and about 3 m (10 ft) deep. Rarely, Coyotes have been known to den in an abandoned car, a hollow tree trunk or a dense brush pile.

YOUNG: A litter of 3 to 10 (usually 5 to 7) pups is born between late March and late May, after a gestation of about two months. The furry pups are blind at birth. Their eyes open after about 10 days, and they leave the den for the first time when they are three weeks old. The young coyotes fight with each other and establish dominance and social position at just three to four weeks of age.

foreprint

gallop group

SIMILAR SPECIES: The Grey Wolf (p. 122) is generally larger, has much bigger feet and longer legs and carries its tail straight back when it runs. The Red Fox (p. 130) is generally smaller and has a white tail tip and black forelegs. Coyote-like domestic dog breeds generally have more bulging foreheads and usually carry their tails straight back when they run.

Grey Wolf

Grey Wolf
Canis lupus

For many Albertans, the Grey Wolf represents the apex of wilderness, symbolizing the pure, yet hostile, qualities of all that remains wild. Other people continue to disparage this iconic representation, characterizing the Alberta wolf as a blood-lusting enemy of range animals and the ranchers who care for them. Objective opinions about the Grey Wolf are few; caricatures, whether positive or negative, abound. Truth probably lies in the words of Aldo Leopold: "Only the mountain has lived long enough to listen objectively to the howl of a wolf."

After studying and following wolves, some people have postulated that human society has a near equal in the social structure of the wolf pack. A pack behaves like a "super organism," cooperatively making it possible for more animals to survive. By hunting together, pack members can catch and subdue much larger prey than if they were acting alone. A social hierarchy is strictly followed in the pack, and moments of tension rarely break the orderly, communal pack scene. Often, only the top animals (called the "alpha male" and "alpha female" by wolf biologists) will reproduce, but other pack members help with bringing food to the pups and defending the group's territory against the intrusions of other wolves.

A wolf pack generally occupies such a large territory—usually 250–730 km^2 (97–282 mi^2)—that individual densities are extremely low. Howling is an effective way for wolves to keep in contact over long distances, and it appears to play an important role in communication among pack members and between adjacent packs. Howling also conveys a powerful message to people wishing to realign

Total Length: 1–2 m (3½–6½ ft)
Shoulder Height: 66–97 cm (26–38 in)
Tail Length: 35–50 cm (14–20 in)
Weight: 26–79 kg (57–174 lb)

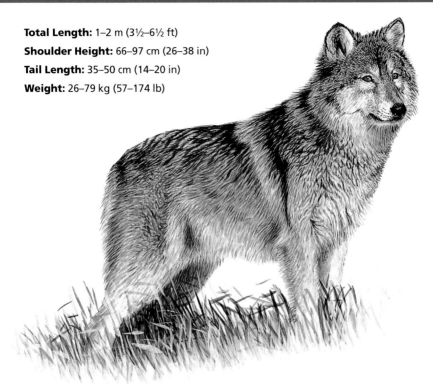

themselves with the wild. In the sound of a wolf's long, drawn-out howl is the spirit of the untameable and the independence of all wild animals. When you are next in wild country, cup your hands and offer your best howl to the night sky—and hope for the numbing wilderness reply.

DESCRIPTION: Most wolves resemble a long-legged German Shepherd with extra large paws. Although typically thought of as being a grizzled grey, the coat colour ranges from coal black to creamy white. Black wolves are most common in dense forests; whitish wolves are characteristic of high Arctic tundra. The bushy tail is carried straight behind the wolf when it runs. In social situations, the height of the tail generally relates to the social status of that individual.

DID YOU KNOW?

Wolves routinely prey on large, big-boned hoofed mammals, and their jaws have twice the crushing power of a similar-sized German Shepherd's jaws.

BEST SITES: Wood Buffalo NP (near bison herds); eastern half of Jasper NP; Lake Minnewanka area, Banff NP.

RANGE: Much reduced from historic times in North America, the Grey Wolf's range extends through most of Alaska and Canada, except on the prairies and in southeastern Canada. It extends south into Minnesota, Wisconsin, Idaho and Montana. The Grey Wolf was recently re-introduced from Alberta into Yellowstone National Park.

HABITAT: Although wolves formerly occupied grasslands, they are now mostly restricted to forested areas.

FOOD: Because large carnivores customarily eat large herbivores, wolves are destined to eat cervids and Bighorn Sheep. Although large mammals typically comprise about 80 percent of the diet, wolves also devour rabbits, mice, nesting birds and carrion when it is available. Where humans leave livestock unguarded, wolves may take cattle, sheep, goats, horses, dogs, cats or pigs.

DEN: Usually located on a rise of land near water, most dens are bank burrows, often adapted by enlarging the den of a fox or burrowing mammal. Sometimes a rock slide, hollow log or natural cave is used. Sand or soil scratched out of the entrance by the female is usually evident as a large mound. The burrow opening is generally about 50 x 65 cm (20 x 26 in), and the burrow extends back 2–10 m (6½–33 ft) to a dry natal chamber with a floor of packed soil. The beds from which adults can keep watch are generally found above the entrance.

YOUNG: A litter generally contains five to seven pups (with extremes of 3 to 13), which may be of different colours. The newborn pups resemble domestic dogs in their development: their eyes open at 9 to 10 days, and they are weaned at six to eight weeks. The pups are fed regurgitated food until they begin to accompany the pack on hunts. Wolves become sexually mature a couple of months before their third birthdays, but their first incidence of mating is largely determined by the pack hierarchy.

foreprint

hindprint

SIMILAR SPECIES: The Coyote (p. 118) is smaller, with much smaller feet and shorter legs, it has a reddish patch on its nose, and it runs with its tail angled down.

Coyote

Arctic Fox

Alopex lagopus

Arctic Foxes typically occur north of treeline, creatively surviving on Polar Bear kills, lemmings and ground-nesting birds and eggs. Every winter a small number of these polar specialists cross into the northeastern corner of Alberta as they retreat from the extreme conditions of the barrens, justifying their inclusion in our faunal list. They likely follow the migratory Caribou herds south into northern Alberta and Saskatchewan. It is likely within these herds that the dispersing foxes hold their ticket in the winter lottery; disease, starvation and wolves undoubtedly follow these hoofed buffets as well, leaving scraps upon which the Arctic Foxes can dine. Once the snows begin to melt in earnest from the stunted northern spruce, Arctic Foxes, fuelled by visions of the bounty of an Arctic summer, may return north with the Caribou.

The Arctic Fox's winter stay in the political region known as Alberta is brief, and it is inconsequential to most Arctic Foxes and the biologists who study them. Almost every year, however, trappers collect a half-dozen or so skins, confirming this movement. Trapping records and personal accounts suggest that these foxes typically remain north of Lake Athabasca, but some people think that individuals occasionally move as far south as Fort McMurray. The animals that come south are likely more susceptible to traps; wandering individuals are quite likely starving, weakened by a scarcity of food.

DESCRIPTION: This cat-sized fox is the only canid with distinct seasonal pelages. The summer coat is generally brownish grey above and light or white below, with some white hairs on the head and shoulders, but most summer patterns are unique. The forelegs are brown and the tail is brownish above and lighter below, often with some long, white hairs. In winter, only the brownish-yellow eyes and black nose contrast with the long white coat and bushy white tail. On rare occasions, the winter pelage of an Arctic Fox is the "blue" phase: the white-frosted

Total Length: 75–91 cm (30–36 in)
Shoulder Height: 25–30 cm (9¾–12 in)
Tail Length: 27–34 cm (11–13 in)
Weight: 1.8–4.1 kg (4–9 lb)

summer colours

coat is blue-black to pearl grey. The ears are short and rounded, and the soles of the feet sport abundant hair between the toe pads.

HABITAT: Typically occurring in the treeless Arctic tundra or out on the polar ice, some Arctic Foxes may move south into the northern forests in winter.

FOOD: Arctic Foxes feed avidly on rodents, which they may dig up from under the snow. Their diet also includes birds, eggs, young hares, insects, carrion and the scraps left by bears or wolves.

DEN: On the tundra, Arctic Foxes make their dens under rocks or in banks or hillsides, often with multiple entrances.

DID YOU KNOW?

In Siberia, Arctic Foxes have been known to travel as much as 1200 km (750 mi) south during winter.

BEST SITES: North of Lake Athabasca and east of the Slave River.

RANGE: In North America, the circumpolar Arctic Fox ranges throughout the Arctic tundra, from western Alaska to Labrador. Extralimital records in Ontario approach the 49th parallel, and it has been seen as far north as 88° N on the polar ice.

The area around the entrance may be littered with feathers and bits of bone; sometimes rather large Muskox bones are carried to the den. In winter, the only time they occur in Alberta, they may tunnel into snowbanks.

YOUNG: When there is an abundance of food, Arctic Foxes may mate as early as mid-February, but breeding is more typically delayed until late March or, if food is scarce, late April. In times of extreme hardship, Arctic Foxes might not mate at all. After a gestation of 1½ to 2 months, the vixen usually gives birth to six to nine helpless kits. Instances where up to 25 pups are found in a den may represent multiple litters. The young are weaned at two to four weeks. If food becomes scarce, the stronger pups may attack, kill and devour their siblings. The parents continue to feed their pups until mid-August. Arctic Foxes are sexually mature before their first birthday.

SIMILAR SPECIES: There is no other mammal that resembles an Arctic Fox in its white winter coat. The Red Fox (p. 130) has taller ears, is generally reddish and has black forelegs and a white tail tip.

foreprint

Common Grey Fox
Urocyon cinereoargenteus

While most books on Alberta mammals include the Common Grey Fox in their accounts, its inclusion has little zoogeographic value. The closest known population of Common Grey Foxes occurs sporadically in Manitoba, more than 1000 km (620 mi) from Alberta's single specimen record, which was trapped at Old Fort Point on Lake Athabasca in 1950. The tattered skin, which did not have guard hairs, and skull of this animal were quickly attributed to this species, but no evidence has since appeared to explain this most unusual, and unique, record.

Total Length: 80–113 cm (31–44 in)

Shoulder Height: 36–38 cm (14–15 in)

Tail Length: 28–44 cm (11–17 in)

Weight: 3.4–5.9 kg (7½–13 lb)

Red Fox
Vulpes vulpes

More than Alberta's other native canids, the Red Fox has received some favourable presentations in literature and modern culture. From Aesop's fables to construction yard compliments, the fox is often symbolized as a cunning, intelligent, attractive and noble animal. Its signature, bushy tail helps balance the fox when it is running or jumping, and during cold weather the fox wraps it over its face. The fox's wide-ranging diet, undeniable cuteness and positive impact upon most farmlands have endeared it to many people who otherwise do not care for wildlife.

Despite its vast range and moderate densities, the Red Fox is not often seen by Albertans. Its primarily nocturnal activity is probably the main culprit, but a fox's keen senses of sight, hearing and smell, with which it can usually detect humans long before we see it, enhance its elusive nature. Winter may be the best time to see a fox: it is more likely to be active during the day, and it tends to stand out when it's mousing in a snow-covered field.

Young foxes are most often seen in early June: by that time they have become quite active but they have not fully absorbed the cryptic training of their mothers. These sightings are often surprisingly close to houses, roadways, golf courses and industrial yards—these structures and their associated human activity give foxes refuge from Coyotes.

The Red Fox has become increasingly common in agricultural landscapes, particularly in the extreme southern parts of Alberta, and it is re-entering areas that have not supported foxes for many years. The Red Fox stronghold, however, remains northern Alberta, where these diminutive carnivores live on mice and carcasses in the shadow of the Grey Wolf.

Total Length: 90–113 cm (35–44 in)
Shoulder Height: 38–41 cm (15–16 in)
Tail Length: 35–44 cm (14–17 in)
Weight: 3.6–5.8 kg (8–13 lb)

DESCRIPTION: This small, slender, dog-like fox has an exceptionally bushy, long tail. Its upperparts are usually a vivid reddish orange, with a white chest and belly, but there are many colour variations: there is a Coyote-coloured phase in parts of the Rocky Mountains; the "cross fox" (shown on p. 133) has darker hairs along the back and across the shoulder blades; and the "silver fox," which is more frequently encountered on the prairies, is mostly black with silver-tipped hairs. In all colour phases the tail has a white tip and the backs of the ears and fronts of the forelegs are black.

HABITAT: Year-round, the Red Fox prefers open habitats interspersed with

DID YOU KNOW?

A Red Fox will often travel up to 8 km (5 mi) during the night, searching out potential prey with its keen senses.

BEST SITES: Gaetz Lake Sanctuary, Red Deer; Police Point Park, Medicine Hat; Lethbridge, Calgary and Edmonton river parks; Wood Buffalo NP; Cold Lake PP.

RANGE: In North America, this holarctic species occurs throughout most of Canada and the U.S., except for the high Arctic, northwestern British Columbia and much of the western U.S.

brushy shelter. It avoids extensive areas of dense, coniferous forests with heavy snowfall.

FOOD: This opportunistic feeder usually stalks its prey and then pounces on or captures it after a short rush. In winter, small rodents, rabbits and birds make up most of the diet, but dried berries are also eaten. In more moderate seasons, invertebrates, birds, eggs, fruits and berries supplement the basic small-mammal diet.

DEN: The Red Fox generally dens in a burrow, which the vixen either digs herself or, more usually, makes by expanding a marmot or badger hole. The den is sometimes located in a hollow log, in a brush pile or beneath an unoccupied building.

YOUNG: A litter of 1 to 10 kits is born in April or May after a gestation of about 7½ weeks. The kits weigh about 100 g (3½ oz) at birth. Their eyes open after nine days, and they are weaned when a month old. The parents first bring the kits dead food, and later crippled animals. The father may bring back to the

den several voles, or perhaps a hare and some mice, at the end of a single hunting trip. After the kits learn to kill, the parents start taking them on hunts. The young disperse when they are three to four months old; they become sexually mature well before their first birthdays.

foreprint

hindprint

SIMILAR SPECIES: The Coyote (p. 118) is generally larger, has a dark tail tip and does not have black forelegs. The Swift Fox (p. 134) has a very limited distribution in Alberta, is smaller and has a dark-tipped tail and light-coloured feet.

Coyote

Swift Fox

Vulpes velox

There are precious few conservation success stories in Alberta, but the ongoing re-establishment of the Swift Fox is one achievement to be celebrated. Historically, the Swift Fox was found throughout the Great Plains, ranging as far north as the Red Deer River in Alberta. Its provincial numbers declined as a result of habitat loss and deaths from traps and poison set for Grey Wolves and Coyotes. The last wild Swift Fox in Alberta, prior to their re-establishment, was seen near the prairie outpost of Manyberries in 1938.

The case for re-establishing the Swift Fox into areas of Alberta was strong—some relatively pristine grasslands remained, wild populations still occurred to the south, and the primary causes for its initial decline were eliminated—and the reintroduction initiative, which began in 1983, has been largely successful. Many of the first animals that were released were captive-raised in Alberta, but few, if any, of these animals survived long after their release. Now the emphasis is on wild-born animals transported from the northern U.S. These later introductions have survived and reproduced successfully, resulting in a small, but so far continuing, population. Through the enthusiasm of private stewards and the diligence of government biologists, there are now about 200 Swift Foxes in Alberta, tightly framed by the U.S. and Saskatchewan borders.

Re-introduction into the wild is no guarantee for the Swift Fox's survival in

Total Length: 60–80 cm (24–31 in)
Shoulder Height: 28–31 cm (11–12 in)
Tail Length: 23–30 cm (9–12 in)
Weight: 1.4–2.7 kg (3–6 lb)

Alberta. This cat-sized canid has high mortality rates, especially from larger grassland predators—ignoring its family ties, the Coyote is the Swift Fox's main predator and accounts for the majority of known deaths. To avoid Coyote predation, the Swift Fox tends to den in areas with sweeping vistas, which give denning foxes ample visual warning of approaching danger. These innate adaptations, coupled with a progressive implementation of effective conservation strategies, will hopefully ensure that future generations of Swift Foxes will have a secure place in Alberta's grassland community.

DESCRIPTION: The summer coat of this tiny fox closely matches its prairie environment: the back is mainly pale

DID YOU KNOW?

Within the first decade of their re-establishment into Alberta, over 200 kits had been born in the wild to released parents. The average litter size of these foxes in Alberta is about four, which corresponds with populations elsewhere.

BEST SITES: Native prairies southeast of Manyberries.

RANGE: The former range included the arid regions of Alberta, Saskatchewan and Manitoba south through eastern Montana and the Dakotas to northern Texas. Although its number are greatly reduced, the Swift Fox may still be found sprinkled throughout this range.

rufous or buffy grey, and the sides are a lighter yellowish buff. The long guard hairs are white- or black-tipped, giving the fox an overall grizzled appearance. Each side of the muzzle bears a distinct black spot, and the neck, backs of the ears and legs have orange highlights. The tail is large and has a noticeable black tip.

HABITAT: This open-country fox inhabits prairies, badlands and other arid areas.

FOOD: Rabbits and small rodents make up the bulk of the diet, but Swift Foxes also eat birds, insects and even grasses or berries. It also consumes carrion in significant amounts.

DEN: A Swift Fox's fairly complex burrow usually has four or five entrances. The same burrow is used throughout the year, and perhaps even for a lifetime.

YOUNG: Swift Foxes usually form lifelong pair bonds. Mating in already-paired foxes begins with courtship in January. Foxes courting for the first time begin later in the season. The kits are born in a small, bare chamber of the burrow after a gestation of about seven to eight weeks. The litter of three to six young requires great care for the first few weeks. The kits open their eyes and ears at two weeks, and they are weaned at six weeks. They disperse in the fall and breed before they are one year old.

trotting trail

SIMILAR SPECIES: The Red Fox (p. 130) is larger and has black forelegs and a white-tipped tail. The Coyote (p. 118) is much larger and has a tawny patch on the upper-surface of its snout.

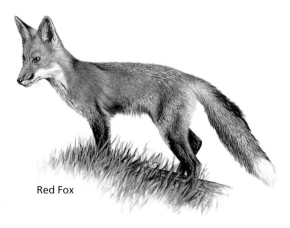

Red Fox

RODENTS

In terms of sheer numbers, rodents are the most successful order of mammals in Alberta. They are often regarded negatively by humans because of the group's association with its best-known members, rats and mice. One must remember, however, that chipmunks, marmots, beavers, lemmings and flying squirrels are also rodents. Most rodents are relatively small mammals, but the American Beaver and the Common Porcupine can grow quite large.

All rodents have upper and lower pairs of protruding incisor teeth that continue to grow throughout the animal's life. These four teeth have pale yellow to burnt orange enamel only on their front surfaces; the softer dentine at the rear of each tooth is worn away against its opposing tooth so that the teeth retain knife-sharp cutting edges.

Common Porcupine

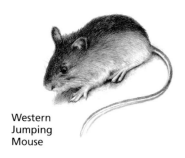

Western Jumping Mouse

Western Harvest Mouse

Porcupine Family
(Erethizontidae)

The stocky-bodied Common Porcupine has some of its hairs modified into sharp-pointed quills that it uses in defence. The sharp, curved claws and rough soles of its feet are adapted for climbing.

Jumping Mouse Family
(Zapodidae)

Jumping mice are so called because they make long leaps when they are startled. Their hindlegs are much longer than their forelegs, and the tail, which is longer than the combined length of the head and body, serves as a counterbalance during jumps. Jumping mice are almost completely nocturnal.

Mouse Family
(Muridae)

This diverse group of rodents is the largest and most successful mammal family in the world. Its members include the familiar rats and mice, as well as voles and lemmings. The Albertan representatives vary in size from the tiny Western Harvest Mouse to the Common Muskrat.

Beaver Family
(Castoridae)

The American Beaver accounts for half the worldwide species in this family. It is the largest North American rodent, and it is one of the most visible mammals in the province. After humans, it is probably the animal with the biggest impact on the landscape of Alberta.

American Beaver

Pocket Mouse Family
(Heteromyidae)

Pocket mice and kangaroo rats make up a group of small to medium-sized rodents that are somewhat adapted to a subterranean existence. They feed mainly on seeds, and they use their fur-lined cheek pouches to transport food to caches in their burrows. Typically occurring in dry environments, many of them can live for a long time without free water.

Olive-backed Pocket Mouse

Pocket Gopher Family
(Geomyidae)

Almost exclusively subterranean, all pocket gophers have small eyes, tiny ears, heavy claws, short, strong forelegs and a short, sparsely haired tail. Their fur-lined cheek pouches, or "pockets," are primarily used to transport food. The lower jaw is massive, and the incisor teeth are used in part for excavating tunnels.

Northern Pocket Gopher

Squirrel Family
(Sciuridae)

This family, which includes chipmunks, tree squirrels, flying squirrels, marmots and ground squirrels in Alberta, is considered the most structurally primitive group of rodents. All its members, except the flying squirrels, are active during the day, so they are among the most frequently seen rodents.

Red-tailed Chipmunk

Common Porcupine
Erethizon dorsatum

Although it is aggressiveness that is most often celebrated among Alberta's mammals, the trademark of the Common Porcupine is its unsurpassed defensive armoury. A porcupine's formidable quills, numbering about 30,000, are actually modified, stiff hairs with overlapping, shingle-like barbs at their tips.

Contrary to popular belief, a porcupine cannot throw its quills, but if it is forced to fight it will lower its head in a defensive posture and lash out with its tail. The loosely rooted quills detach easily, and they may be driven deeply into the attacker's flesh. The barbs expand with the body heat and blood, making the quills even harder to extract. Quill wounds may fester, or, depending on where the quills strike, they can blind an animal, prevent it from eating or even puncture a vital organ.

Porcupines are strictly vegetarian, and they are frequently found feeding in agricultural fields, willow-edged wetlands and forests. The tender bark of young branches seems to be a porcupine delicacy, and although you wouldn't think it from their size, porcupines can move far out on very thin branches with their deliberate climbing. Accomplished, if slow, climbers, porcupines use their sharp, curved claws, the thick, sand-papery soles of their feet and the quills on the underside of the tail to reach great heights in trees. These large, stocky rodents often remain in individual trees and bushes for several days at a time, and when they leave a foraging site, the naked, cream-coloured branches are clear evidence of their activity.

The Common Porcupine is mostly nocturnal, and it often rests by day in a hollow tree or log, in a burrow or in a treetop. It is not unusual to see a porcupine abroad by day, however, either in an open field or in a forest. It often chews bones or fallen antlers for calcium, and the sound of a porcupine's gnawing can sometimes be heard at a considerable distance.

Unfortunately for the Common Porcupine, its armament is no defence against vehicles—highway collisions are a major cause of porcupine mortality—and most Albertans see many more porcupines at the side of a road than alive in the wild. Perhaps that is why some unkind people call them "Alberta speed bumps."

DID YOU KNOW?

The name "porcupine," which comes from the Vulgar Latin porcospinus *(spiny pig), underwent serveral variations—Shakespeare used the word "porpentine"—before settling on its current spelling in the 17th century.*

BEST SITES: Roadways in the Eastern Irrigation District; Elk Island NP.

RANGE: The porcupine is widely distributed from Alaska across Canada to Pennsylvania and New England and south through most of the West into Mexico.

Total Length: 53–94 cm (21–37 in)
Tail Length: 14–28 cm (5½–11 in)
Weight: 1–12 kg (2¼–26 lb)

DESCRIPTION: This large, stout-bodied rodent has long, white-tipped guard hairs surrounding the centre of the back, where abundant, long quills criss-cross one another in all directions. The young are mostly black, but adults are variously tinged with yellow. The upper surface of the powerful, thick tail is amply supplied with the dark-tipped, white to yellowish quills. The front claws are curved and sharp. The skin on the soles of the feet is covered with tooth-like projections. There may be grey patches on the cheeks and between the eyes.

FOOD: Completely herbivorous, the Common Porcupine is like an arboreal counterpart of the American Beaver. It eats leaves, buds, twigs and especially young bark or the cambium layer of both broadleaf and coniferous trees and shrubs. During spring and summer it eats considerable amounts of herbaceous vegetation. The porcupine typically puts on weight during spring and summer and loses it during fall and winter. It seems to have a profound fondness for salt, and it will chew and devour wood handles, boots and other materials that are salty from sweat or urine.

DEN: Porcupines prefer caves or shelters along watercourses or beneath fallen rocks, but they sometimes move into abandoned buildings, especially in winter. They are typically solitary animals, denning alone, but they may share a den during particularly cold weather. Sometimes a porcupine will sleep in a treetop for weeks, avoiding any den site, while it completely strips the tree of bark.

YOUNG: The porcupine's impressive armament inspires many questions about how it manages to mate. The female docs most of the courtship, although males may fight with one another, and she is apparently stimulated by having the male urinate on her. When she is sufficiently aroused, she relaxes her quills and raises her tail over her back so that mating can proceed.

141

Following mating in November or December and a gestation period of 6½ to 7 months—unusually long for a rodent—a single precocious porcupette is born in May or June. The young porcupine is born with quills, but they are not dangerous to the mother: the baby is born headfirst in a placental sac with its soft quills lying flat against its body. The quills harden within about an hour of birth. Porcupines have erupted incisor teeth at birth, and although they may continue to nurse for up to four months, they begin eating green vegetation before they are one month old. Porcupines become sexually mature when they are 1½ to 2½ years old.

right hindprint

walking trail

SIMILAR SPECIES: No other Albertan animal closely resembles the Common Porcupine, but there is a small chance that, in a nocturnal sighting, the Common Raccoon (p. 106) could be mistaken for a porcupine.

Common Raccoon

Meadow Jumping Mouse
Zapus hudsonius

Total Length: 19–22 cm (7½–8¾ in)

Tail Length: 11–14 cm (4¼–5½ in)

Weight: 14–24 g (½–⅞ oz)

On the rare occasions when these fascinating mice are encountered, their method of escape belies their true identities: startled from their sedgy homes, jumping mice hop away in a manner befitting a frog.

Jumping mice spend up to nine months of the year in hibernation, giving them activity patterns like those of some marmots and ground squirrels. This situation is not surprising, however, because jumping mice rarely venture far from wet areas—they spend their entire lives in a landscape that is almost wholly frozen for much of the year. Adults all seem to be underground by the end of August; only a few small juveniles that have not yet reached their minimum hibernation weight may be aboveground until mid-September.

DESCRIPTION: The back is brownish, the sides are yellowish, and the belly is whitish. Juveniles are much browner

dorsally than adults. The long, naked tail is distinctly bicoloured: dark above; pale below. The hindfeet are greatly elongated.

HABITAT: Moist fields are preferred, but it also occurs in brush, marshes, brushy fields or even woods with thick vegetation.

FOOD: In spring, insects account for about half the diet. The seeds of grasses and many forbs are eaten as they ripen. In summer and fall, subterranean fungi form about an eighth of the diet.

DEN: This jumping mouse hibernates in a nest of finely shredded vegetation in a burrow or other protected site. Its summer nest is built aboveground on the surface or in a small shrub.

YOUNG: Mating occurs within a week of the female's emergence from hibernation, typically in May. She bears two to nine young after a 19-day gestation. The eyes open after two to five days, and nursing continues for a month. The young must achieve a certain minimum weight or they will not survive the lengthy hibernation. Most females have a second litter after the first one leaves.

SIMILAR SPECIES: The Western Jumping Mouse (p. 145) has white edges on its ears and generally has a more southern range.

BEST SITES: Tall grass and shrubs near wet areas; Wolf Creek, near Edson.

RANGE: This jumping mouse is found from southern Alaska across most of southern Canada (except the prairies) and south to northeastern Oklahoma in the West and northern Georgia in the East.

Western Jumping Mouse
Zapus princeps

Total Length: 20–26 cm (7¾–10 in)
Tail Length: 12–15 cm (4¾–6 in)
Weight: 19–33 g (¹¹⁄₁₆–1⅛ oz)

Let's face it, Alberta's two species of jumping mice are virtually indistinguishable from each other, which may create some confusion in the parts of central Alberta where their ranges overlap. Their hopping escapes and supremely long tails, however, are sufficiently distinctive for novice naturalists to identify an animal as a jumping mouse, even if they can't tell exactly which one it is.

DESCRIPTION: A broad, dark, longitudinal band extends from the nose to the rump. The sides of the body are yellowish olive, often with some orangish hairs. The belly is a clear creamy white. The flanks and cheeks are golden yellow. The naked tail is olive brown above and whitish below. The hindfeet are greatly elongated.

HABITAT: This jumping mouse prefers areas of tall grass, often near streams, that may have brush or trees. In the mountains, it ranges from valley floors up into tundra sedge meadows. It frequently enters the water and appears to swim well, diving as deep as 1 m (3½ ft).

FOOD: In spring and summer it eats berries, tender vegetation, insects and a few other invertebrates. As fall approaches, grass seeds and the fruits of forbs are taken more frequently. Subterranean fungi are also favoured.

DEN: The hibernation nest, made of finely shredded vegetation, is 30–60 cm (1–2 ft) below the surface in a burrow that is 1–3 m (3½–10 ft) long. The breeding nest is typically built amongst interwoven, broad-leaved grasses or in sphagnum moss in a depression.

YOUNG: Breeding takes place within a week after the female emerges from hibernation. Following an 18-day gestation period, four to eight young are born in late June or early July. The eyes open after two to five days. The young nurse for one month. Some females have two, or even three, litters a year.

SIMILAR SPECIES: The Meadow Jumping Mouse (p. 144) lacks the black hairs in the dorsal stripe and generally has a more northern range.

BEST SITES: Tall grasses and shrubs near wet areas; Elk Creek, west of Sundre.

RANGE: This western species is found from the southern Yukon southeast to North Dakota and south to central California and northern New Mexico.

Western Harvest Mouse
Reithrodontomys megalotis

In contrast to the comparative ferocity of many mice, the Western Harvest Mouse has an angelic disposition. It is very tolerant of crowding, and individuals are known to huddle together to conserve heat in winter—the Western Harvest Mouse does not hibernate. This diminutive mouse appears to be inoffensive not only towards other harvest mice, but even towards other species. A female harvest mouse will tolerate having a male in her nest, and even strange mice may be introduced to the group without incident.

Leading candidates for the title of smallest Alberta rodents, Western Harvest Mice are most active during the two hours after sunset, but their activity may continue almost until dawn, particularly on dark, moonless nights. They often use vole runways through thick grass to reach foraging areas, and harvest mice are named for their habit of collecting grass cuttings in mounds along their trail networks. Western Harvest Mice do not store food in any great quantities, however, which is understandable for a species that usually lives for less than a year.

Alberta's Western Harvest Mice are at the northern limit of this species' range—since the retreat of the Wisconsonian ice sheets, this species has been expanding its range north and east from the deserts of northern Mexico—and they are among the rarest of western Canadian mammals. Even in the more southern parts of its range, the Western Harvest Mouse is rarely as plentiful as other native mice.

DESCRIPTION: This native mouse closely resembles the House Mouse: it is small and slim, with a small head and pointed nose, and it has a conspicuous, long, sparsely haired tail and large, naked ears. The bicoloured tail is greyish above and lighter below. The upperparts are brownish, darkest down the middle of the back and on the ears. The underparts are greyish white, sometimes with a pale cinnamon wash, and they blend imperceptibly into the buffy tones on the cheeks, flanks and sides.

HABITAT: Harvest mice occur in both arid and moist places—grasslands, sagebrush, weedy waste areas, fence lines and

---

DID YOU KNOW?

The reproductive potential of harvest mice is remarkable, although high densities of the species have never been reported in Alberta. Two females once produced 14 litters in 11 and 12 months respectively, with the total numbers of young being 57 and 58.

BEST SITES: Suffield military reserve; native grasslands southeast of Manyberries.

RANGE: From extreme southern Alberta and Saskatchewan and south-central British Columbia, this mouse ranges south through most of the western U.S. It is absent from most of the Rockies and Cascades, and has an eastward extension into Wisconsin, Illinois and Missouri.

Total Length: 11–15 cm (4¼–6 in)
Tail Length: 5.9–7.8 cm (2⅜–3⅛ in)
Weight: 9–24 g (⁵⁄₁₆–⅞ oz)

even cattail-choked marsh edges—as long as there is abundant overhead cover.

FOOD: This harvest mouse eats lots of green vegetation in spring and early summer, and at those times of year its runways may sport piles of grass cuttings. During most of the year, however, the seeds of grasses, legumes, mustards and grains predominate in the diet. Many grasshoppers, beetles, weevils and green sedges are also eaten throughout the year. The Western Harvest Mouse apparently does not store food.

DEN: This mouse builds its ball-shaped nest, which is about 7.5 cm (3 in) in diameter, either on the ground or low in a shrub or weeds. It builds the nest with grass and other plant fibres and usually lines the central chamber, which is about 3.5 cm (1⅜ in) across, with finer downy material, such as cattail or milk-

weed fluff. The nest has one or more entrances, each about 1 cm (⅜ in) across, on the underside. A single nest may house 2 to 10 of these docile mice.

YOUNG: Reproduction is concentrated in the warmer months, but if conditions are right adult females may be almost continuously pregnant. The average litter of four is born after a 23- to 24-day gestation. At 4 days the incisors erupt; the hair is visible by day 5; the eyes open after 10 to 12 days; and at 19 days the young are weaned. The female becomes sexually mature at four to five months.

SIMILAR SPECIES: The House Mouse (p. 156) is generally larger, its tail is grey-brown, it has a faint black mid-dorsal stripe from head to tail and it does not have the buffy tones on the cheeks and flanks.

Deer Mouse

Peromyscus maniculatus

To even the most committed mouse-o-phobe, the Deer Mouse looks cute. Its large, protruding, coal black eyes give it a justifiably inquisitive look, while its dainty nose and long whiskers continually twitch, sensing odorous changes in the wind.

Wherever there is groundcover, from thick grass to deadfall, Deer Mice scurry about with great caution. These small mice are omnipresent over much of the province, and they may well be the most numerous mammals in Alberta. When you walk through Alberta's wild areas, they are in your company, even if their presence remains hidden.

Deer Mice most frequently forage along the ground, commuting between piles of ground debris, but they are known to climb trees and shrubs to reach food. During winter, Deer Mice are the most common of the small rodents to travel above the snow. In doing so, however, characteristically bounding along and leaving four neat little footprints, Deer Mice are vulnerable to predators. The tiny skulls of these rodents are among the most common remains in the regurgitated pellets of owls, which is a testament to their irreplaceable role in Alberta's food web.

The Deer Mouse, which is named for the similarity of its colouring to that of the White-tailed Deer, commonly occupies farm buildings, garages and storage sheds, often alongside the House Mouse. There have been a few high-profile cases in Alberta of people dying from the Hanta virus, which can be associated with the feces and urine of the Deer Mouse. The virus can become airborne, so if you find Deer Mouse droppings, it is best to wear a mask while spraying the area with water and bleach before attempting to remove the animal's waste.

DESCRIPTION: All Deer Mice have large ears, a pointed nose, long whiskers, bright white undersides and feet, a cluster of whitish hairs at the front of each ear base, protruding, black, lustrous eyes and a sharply bicoloured tail with a dark top and light underside. In contrast to these constant characteristics, the colour of the adult's upperparts is quite variable: yellowish buff, tawny brown, greyish brown or blackish brown. A juvenile has uniformly grey upperparts.

DID YOU KNOW?

Adult Deer Mice displaced a mile from where they were trapped were generally able to return to their home burrows within 24 hours. Perhaps they ranged so widely in their regular travels that they recognized where they were and simply scampered home.

BEST SITES: Under boards or in barns and other storage facilities on your friend's or relative's farm.

RANGE: This rodent is the most widespread mouse in North America. Its range extends from Labrador almost to Alaska and south through most of North America to south-central Mexico.

Total Length: 14–21 cm (5½–8¼ in)
Tail Length: 5.4–10 cm (2⅛–4 in)
Weight: 18–34 g (⅝–1¼ oz)

HABITAT: These ubiquitous mice occupy a variety of habitats, including prairie grasslands, mossy depressions, brushy areas, tundra and heavily wooded regions. Another habitat that these little mice have a profound tendency to enter is the human building—our warm, food-laden homes are palatial residences to Deer Mice.

FOOD: Deer Mice use their internal cheek pouches to transport large quantities of seeds from grasses, grains, chokecherries, buckwheat and other weeds to their burrows. They also eat insects.

DEN: As the habitat of this mouse changes, so does its den type: in prairies and meadows it nests in a small burrow or makes a grassy nest on raised ground; in wooded areas it makes a nest in a hollow log or under debris. Nests can also be made in rock crevices, and certainly in human structures.

YOUNG: Breeding takes places between March and October, and gestation lasts for three to four weeks. The helpless young number one to nine (usually four or five) and weigh about 1.7 g (1/16 oz) at birth. They open their eyes between days 12 and 17, and about four days after that they venture out of the nest. At three to five weeks the young are completely weaned and are soon on their own. The female is sexually mature in about 35 days; the male in about 45 days.

SIMILAR SPECIES: The House Mouse (p. 156) and the Western Harvest Mouse (p. 146) lack the distinct white belly. The Bushy-tailed Woodrat (p. 152) is much larger. Jumping mice (pp. 144–45) have much longer tails.

Northern Grasshopper Mouse
Onychomys leucogaster

The Northern Grasshopper Mouse is the bulldog of Alberta mice. It is a thick-legged, chunky resident of sandy parts of the province, often living in close association with the equally specialized Ord's Kangaroo Rat. The stocky form of the Northern Grasshopper Mouse befits its predatory nature: up to 90 percent of its diet consists of animals, primarily grasshoppers, but also including prey as large as mice and voles.

This mouse is also reputed to have a fierce disposition towards non-prey species, frequently usurping the burrows of other small mammals and modifying them for its own needs. Its nest burrow tends to be U-shaped: a tunnel leading only a few centimetres down from the surface; then levelling out to a nest; then returning to the surface. The burrow is built in loose, dry, sandy soil, which is also ideal for dust bathing—a grasshopper mouse's form of sanitation to shampoo the naturally oily fur.

In contrast to its attitude towards strangers, the Northern Grasshopper Mouse seems to make a devoted parent; both the male and female care for the young, bringing food to the nest until their offspring become self-sufficient, mini-mauraders of the sands.

DESCRIPTION: The back is grey to yellowish buff and the entire belly is white. The nose is pointed, the dark, lustrous eyes protrude noticeably, and the ears are large. The short tail—it is less than twice the length of the hindfoot—is thick, sharply bicoloured (darker above, white below) and has a white tip. The thick legs, broad feet and broad shoulders of this mouse give an impression of burliness. Animals seen in the wild may appear rumpled.

HABITAT: This mouse occurs in a wide variety of open habitats with sandy or gravelly soils, from grasslands to sandy brushlands, but it avoids alkali flats, marshy areas and rocky sites.

FOOD: Only a little more than 10 percent of the summer diet consists of vegetation, mostly the seeds of grasses and forbs; grasshoppers, crickets and beetles make up about 60 percent. In winter, up to 40 percent of the diet is composed of seeds and vegetation. This fierce little predator may also take scorpions, spi-

DID YOU KNOW?

The Northern Grasshopper Mouse has the ability to produce complex vocalizations. Mated pairs hunt simultaneously, and they apparently keep in contact with frequent, variable, bird-like calls.

BEST SITES: Sandhills in the Empress, Bindloss and Suffield areas.

RANGE: This grasshopper mouse ranges through much of the Great Plains, Rocky Mountains and Great Basin, from southern Alberta and Saskatchewan south into northern Mexico.

Total Length: 13–15 cm (5–6 in)
Tail Length: 3–4 cm (1⅛–1⅝ in)
Weight: 20–52 g (^{11}⁄₁₆–1⅞ oz)

ders, moths and butterflies. It can even overpower and kill mice and birds up to three times its own weight.

DEN: Nest burrows are U-shaped and about 4 cm (1½ in) in diameter. The nest is located about 15 cm (6 in) below the surface. The entrance is plugged by day to retain moisture. Nests may also be built under vegetation or debris, or in holes dug by other animals.

YOUNG: Breeding occurs between March and August. A female's first pregnancy lasts about one month, but subsequent litters are typically born 32 to 38 days after mating. A litter usually contains three or four young, which weigh 1.7–2.7 g (¹⁄₁₆–⅛ oz) and are naked and blind at birth. The incisors begin to erupt at nine days, the eyes open at two to three weeks, and weaning follows by day 24. Most females breed during the spring following their birth, as do males,

and they may bear two or three litters each summer.

SIMILAR SPECIES: The Deer Mouse (p. 148) has similar coloration but lacks the burly proportions and has a thinner, longer tail.

running group

Bushy-tailed Woodrat
Neotoma cinerea

While most Albertans have heard of "packrats," few of them know that a species lives in their own province. The Bushy-tailed Woodrat is a fine representative of packrats, animals that are widely known for their habit of collecting all kinds of objects into a messy heap. Woodrats are also sometimes called "trade rats," because they are nearly always carrying something in their teeth and dropping that item to take something else. Thus, camping gear, false teeth, tools or even jewellery may disappear from a campsite, with sticks, bones or pinecones kindly left in their place.

Bushy-tailed Woodrats have a limited range in Alberta, and they are common in very few places in the province. They tend to nest in rocky areas, and because their nests are large and messy, woodrat homes are easier to find than the woodrats themselves. The areas in which woodrats can build their nests are prized real estate, and rival males fiercely fight over their houses. Female woodrats are likely attracted to males who have secure nests, and several females may be found nesting with a single male.

The Bushy-tailed Woodrat may have proportionally the longest whiskers of any Alberta mammal. Extending well over the width of the animal's body on either side, a woodrat's whiskers serve it well as it feels its way around in the darkness of caves, mines and the night.

Woodrats are most active after dark, so a late-night prowl with flashlights in hand may catch the reflective glare of woodrat eyes as the animals investigate their territories. These are among the most endearing of all Alberta's rodents, and it is unfortunate that their name brings with it the negative connotations of the word "rat."

DESCRIPTION: The back is grey, pale pinkish or grizzled brown. The long, soft, dense, buffy fur is underlain by a short, soft underfur. The belly is white. The long, bushy, almost squirrel-like tail is grey above and white below. There are distinct juvenile and sub-adult pelages: the juvenile's back is grey, and its has short tail hairs; the subadult has brown hues in its back, and the tail has bushy guard hairs; the tawny adult pelage is developed in fall. All woodrats have large, protruding, black eyes, big,

---

DID YOU KNOW?

When a very old woodrat nest in a decrepit cabin near the Banff Springs Hotel was torn apart some years ago, a complete collection of hotel silverware dating back to the earliest days of the establishment was discovered.

BEST SITES: Writing-on-Stone PP; low-elevation rock piles from Waterton Lakes to Jasper NPs.

RANGE: The Bushy-tailed Woodrat is the most northerly species of woodrat; its range extends from the southern Yukon southeast to western North Dakota and south to central California and northern New Mexico.

Total Length: 29–45 cm (11–18 in)
Tail Length: 11–22 cm (4¼–8¾ in)
Weight: 80–520 g (2⅞–18 oz)

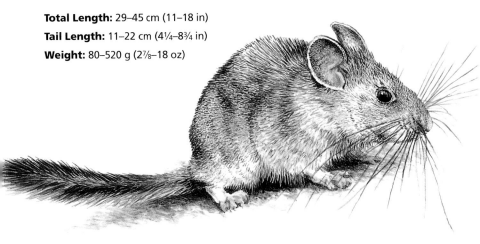

fur-covered ears and long, abundant whiskers.

HABITAT: This woodrat's domain usually includes rocks and shrubs or abandoned buildings, mine shafts or caves. It has a greater altitudinal range than other woodrats, extending from the prairies to alpine mountain regions.

FOOD: The leaves of shrubs are probably the most important component of the diet, but conifer needles and seeds, juniper berries, mushrooms, fruits, grasses, rootstocks and bulbs are all eaten or stored for later consumption. To provide adequate winter supplies, a woodrat gathers and stores about 8 *l* (2 gal) of food. One woodrat may make several caches.

DEN: Large quantities of sticks, plus a large variety of bark, dung and other materials, are piled in a rock cleft or talus near the nest site. There are often no inner passages or chambers in this accumulation; instead, a lined, ball- or cup-shaped nest is built of fibrous material and situated nearby, usually more than 3.5 m (11 ft) above the ground, either in a narrow crevice, in the fork of a tree, on a shelf or sometimes in a stove in an abandoned cabin.

YOUNG: Mating usually takes place between March and June. Following a 27- to 32-day gestation, three or four helpless young are born. They are 12–17 g (⁷⁄₁₆–⅝ oz) at birth and their growth is rapid. Special teeth help them hold on to their mother's nipples almost continuously. Their incisors erupt at 12 to 15 days and the eyes open on day 14 or 15. They first leave the nest at about 22 days, and they are weaned at 26 to 30 days. The young reach sexual maturity the spring following their birth. Some females bear two litters in a season.

SIMILAR SPECIES: No other Alberta mammal of comparable size resembles this woodrat. The American Pika (p. 207) has no visible tail and its whiskers are dark. The Deer Mouse (p. 148) is similarly coloured, but it is much smaller.

right hindprint

Norway Rat
Rattus norvegicus

While it is said that absence makes the heart grow fonder, it's a sure bet that no Albertans miss rats. As most every Albertan knows, our province is one of the few areas of the world that is free of these highly successful animals. This distinction is hard earned: control programs have been in place for decades to maintain our rat-free status. Even today, the famed Alberta Rat Patrol works our borders, eradicating every reported population of these rodents.

Alberta's geographic position has done as much as human management efforts to limit the spread of rats into the province. Our western boundary has the Rocky Mountains as an effective barrier, and the northern half of the province's boreal regions is equally inhospitable to the animals. Only along the southern and southeastern borders can rats enter the province on their own. Farms and ranches in the area are large, however, which limits rat dispersal. The greatest influx of rats arrives courtesy of modern transport: rats hitch-hiking on trucks and trains are of concern, and they have taken up temporary residence in some areas before their elimination.

Norway Rats are viewed with disgust by most people. They are described as filthy, loathsome creatures for their habit of eating vast quantities of stored food and living in the sewers, docks and warehouses of all major international cities. Without these occurrences in Alberta, the most significant provincial concentrations of rats occur in scientific laboratories. As one of the world's most studied and manipulated animals, much of our biomedical and psychological knowledge can be directly attributed to experiments involving these animals—a rather significant contribution for a lowly pest.

DESCRIPTION: The back is grizzled brown, reddish brown or black in colour. The paler belly is greyish to yellowish white. The long, round, tapered tail is darker above and lighter below. It is sparsely haired and scaly. The prominent ears are covered with short, fine hairs. Occasionally, someone releases albino, white or piebald Norway Rats that had been kept in captivity.

HABITAT: Norway Rats nearly always live near human habitations. Where

---

BEST SITES: British Columbia, Saskatchewan, Montana, Toronto, Ottawa.

RANGE: Apart from Alberta, the Norway Rat occurs across southern Canada and south through the entire U.S. in scattered populations that are concentrated in towns, cities and ranches. In can disperse 5–8 km (3–5 mi) in a summer, but if sufficient shelter is not available, winter temperatures of –18° C (0° F) are fatal.

Total Length: 32–46 cm (13–18 in)
Tail Length: 12–22 cm (4¾–8¾ in)
Weight: 200–490 g (7–17 oz)

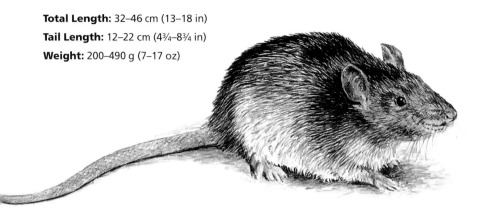

they are found away from buildings, they prefer thickly vegetated regions with abundant cover.

FOOD: This rat eats a wide variety of grains, insects, garbage and carrion; it may even kill young chickens, ducks, piglets and lambs. Green legume fruits are also popular items, and some shoots and grasses are consumed.

DEN: A cavity scratched beneath a fallen board or a space beneath an abandoned building may hold a bulky nest of grasses, leaves and often paper or chewed rags. Although the Norway Rat is cap-able of burrowing, it seldom digs a long burrow.

YOUNG: After a gestation of three weeks, the female bears 6 to 22 pink, blind babies. They open their eyes after 10 days and are sexually mature in about three months. A female may have several litters in a season.

SIMILAR SPECIES: The Bushy-tailed Woodrat (p. 152) has a white belly and its tail is covered with long, bushy hair. The Common Muskrat (p. 166) is generally larger and has a laterally compressed tail.

Black Rat
Rattus rattus

Total Length: 33–46 cm (13–18 in)
Tail Length: 16–26 cm (6¼–10 in)
Weight: 120–350 g (4¼–12 oz)

The Black Rat is generally restricted to the southern and coastal U.S., and the small numbers that have been captured in Edmonton and Calgary arrived via human transport. It is very similar in appearance to the Norway Rat, although generally slimmer and with a longer tail.

House Mouse
Mus musculus

Thanks to its habit of catching rides with humans, first aboard ships and now in train cars, trucks and containers, the House Mouse is found in most countries of the world. In fact, the House Mouse's dispersal closely mirrors the agricultural development of humankind. As we began growing crops on the great sweeping plains of middle Asia, this mouse, native to that region, began profiting from our storage of surplus grains and our concurrent switch from a nomadic to a relatively sedentary lifestyle. Within the short span of a few hundred human generations, farmed grains began to find their way into Europe and Africa for trade. Along with these grain shipments, stowaway House Mice were spread to every corner of the globe. Even in Alberta, where we are proud of our rat-free status, the House Mouse is found wherever humans provide it free room and board.

House Mice are known to most Albertans who have spent some time on farms or in warehouses, university labs and other disorderly places. The white mice commonly used as laboratory animals are an albino strain of this species.

Unlike many of the introduced animals in the province, House Mice seem to have had a minimal negative impact on native animal populations. Although the great agricultural plains of Alberta are a long way from central Asia, they must be deceptively similar to this mouse's original home.

DESCRIPTION: The back is yellowish brown, grey or nearly black, the sides may have a slight yellow wash, and the underparts are light grey. The nose is pointed and surrounded by abundant whiskers. There are large, almost hairless ears above the protruding black eyes. The long, tapered tail is hairless, grey and slightly lighter below than above. The brownish feet tend to be whitish on the terminal portion.

HABITAT: This introduced mouse inhabits homes, outbuildings, barns, granaries, hay stacks and trash piles. It cannot tolerate temperatures below –10° C (14° F) around its nest and seems to be unable to survive winters in the northern forests without access to heated buildings or haystacks. In summer, it may disperse slightly more than 3.5 km (2 mi) from its

---

DID YOU KNOW?

The word "mouse" probably derives from the Sanskrit mus—*also the source, via Latin, of the genus name—which itself came from* musha, *meaning "thief."*

BEST SITES: Barns, warehouses and garages.

RANGE: The House Mouse is widespread throughout North America, inhabiting nearly every city, hamlet or farm from the Atlantic to the Pacific and north to the tundra.

Total Length: 13–20 cm (5–7¾ in)
Tail Length: 6.5–10 cm (2½–4 in)
Weight: 14–24 g (½–⅞ oz)

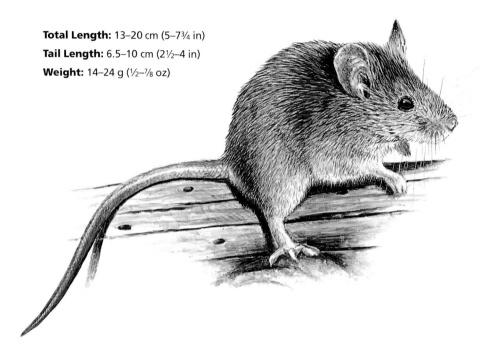

winter refuge into fields and prairies, only to succumb the following winter. Cabins in Alberta that are only occupied in summer are far more likely to be invaded by Deer Mice than by House Mice.

FOOD: Seeds, stems and leaves comprise the bulk of the diet, but insects, carrion and human food are eagerly consumed, including meat and milk.

DEN: The nest is constructed of shredded paper and rags, vegetation and sometimes fur combined into a 10-cm (4-in) ball beneath a board, inside a wall, in a pile of rags or in a haystack. It may occur at any level in a building. House Mice sometimes dig short tunnels, but they generally do not use tunnels as nest sites.

YOUNG: If abundant resources are available, as in a haystack, breeding may occur throughout the year, but populations away from human habitations seem to breed only during the warmer months. The gestation period is usually three weeks, but it may be extended to one month if the female is lactating when she conceives. The litter usually contains four to eight helpless, pink, jellybean-shaped young. Their hair begins to grow at two to three days, the eyes open at 12 to 15 days, and they are weaned at 16 to 17 days. At six to eight weeks the young become sexually mature.

SIMILAR SPECIES: The Western Harvest Mouse (p. 146) looks very similar, but it has a clearly bicoloured tail (lighter below) and a distinct longitudinal groove on the outside of each upper incisor tooth. The Deer Mouse (p. 148) has a bright white belly and distinctively bicoloured tail.

Southern Red-backed Vole
Clethrionomys gapperi

Total Length: 12–16 cm (4¾–6¼ in)

Tail Length: 3–5.7 cm (1⅛–2¼ in)

Weight: 13–44 g (⁷⁄₁₆–1½ oz)

Although these handsome little voles, which are active both day and night, can be heard in the leaf litter of just about every sizeable forest in Alberta, they are almost never seen as they scurry along on their short legs through almost invisible runways.

The Southern Red-backed Vole is a typical subnivean wanderer: a small mammal that lives out Alberta's cold winters between the snowpack and the frozen ground. At ground level, snow changes into easily penetrated depth-hoar, forming a narrow, relatively warm layer within which these small rodents spend the winter. Red-backed voles do not even cache food; instead they forage widely under the snow for vegetation or any other digestible foods.

DESCRIPTION: Reddish dorsal stripes make this species one of the easiest voles to recognize. On rare occasions, the dorsal stripe is a rich brownish black or even

slate brown. The sides are greyish buff, and the undersides and feet are greyish white. The short tail is slender and scantily haired. The ears are rounded and project somewhat above the thick fur.

HABITAT: This vole is found in a variety of habitats, including damp and coniferous forests, bogs and sometimes drier aspen forests.

FOOD: Green vegetation, grasses, berries, lichens, seeds and fungi form the bulk of the diet.

DEN: Summer nests, made in shallow burrows, rotten logs or rock crevices, are lined with fine materials, such as dry grass, moss and lichens. Winter nests are subnivean: above the ground but below the snow.

YOUNG: Mating occurs between April and October. Following a gestation period of about 20 days, two to eight pink, helpless young are born. They nurse almost continuously, and by two weeks they are well-furred and have opened their eyes. Once the young are weaned they are driven from the nest. This vole reaches sexual maturity at two to three months.

SIMILAR SPECIES: The Long-tailed Vole (p. 162) has a longer tail, and both it and the Meadow Vole (p. 161) lack the reddish dorsal stripe.

BEST SITES: Montane and mixedwood forests and aspen parklands.

RANGE: This vole is widespread across the southern half of Canada. It ranges south through the Cascades and Rocky Mountains as far as northern New Mexico and through the Appalachians to North Carolina.

Western Heather Vole
Phenacomys intermedius

The Western Heather Vole generally occupies the alpine tundra, but it also occurs in the same northern woodlands as its red-backed kin, and skulls of both species are not infrequently found in the same owl pellets.

This vole's common name is slightly misleading, because heather makes up little of either its dietary or habitat preferences. "Bark Vole" might have been a better label: this small rodent consumes a high percentage of bark seasonally and has a ceacum (a functional appendix) with 1-cm (⅜-in) villi that are modified to handle this fibrous food.

DESCRIPTION: This gentle species has a short, thin, bicoloured tail that is slate grey above and white below. The tops of the feet are silvery grey and the belly hairs have light tips, giving the entire undersurface a light grey hue. The most common dorsal colour is a grizzled buffy brown. The ears are roundish, and scarcely extend above the fur. There is tawny or orangish hair in front of the ear.

HABITAT: Found in a variety of habitats, this vole seems to prefer open areas in the mountains, including alpine tundra, and coniferous forests.

FOOD: This vole primarily feeds on green vegetation, grasses, berries, lichens, seeds and fungi, including the inner bark of various shrubs from the heather family.

Total Length: 11–16 cm (4¼–6¼ in)

Tail Length: 2.5–4.1 cm (1–1⅝ in)

Weight: 25–48 g (⅞–1¾ oz)

DEN: The summer nest is made in a burrow up to 20 cm (8 in) deep, and it is lined with fine dry grass and lichens. In winter, the nest is built on the ground in a snow-covered runway.

YOUNG: Mating occurs between April and October. Following a gestation period of about three weeks, one to eight (usually four or five) pink, helpless young are born. By two weeks, they are well-furred and have opened their eyes. This vole becomes sexually mature after two to three months, but young males do not breed in their first years.

SIMILAR SPECIES: The Long-tailed Vole (p. 162) has a longer tail, and both it and the Meadow Vole (p. 161) have slate grey hindfeet.

BEST SITES: Open areas, including tundra, in the foothills and mountains.

RANGE: This vole occurs across Canada, from the southern Yukon to northern Labrador, and south through the western mountains to central California and northern New Mexico.

Water Vole

Microtus richardsoni

Total Length: 19–27 cm (7½–11 in)
Tail Length: 5.4–9.8 cm (2⅛–3⅞ in)
Weight: 32–120 g (1⅛–4¼ oz)

HABITAT: True to its name, this vole lives primarily along alpine and subalpine streams and lakes. It favours clear, swift streams with gravelly bottoms.

O n hikes along high-country trails, if you linger by the creeks you may have an opportunity to become familiar with the Water Vole. This large vole is like an alpine muskrat that dives and forages with ease in the icy snowmelt creeks. The Water Vole creates diagnostic runways, criss-crossing the margins of alpine streams, often in such close proximity to the water that one expects the burrows to flood with each rainfall. Water Voles appear to abandon these tunnel networks through the winter months, remaining adequately protected from the winter's chill by the snows that deeply coat and insulate the rodent's habitat.

DESCRIPTION: This large vole is brownish black above, with paler grey sides. The underparts are grey with a greyish-white wash. The tail is blackish above and dark grey below. The ears are rounded and scarcely extend above the thick fur. The eyes are small, black and protruding. The hindfoot is more than 2.5 cm (1 in) long.

FOOD: In summer, Water Voles feed on the shoots and culms of various sedges and grasses, plus the leaves, stems, roots and flowers of forbs. Winter foods include the bark of willows and bog birch, and the fruits and seeds of available green vegetation.

DEN: This vole digs extensive burrow systems about 6–10 cm (2¼–4 in) in diameter through moist soil at the edges of streams or waterbodies. The nest chamber is lined with moss and dry grass or leaves. Winter nests may be made aboveground, under the snow.

YOUNG: Breeding seems to occur periodically from May to September, with usually two litters of 2 to 10 young. The gestation period is about 22 days. The young are helpless at birth, but they grow rapidly, reaching maturity quickly and even breeding in their birth year.

SIMILAR SPECIES: The long hindfoot of the Water Vole distinguishes it from all other terrestrial voles.

BEST SITES: Beside streams in the alpine tundra of Jasper, Banff and Waterton Lakes NPs and Kananaskis Country.

RANGE: The Water Vole has two disjunct populations, each associated with mountains: the western population extends along the Cascade Mountains from central British Columbia to southern Oregon; the eastern population occurs in the Rocky Mountains from central Alberta to south-central Utah.

Meadow Vole
Microtis pennsylvanicus

W hen the snows recede from Alberta fields every April, an elaborate network of Meadow Vole activity is exposed to the world. Highways, chambers and nests, previously insulated from the winter's cold by deep snows, await the growth of spring vegetation to conceal them once again.

Many Meadow Voles die in their first months, and very few voles seem to live longer than a year. With two main reproductive cycles a year, it is unlikely that many voles get to experience all seasons. During peaks in these cycles, a walk through any pasture will likely result in at least a fleeting glimpse of this ecologically important animal.

Total Length: 13–19 cm (5–7½ in)

Tail Length: 3.3–4.6 cm (1¼–1¾ in)

Weight: 17–64 g (⅝–2¼ oz)

DESCRIPTION: The body is brown to blackish above and grey below. The rounded ears are mostly hidden in the long fur of the rounded head. The tops of the feet are blackish brown. The tail is about twice as long as the hindfoot.

HABITAT: The Meadow Vole can be found in a variety of habitats, including alpine tundra, taiga, deciduous forests, open plains, cultivated fields and around marshes, waterbodies and areas with dense herbaceous shrubs.

FOOD: The green parts of sedges, grasses and some forbs make up the bulk of the spring and summer diet. In winter, large amounts of seeds, some bark and insects are eaten. Other foods include ground beans, grains, roots and bulbs.

DEN: The summer nest is made in a shallow burrow and lined with fine materials, such as dry grass, moss and lichens. The winter nest is subnivean: above the ground but below the snow.

YOUNG: Spring mating typically occurs with the appearance of green vegetation between late March and the end of April. Gestation is about 20 days, and the average litter size is four to eight. The young nurse almost constantly to support their rapid growth. Their eyes open in 9 to 12 days, and they are weaned at 12 to 13 days. At least one more litter is born, usually in fall.

SIMILAR SPECIES: The Prairie Vole (p. 164) has buffier underparts and a shorter tail.

BEST SITES: Ungrazed pastures and prairies throughout Alberta.

RANGE: Essentially a northern vole, this species occurs from central Alaska to Labrador and south to Idaho in the West and to Georgia in the East. A disjunct population occurs in Arizona, New Mexico, Colorado and Nebraska.

Long-tailed Vole
Microtus longicaudus

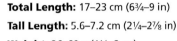

Total Length: 17–23 cm (6¾–9 in)
Tail Length: 5.6–7.2 cm (2¼–2⅞ in)
Weight: 36–60 g (1¼–2 oz)

Long-tailed Voles have a very odd distribution in the province: these voles are among the alpine elite, thriving above treeline in the mountain parks; they also live among their flatland kin on grassland plateaus. In both communities, Long-tailed Voles choose to live in wet meadows with stunted thickets and shrubs. Their night-time scurrying occurs widely; it is not restricted to well-defined trails.

DESCRIPTION: The upperparts are variously coloured, ranging from grizzled greyish to dark grey-brown, but the black tips on the guard hairs may give this vole a dark appearance. The sides are paler than the back, and the undersides are paler still. The tail of this vole is indistinctly bicoloured, and it is about 6 cm (2⅜ in) long. The uppersides of the feet are grey.

HABITAT: This vole lives in a variety of habitats, including dry grassy areas, mountain slopes, coniferous forests, alpine tundra and among alders or willows in the vicinity of water.

FOOD: Summer foods consist of green leaves, grass shoots, fruits and berries. In winter, this vole relies on the bark of heaths, willows and trees.

DEN: The simple burrows made by this vole under logs or rocks are often poorly developed. The nest chamber is lined with fine, dry grass, moss or leaves. The winter nest is subnivean.

YOUNG: Mating is presumed to occur from May to October, with the females often having two litters a year. A litter of two to eight (usually four to six) young is born after a gestation of about three weeks. The young are helpless at birth, but at about the same time as their eyes open, at two weeks old, they are weaned and leave the nest. Some young females have their first litter when they are only six weeks old.

SIMILAR SPECIES: The Meadow Vole (p. 161) has a shorter tail and dark feet.

BEST SITES: Minnewanka Lake, Banff NP.

RANGE: The Long-tailed Vole ranges south from eastern Alaska and the Yukon along the Rocky Mountains to New Mexico and Arizona. From this eastern limit, it occurs to the Pacific Ocean from Washington to California.

Yellow-cheeked Vole
Chestnut-cheeked Vole • Taiga Vole
Microtus xanthognathus

Total Length: 19–23 cm (7½–9 in)
Tail Length: 4.5–5.3 mm (1¾–2⅛ in)
Weight: 52–170 g (1⅞–6 oz)

The Yellow-cheeked Vole is an enigma among Alberta's mammals. Verified specimens were historically taken along the Athabasca River in Alberta, but not since 1904, and there is a good chance that the records were from spurious locations. Elsewhere, Yellow-cheeked Voles are found to be very active and inquisitive, chirping, in ground squirrel manner, at the approach of intruders.

Skulls of this species have been discovered in Virginia. These remains were 11,000 years old, which reinforces the notion that many of the species we now attribute to northern Canada were found much farther south during periods of extensive glaciation.

DESCRIPTION: The back is a dark greyish brown with intermixed coarse, black hairs. The short tail is blackish on top and dusky grey below. The breast and the tops of the feet are sooty. The belly is dusky grey. Bright rusty-yellowish patches appear on the nose and in front of each long ear.

HABITAT: This vole seems to favour forests in post-fire successional stages with heavy moss groundcover. It can also be found occupying upland grassy slopes in aspen-spruce and shrubby evergreen communities.

FOOD: In summer, this species feeds on horsetails, berries, some grasses, willows and lichens. The winter diet is from stores of the rhizomes of horsetails and fireweed.

DEN: These voles dig deep, extensive burrows in loose colonies. Only one pair of voles occupies each burrow. The burrows have conspicuous spoil piles at the entrances. The nest chamber is lined with dry grass, lichens or moss.

YOUNG: The first of two annual matings occurs in May or June. The litter of 6 to 13 helpless young is born after a gestation of about three weeks. The young grow rapidly, but they do not reach sexual maturity in their first summer.

SIMILAR SPECIES: The Water Vole (p. 160) has a much longer hindfoot.

BEST SITES: Athabasca River (if you're extremely optimistic).

RANGE: This vole's former range was from central Alaska east to northern Manitoba and south to central Alberta. There are, however, no recent records from Alberta or Manitoba—it appears to have abandoned the southern and eastern portions of its historic range.

former range

Prairie Vole
Microtus ochrogaster

Total Length: 12–17 cm (4¾–6¾ in)

Tail Length: 2.5–4.1 cm (1–1⅝ in)

Weight: 20–58 g (¹¹⁄₁₆–2 oz)

Although it bears a name that suggests Alberta's southlands, the Prairie Vole has primarily been recorded from the aspen parklands of east-central Alberta.

Prairie Voles seem to be less antagonistic towards one another than other voles, and small aggregations have even been noted, typically during fall and winter. These groups may be families using the same runways, tunnels and nests within a total home range that is often no larger than a tennis court.

Native peoples of the Great Plains habitually gathered the Prairie Vole's fall caches. These larders would often yield several pounds of desirable grass seeds, ground beans and Jerusalem artichoke rhizomes.

DESCRIPTION: This medium-sized vole has short legs and short, rounded ears that scarcely protrude from its fur. The upperparts are dull grey with cinnamon highlights. The underparts are yellowish grey. The tail, which is about twice as long as the hindfoot, is indistinctly bicoloured: dark above and light below.

HABITAT: The preferred habitats are arid grassland regions and sagebrush flats.

FOOD: The new green shoots of grasses and the flowers and leaves of forbs comprise the bulk of the spring and summer diet. In fall and winter, this vole relies on ripened fruits, seeds, bulbs, roots, the inner bark of shrubs and corms.

DEN: This vole digs shallow but extensive burrows in damp soils following rains. The tunnels lead to grass-lined nest chambers, which are the hub of the network of burrows and runways.

YOUNG: Mating occurs mainly between April and September. After a gestation period of about three weeks, an average litter of three or four helpless young is born. The young grow extremely rapidly, and they are weaned and out of the nest before they are three weeks old.

SIMILAR SPECIES: The Meadow Vole (p. 161) has a slightly longer tail and greyish underparts.

BEST SITES: Fencerows and ungrazed pastureland near Kitscoty.

RANGE: This open-country vole occurs from east-central Alberta south to Oklahoma and southeast to Tennessee and West Virginia.

Sagebrush Vole
Lemmiscus curtatus

Total Length: 11–14 cm (4¼–5½ in)
Tail Length: 1.8–2.7 cm (¹¹⁄₁₆–1⅛ in)
Weight: 21–39 g (¾–1⅜ oz)

Decades of walking through prime Sagebrush Vole habitat, will, on very rare occasions, produce encounters with this secretive animal. The arid shortgrass prairie seems to offer little concealment for even this small rodent, but its pale colours help it blend in with the surroundings. Years of very low vole densities may also account for the difficulty in spotting one, but infrequent population irruptions can result in a 10-fold increase in numbers.

Prairie Rattlesnakes seem to have little trouble finding Sagebrush Voles. A recent study found that in some areas of Alberta this dryland rodent makes up about one-fifth of the snake's diet.

DESCRIPTION: This small, stout vole has short ears and legs and long, lax hair. It is very pale ashy grey in colour, with buffy tinges around the ears and nose. The undersides are silvery. The tail is not much longer than the hindfoot and is dark above and light below.

HABITAT: In keeping with its name, the Sagebrush Vole thrives in arid grassland regions and sagebrush flats.

FOOD: The spring and summer diets include a variety of plant and some insect material, especially the new green shoots of grasses and the flowers and leaves of forbs. In fall and winter, the diet switches to ripened fruits, seeds, bulbs, roots, corms and the inner bark of shrubs.

DEN: Shallow but extensive burrows lead to grass-lined nest chambers.

YOUNG: Mating occurs mainly between April and September. After a gestation of about 25 days, a litter of about 1 to 13 helpless young is born. The young grow extremely rapidly, and they are weaned and out of the nest within three weeks.

SIMILAR SPECIES: The Long-tailed (p. 162), Meadow (p. 161) and Prairie (p. 164) voles all have tails that are longer than 2.5 cm (1 in).

BEST SITES: Shortgrass flats around Suffield, Onefour and Manyberries.

RANGE: The U-shaped range, which skirts much of western Montana and northern Idaho, extends from southern Alberta east to North Dakota, south to northern Colorado, southwest to southern Nevada and north to central Washington.

Common Muskrat
Ondatra zibethicus

After a long Alberta winter, which restricts Common Muskrats to a life beneath the ice, the first few weeks of spring find many of these animals stretching their legs on land. It is usually in early May that many first-year animals, now sexually mature, venture from their birth ponds to establish their own territories. These muskrats are commonly seen travelling over land, which is a tragic event for many—their numbers can be all too easily tallied on May roadkill surveys.

The Common Muskrat is not a "mini-beaver," nor is it closely related to that large rodent; rather, it is a highly specialized, aquatic vole that shares many features with the American Beaver as a result of their similar lifestyles. Like a beaver, a muskrat can close its lips behind its large, orange incisors so it can chew underwater without getting water or mud in its mouth. A muskrat's eyes are placed high on its head, and it can often be seen swimming with its head and sometimes its tail abovewater. The Common Muskrat dives with ease; according to reports, it can remain submerged for over 15 minutes and can swim the length of a football field before surfacing.

Muskrats lead busy lives. They are continuously gnawing cattails and bulrushes, whether eating the tender shoots or gathering the coarse vegetation for home building. Muskrat homes rise above shallow waters throughout Alberta, and they are of tremendous importance not only to these aquatic rodents, but also to geese and ducks, which make use of the muskrats' homes as nesting platforms.

Both sexes have perineal scent glands that enlarge and produce a distinctly musk-like discharge during the breeding season. Although this scent is by no means unique to the Common Muskrat, its potency is sufficiently notable to have influenced this animal's common name. An earlier name for this species was "musquash," from the Abnaki *moskwas*, but through the association with musk the name changed to "muskrat."

DESCRIPTION: The coat generally consists of long, shiny, tawny to nearly black guard hairs overlying a brownish-grey undercoat. The flanks and sides are lighter than the back. The underparts

---

DID YOU KNOW?

Muskrats are highly regarded by native peoples. In one story, it was Muskrat who was able to bring some mud from the bottom of the flooded world to the water's surface. This mud was spread over a turtle's back, thus creating all the dry land we now know.

BEST SITES: Prairie potholes; Elk Island NP.

RANGE: This wide-ranging rodent occurs from the southern limit of the Arctic tundra across nearly all of Canada and the lower 48 states except most of Florida, Texas and California.

Total Length: 46–62 cm (18–24 in)
Tail Length: 20–28 cm (7¾–11 in)
Weight: 0.8–1.6 kg (1¾–3½ lb)

are grey with some tawny guard hairs. The long tail is black, nearly hairless, scaly and laterally compressed with dorsal and ventral keels. The legs are short. The large hindfeet are partially webbed and have an outer fringe of stiff hairs. The tops of the feet are covered with short, dark grey hairs. The claws are long and strong.

HABITAT: Muskrats occupy sloughs, lakes, marshes and streams that have cattails, rushes and open water. They are not present in the high mountains.

FOOD: The summer diet includes a variety of emergent herbaceous plants. Cattails, rushes, sedges, irises, water lilies and pondweeds are staples, but a few frogs, snails and an occasional fish may be eaten. In winter, muskrats feed on submerged vegetation.

DEN: Muskrat houses are built entirely of herbaceous vegetation, without the branches or mud of beaver lodges. The dome-shaped piles of cattails and rushes have an underwater entrance. In places, muskrats may dig bank burrows, which are 5–15 m (16–49 ft) long and have entrances that are below the usual water level.

YOUNG: Breeding takes place between March and September. Each female produces two or sometimes three litters a year. Gestation lasts 25 to 30 days, after which six to seven young are born. The eyes open at 14 to 16 days, the young are weaned at three to four weeks, and they are independent at one month old. Both males and females are sexually mature the spring after their birth.

SIMILAR SPECIES: The American Beaver (p. 170) is larger and has a broad, flat tail, and typically only its head is visible abovewater when it swims.

Brown Lemming
Lemmus trimucronatus

Total Length: 10–17 cm (4–6¾ in)

Tail Length: 1.1–2.9 cm (⁷⁄₁₆–1⅛ in)

Weight: 48–113 g (1¾–4 oz)

The Brown Lemming is a colourful Arctic furball that tolerates some of the most inhospitable environments in North America. In Alberta, it is only known to occur in the alpine tundra of our northernmost Rocky Mountains. Every part of the body is covered with a long coat—most appropriate for an animal that typically lives in the tundra—that provides the lemming with excellent buoyancy when it swims.

DESCRIPTION: The body, ears, feet, head and stubby tail are all completely covered with long, lax fur. In summer, the lower back is chestnut coloured, grading to grizzled grey over the head and shoulders. The rump is a lighter brown, and the cheeks and sides are tawny. The undersides are primarily light grey. In autumn, the lemming moults into a longer, greyer coat. The strong, curved claws aid in digging the elaborate winter runways.

HABITAT: Bogs, alpine meadows and tundra may support large colonies.

FOOD: Grasses, sedges and other mono-cotyledonous plants form the bulk of the diet. In times of scarce vegetation, any emergent plant is eaten down to the surface.

DEN: Summer nests are located 5–30 cm (2–12 in) underground in tunnels. The nests are made of dry grass and fur, with nearby chambers for wastes. Winter nests are subnivean: above the ground but below the snow.

YOUNG: Breeding occurs from spring through fall, and sometimes in winter. Gestation is about three weeks, after which four to nine young are born. Lemmings resemble pink jelly beans at birth, but their growth is rapid: at 7 days they are furred, the ears open at 8 to 9 days, and the eyes open at 10 to 12 days. The young are weaned at 16 to 21 days, and they are probably sexually mature soon thereafter.

SIMILAR SPECIES: The Northern Bog Lemming (p. 169) is generally smaller and has a bicoloured tail and grooved upper incisors. The Long-tailed Vole (p. 162) and the Meadow Vole (p. 161) have longer, bicoloured tails.

BEST SITES: Willmore Wilderness Park.

RANGE: The Brown Lemming primarily inhabits Alaska, the Yukon and the Northwest Territories, ranging south into northern British Columbia and western Alberta.

Northern Bog Lemming
Synaptomys borealis

Total Length: 9–15 cm (3½–6 in)

Tail Length: 1.2–2.7 cm (½–1⅛ in)

Weight: 15–33 g (½–1⅛ oz)

The Northern Bog Lemming has a very patchy distribution in the province. Its favoured habitat is cool sphagnum bogs, but black spruce forests, subalpine meadows and tundra sedge meadows can hold populations. Although the animals are rarely seen, their workings are easy enough to identify. Their mossy runways are frequently lined with evenly clipped grasses, which are piled neatly at points along the trails like harvested trees awaiting logging trucks along haulroads.

DESCRIPTION: The ears of this stout lemming scarcely project above the fur of the head. The whole body is covered in thick fur. Although there are various colour phases, the sides and back are usually chestnut or dark brown, and the underparts are usually greyish. There is a little patch of tawny-coloured hairs just behind the ears. The claws are strong and curved; the claws on the middle two front toes become greatly enlarged in winter to aid in digging in frozen conditions.

HABITAT: This lemming thrives in wet tundra conditions, such as tundra bogs, alpine meadows and even spruce woods.

FOOD: The diet is primarily composed of grasses, sedges and similar plants. If this vegetation is scarce, other emergent plants are eaten.

DEN: In summer, nests are located in tunnels about 15 cm (6 in) underground. The nests are made of dry grass and fur, and there are nearby chambers for wastes. In winter, the nests are located aboveground, under the snow.

YOUNG: Little is known about the Northern Bog Lemming, but it is thought to breed between spring and fall, with a gestation of about three weeks. The litter contains about two to six helpless young. Growth is rapid: they are furred by one week, weaned by three weeks, and leave to start their own families soon thereafter.

SIMILAR SPECIES: The Brown Lemming (p. 168) is generally larger and has a stubby tail and ungrooved incisors. The Long-tailed Vole (p. 162) and the Meadow Vole (p. 161) have longer tails.

BEST SITES: Subalpine forests in mountain parks.

RANGE: This lemming ranges across most of Alaska and Canada south of the Arctic tundra. It occurs as far south as the northern parts of Washington, Idaho and Montana.

American Beaver

Castor canadensis

The American Beaver is truly a great North America mammal, and Canada was figuratively built upon the back of this large rodent. Even today, the beaver serves as an international symbol for our nation's wild places, and, quite surprisingly to many Albertans, foreign tourists often hold out great hopes of seeing these aquatic specialists during their visits. Fortunately, the American Beaver can be regularly encountered in wet areas of the province (except during winter), where its engineering marvels can be studied in awe-inspiring detail.

Being one of the few mammals that alters its environment to suit its needs, the American Beaver often sets back natural succession and brings about changes in vegetation and animal life. Nothing seems to bother a beaver like the sound of running water, and this busy rodent builds dams of branches, mud and vegetation to slow the flow of water. The deep pools that the beaver's dams create will allow it to remain active beneath the ice in winter. Such achievements require vast amounts of labour—a single beaver can cut down up to 1700 trees each year to ensure its survival.

Beavers live in colonies that generally consist of a pair of mated adults, their yearlings and a set of young kits. This family group occupies a tightly monitored habitat that consists of several dams, terrestrial runways and a lodge. Throughout much of Alberta, the lodge is ingeniously built of branches and mud. Where trees do not commonly grow, beavers tunnel into the banks of rivers for their den sites.

Although the American Beaver is not a fast mover, it more than compensates with its immense strength. It is not unusual for this firmly built rodent to handle and drag—with its jaws—a piece of wood weighing more than a large sack of flour. The beaver's flat, scaly tail, for which it is so well known, increases an animal's stability when it is cutting a tree, and it is slapped on the water or ground to communicate alarm.

Beavers are well adapted to their aquatic lifestyles. They have valves that allow them to close their ears and nostrils when they are submerged, and clear membranes slide over the eyes. Because the lips form a seal behind the incisors, beavers can chew while they are submerged without having water,

---

DID YOU KNOW?

Beavers are bothered by neither lice nor ticks, but there is a tiny, flat beetle that lives nowhere but in beaver fur and feeds on beaver dandruff. The beetle's meanderings probably tickle sometimes, because beavers often scratch when they are out of water.

BEST SITES: Calgary, Red Deer and Edmonton river valleys; Amisk Wutche trail, Elk Island NP; Cottonwoods Slough, Jasper NP; Vermillion Lakes, Banff NP.

RANGE: Beavers can be found from the northern limit of deciduous trees south to northern Mexico. They are absent only from the Great Basin, deserts and extensive prairie areas devoid of trees.

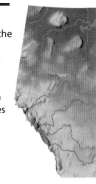

Total Length: 89–120 cm (35–47 in)
Tail Length: 29–53 cm (11–21 in)
Weight: 8–45 kg (18–99 lb)

mud and chips enter the mouth. Beavers have a thick layer of fat to protect them from cold waters, and the oily secretions they continually groom into their coats keep their skin dry.

Truly, the American Beaver is wonderfully adapted animal that shapes, through its industrious workings, the physical settings and subjective feelings of Alberta's wild areas. Although most tree cutting and dam building occurs at dusk or at night, you can sometimes see beavers during the day, if not working, then at least sunning themselves.

DESCRIPTION: This chunky, dark brown rodent has a broad, flat, scaly tail, short legs, a short neck and a broad head with short ears and massive, protruding, orange-faced incisors. The underparts are paler than the back and lack the reddish-brown hue. The nail on the next-to-outside toe of each webbed hindfoot is split horizontally, allowing it to be used as a comb in grooming the fur. The forefeet are not webbed.

HABITAT: Beavers occupy freshwater environments wherever there is suitable woody vegetation. They are sometimes even found feeding on dwarf willows above timberline.

FOOD: Bark and cambium, particularly that of aspen, willow, alder and birch, is favoured, but aquatic pond vegetation is eaten in summer. Beavers sometimes come ashore to eat some grains or grasses.

DEN: Beaver lodges are cone-shaped piles of mud and sticks. Beavers construct a great mound of material first, and then chew an underwater access tunnel into the centre and hollow out a den. The lodge is typically located away from shore in still water; in flowing waters it is generally on a bank. Access to the lodge is from about 1 m (3½ ft) below the water's surface. A low shelf near the two or three plunge holes in the den allows much of the water to drain from the beavers before they enter the den chamber. Beavers often pile more sticks and mud on the outside of the lodge each year, and shreds of bark accumulate on the den floor. Adult males generally do not live in the lodge but dig bank burrows across the water from the lodge entrance. These burrows, the entrances to which are below water, may sometimes be as long as 50 m (164 ft), but most are much shorter.

YOUNG: Most mating takes place in January or February, but occasionally as much as two months later. After a gestation period of four months, a litter of usually four kits is born. The 350–650-g (12–23-oz) kits are fully furred at birth, their incisors are erupted, and their eyes are nearly open. The kits begin to gnaw before they are a month old, and weaning takes place at two to three months. There is evidence from Alberta that a second litter may occasionally be born. Beavers become sexually mature when they are about two years old, at which time they often disperse from the colony.

walking trail

SIMILAR SPECIES: The Common Muskrat (p. 166) is much smaller and its long tail is laterally compressed rather than paddle-shaped. The Northern River Otter (p. 102) has a long, round, fur-covered tail, a streamlined body and a small head.

Common Muskrat

Olive-backed Pocket Mouse
Perognathus fasciatus

While there are some wild mammals in Alberta that literally come to your backdoor, others require a visit to their special places of residence. The Olive-backed Pocket Mouse is one of the latter. A staunch resident of active, open sand dunes, this specialized rodent can only be found in a handful of locales in the province.

Like kangaroo rats, pocket mice have large hindfeet and small forelegs. They tend to sit on their hindlegs outside the burrow, but the body remains horizontal, not upright as in ground squirrels—they stand crouched like an Olympic sprinter ready to explode from the starting blocks. Pocket mice move either in a slow walk or an unusual hop that involves all four limbs. The hop may take them 60 cm (24 in) vertically in response to a sudden alarm.

Pocket mice are fond of dust baths: they roll and dig in the sand; then brush their fur with both their forefeet and hindlimbs. They even invert their cheek pouches to clean them against the substrate.

Unlike most hibernating rodents, pocket mice do not build up a store of fat; instead, they pack their burrows with vast numbers of seeds. When outside food supplies dwindle, whether because of cold winter temperatures or during periods of extreme summer heat, pocket mice retreat to their burrows and enter torpor, a state of dormancy that is not as deep as hibernation. They arouse periodically to urinate and feed on their stored seeds.

Pocket mice require little free water to drink, because they can obtain all the water they need from the metabolism of their food.

DESCRIPTION: This tiny, attractive, docile mouse has a dominant buffy back colour that is modified by blackish or olive-coloured hairs. The dark hairs end abruptly, and the back contrasts with the buffy sides and the white or buffy-white feet and underparts. There is a buffy spot behind each ear. The whole coat is shiny and soft. The antitragus of the ear is not lobed. The tail is long and thin and uniformly coloured.

HABITAT: The Olive-backed Pocket Mouse is restricted to grasslands on light, sandy soils.

DID YOU KNOW?

These tiny little mice use their sharp front claws to glean the tiny seeds of annual weeds from the sand. In one night, a single mouse may gather more than a thousand seeds: some to be eaten, others stored.

BEST SITES: Sandhills around Bindloss, Empress and Suffield; military reserve roads on moonless nights.

RANGE: The range of this pocket mouse extends from southeastern Alberta east to western Manitoba and south to New Mexico.

Total Length: 10–15 cm (4–6 in)
Tail Length: 5.2–7 cm (2–2¾ in)
Weight: 8–14 g (¼–½ oz)

FOOD: Seeds with a higher-than-average oil content, including Russian thistle, knotweed, tumbling mustard, lambsquarter, blue-eyed grass and foxtail, seem to be the mainstay of the diet. Some green vegetation and a few insects are also consumed, and grasshopper eggs may be stored in the burrow.

DEN: Summer tunnels, which are about 2 cm (¾ in) in diameter, form a network of storage and refuge burrows that are 30–45 cm (12–18 in) deep. The tunnel entrances are plugged with soil by day. The summer nesting chamber is bare. Winter burrows may penetrate 2 m (6½ ft) beneath the surface. They contain a grass nest and the first 1 m (3½ ft) of the burrow is plugged with soil. The entire system may have a diameter of 10 m (33 ft).

YOUNG: Breeding begins after the pocket mice emerge in spring. After four weeks of gestation, a litter of usually four to six young is born. There are two litters each season. Young pocket mice become sexually mature the spring after their birth.

SIMILAR SPECIES: The Ord's Kangaroo Rat (p. 176) is larger, has an extremely long tail and rests with its body sitting more vertically over its hindfeet.

bounding trail

Ord's Kangaroo Rat
Dipodomys ordii

Finding sand dunes within this rodent's range is challenging in itself; locating an individual kangaroo rat requires luck and knowledge. This nocturnal hopper is best seen on dark, moonless and overcast nights. If you shine a flashlight across the dunes or drive slowly along sandy road-cuts, this sand-dweller might be revealed. By day, kangaroo rats retire to the coolness of their plugged sand burrows.

Much of a kangaroo rat's food is taken from the sand; it forages slowly, sifting out seeds with its sharp foreclaws. Seeds that are to be eaten immediately are first husked, but those to be stored are left intact. The kangaroo rat transports the food to its burrow in spacious cheek pouches, which can be inverted for cleaning and combing with the foreclaws. The sand is also critical to this mammal's cleanliness: dust bathing is an important part of the kangaroo rat's grooming routine.

The Ord's Kangaroo Rat can live its entire life without having a drink. It can survive on the metabolic water produced through the breakdown of the oils and fats in the seeds it eats. This water is used in digestion, reproduction and milk production. Despite this ability, in the wild, kangaroo rats will opportunistically lap droplets of dew and sometimes eat a bit of green vegetation when it is available.

DESCRIPTION: The back is yellowish buff, with a few black hairs down the centre, the sides are clear buff, and the belly is white. The eyes are large, luminous and protruding. There is a white spot above the eye and behind the brownish-black ear. A black patch on the side of the nose, above the white lip, marks the base of the whiskers. There is a diagonal, white line across the hip. The extremely long hindfeet are white on top and brownish black on their hairy soles. The greatly reduced forelegs are held up and are often not visible in profile as the animal sits hunched over, supporting itself on its hindfeet. The tail, which is at least as long as the body, is tufted at the tip. It has white sides and brownish-black upper and lower surfaces.

HABITAT: This kangaroo rat occupies sandy, grassland and sagebrush semi-desert sites. Disturbed, vegetation-free areas, whether produced by drifting

---

DID YOU KNOW?

The huge auditory bullae of Ord's Kangaroo Rats make up a major rear portion of the skull. Able to hear very low-frequency sounds, kangaroo rats can avoid a rattlesnake's bite, presumably because they are able to hear the snake's movement.

BEST SITES: Sandhills near Bindloss, Empress and Suffield.

RANGE: This widely distributed kangaroo rat occurs from southeastern Alberta and southwestern Saskatchewan south through the Great Plains and western Texas into Mexico, and from eastern Oregon south through the Great Basin and Arizona.

Total Length: 23–28 cm (9–11 in)
Tail Length: 14–16 cm (5½–6¼ in)
Weight: 44–96 g (1½–3⅜ oz)

sand or by road building or traffic, seem particularly attractive.

FOOD: Seeds make up more than three-quarters of the year-round diet. Insects, such as ants, butterfly pupae, adult beetles and larval antlions, account for one-fifth of the diet in spring, and grasshoppers and roots are eaten in summer.

DEN: Burrows, which are usually located in the sides of sand dunes, blowouts, dry eroded channels or road slopes, are about 7.5 cm (3 in) in diameter. The entrances are plugged during the day. The tunnels branch frequently, with some branches used for food storage and at least one as a nesting chamber. Most of the burrow system is often within 30 cm (12 in) of the surface. The burrow is actively defended against other kangaroo rats.

YOUNG: Breeding occurs in early to mid-spring, and sometimes again in mid-summer. After a 29- to 30-day gestation period, a litter of usually three to five young is born in a nest built just beforehand. The helpless newborns, weighing about 6 g (³⁄₁₆ oz), are groomed by the mother. At two weeks their eyes open, and at three weeks they have functioning cheek pouches. After the young reach adult size, at five to six weeks, they

disperse to develop their own burrows. The mortality rate in the first year may be as high as 90 percent.

SIMILAR SPECIES: No other rodent has the extremely long tail and hindlegs, big head and stocky body of the Ord's Kangaroo Rat. The Olive-backed Pocket Mouse (p. 174) is smaller, with a shorter tail, and it usually holds its body more horizontally when it rests on its hindfeet.

hopping trail

Northern Pocket Gopher
Thomomys talpoides

The Northern Pocket Gopher is nature's cantakerous rototiller. This ground-dwelling, myopic rodent is continuously tunnelling through dark, rich soils in Alberta, and one individual is capable of turning over 16 tons of soil every year. Evidence of their workings is commonplace in Alberta, as the freshly churned earth is neatly piled in mounds, or "gopher cores," in ditches, lawns and fields.

Pocket gopher push-ups hide the access holes to a system of burrows. From the rodent's viewpoint, the ground's surface provides a space to dump the dirt from tunnel excavation. Even when the ground is covered by snow, pocket gophers still bring up spoil to the surface and pack it into snow tunnels. When the snow melts, these soil cores, or crotovinas, are left exposed.

There is no mammal in the province better adapted to an underground existence. The Northern Pocket Gopher has small eyes, which it rarely needs in its darkened world; reduced external ears that do not interfere with tunnelling; short, lax fur that does not impede backward or forward movement in the tunnels; and a short, sparsely haired tail that serves as a tactile organ when the animal is tunnel running in reverse. To dig its elaborate burrows, the Northern Pocket Gopher has heavy, stout claws on short, strong forelegs and a massive lower jaw armed with long incisors. Once the soil is loosened with tooth and claw, it is pushed back under the body, initially with the forefeet, and then further with the hindfeet. When sufficient soil has accumulated behind the animal, the gopher turns, guides the mound with its forefeet and head and pushes with its hindlegs until the soil is in a side tunnel or on the surface.

This animal is named for its large, externally opening, fur-lined cheek pouches. As in the related pocket mice and kangaroo rats, these "pockets" are used to transport food, but they have no direct opening to the animal's mouth.

DESCRIPTION: This squat, bullet-headed rodent has visible incisors, long foreclaws and a thick, nearly hairless tail. A row of stiff hairs surrounds the naked soles of the forefeet. The upperparts often match the soil colour—individuals may be black, grey, brown or

---

DID YOU KNOW?

The pocket gopher's incisor teeth grow at a spectacular rate: lower incisors are reported to grow as much as 1 mm (0.04 in) a day; upper incisors grow 0.6 mm (0.02 in) a day. If that rate was continuous, the lower incisors could grow 36 cm (14 in) in a year.

BEST SITES: Pastures and roadsides between Edmonton and Red Deer.

RANGE: This species occupies most of the northern Great Plains and central Rocky Mountains from Manitoba to Alberta, and south to Nebraska, Colorado, northern Arizona and New Mexico. It occurs as far east as western Minnesota, and as far west as western Washington and Oregon.

Total Length: 19–26 cm (7½–10 in)
Tail Length: 4.1–7.7 cm (1⅝–3 in)
Weight: 75–210 g (2⅝–7⅜ oz)

even light grey—and the upperparts are slightly darker than the underparts.

HABITAT: This adaptable animal avoids only dense forest, wet or waterlogged, fine-textured soils, very shallow rocky soil or areas exposed to strong winter freezing of the soil.

FOOD: Succulent underground plant parts are the staple diet, but in summer pocket gophers emerge from their burrows at night to collect green vegetation.

DEN: The burrow system may spread 50–150 m (160–490 ft) laterally and extend 5 cm (2 in) to 3 m (10 ft) deep. A tunnel's diameter is about 5 cm (2 in). Some lateral tunnels serve for food storage, others as latrines. Several nesting chambers, 20–25 cm (7¾–9¾ in) in diameter and filled with fine grasses, are located below the frost line. Spoil from tunnelling is spread fanwise to one side of the burrow entrance. Only a single gopher occupies a burrow system, except during the breeding season, when a male may share a female's burrow for a time.

YOUNG: Breeding occurs once a year, in April or May. Following a 19- to 20- day gestation, three to six young are born in a grass-lined nest. Weaning takes place at about 40 days. When the young weigh about 45 g (1⅝ oz) they leave to either occupy a vacant burrow system or begin digging their own burrows. They are sexually mature the following spring.

SIMILAR SPECIES: Voles (pp. 158–65) do not have the large external cheek pouches or the long front claws of pocket gophers, although the colour patterns are similar. Pocket gophers are incorrectly called "moles" by many people on the Canadian prairies, but Alberta has no true moles, which are more closely related to shrews than rodents.

foreprint

Least Chipmunk
Tamias minimus

The sound of scurrying among fallen leaves and sharp, high-pitched "chips" are often enough clues to direct your attention to the nervous behaviours of a Least Chipmunk. Using fallen logs as runways and the leaf litter as its pantry, this busy animal inhabits most wooded areas of the province. It is the most commonly seen chipmunk in Alberta.

The word "chipmunk" is thought to derive from the Algonkian word for "head first," which is the manner in which a chipmunk descends a tree, but contrary to cartoon-inspired Disney myths, chipmunks spend very little time in high trees in Alberta. They prefer the ground, where they bury food and dig golf ball–sized entrance holes to their networks of tunnels. Chipmunk burrows are known for their well-hidden entrances—they never have piles of dirt to give away their locations.

In a few heavily visited parks and golf courses, Least Chipmunks that have grown accustomed to human handouts can be very easy to approach. These exchanges contrast dramatically with the typically brief sightings of wild chipmunks, which scamper away at the first sight of humans—in the wild, chipmunks rely on their nervous instincts to survive in their predator-filled world.

DESCRIPTION: This tiny chipmunk has three dark and two light stripes on its face, and five dark and four light stripes on its body. The central dark stripe runs from the head to the base of the tail, but the other dark stripes end at the hips. The overall colour is greyer and paler than other chipmunks, and the underside of the tail is yellower. The tail is quite long—more than 40 percent of the total length.

HABITAT: The Least Chipmunk inhabits a wide variety of areas, including open coniferous and aspen forests, sagebrush flats, rocky outcroppings and pastures with small shrubs.

FOOD: This chipmunk loves to dine on ripe berries, such as chokecherries, pincherries, strawberries, raspberries or blueberries. Other staples in the diet include nuts, seeds, grasses, mushrooms and even insects and some other animals.

DEN: The majority of Least Chipmunks live in underground burrows, which

---

DID YOU KNOW?

During summer, a chipmunk's body temperature is 35°–42° C (95°–108° F). While it is hibernating in its burrow during winter, its body temperature drops to 5°–7° C (41°–45° F).

BEST SITES: Edmonton river valleys; Elk Island NP; low elevations in Kananaskis Country and other mountain parks.

RANGE: The extensive range of this species spreads from the central Yukon to western Quebec, and in the U.S from Washington to northern California, from North Dakota to New Mexico, and just west of the Great Lakes.

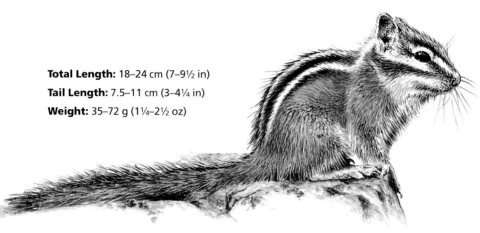

Total Length: 18–24 cm (7–9½ in)
Tail Length: 7.5–11 cm (3–4¼ in)
Weight: 35–72 g (1¼–2½ oz)

have concealed entrances. After a chipmunk excavates its burrow, it seals up the "work hole" and opens new entrances from the inside, so there are no tell-tale piles of dirt on the outside. Some individuals live in tree cavities or even make spherical leaf and twigs nests among the branches in the manner of tree squirrels.

YOUNG: Breeding occurs about two weeks after the chipmunks emerge from hibernation in spring. After about one month of gestation, a litter of two to seven (usually four to six) helpless young is born in a grass-lined nest chamber of the burrow. The young develop rapidly, and the mother may later transfer them to a tree cavity or tree nest.

SIMILAR SPECIES: It is very difficult to distinguish chipmunk species in the field; range maps often help. The Red-tailed Chipmunk (p. 183) has a brick red underside of the tail. The Yellow-pine Chipmunk (p. 182) tends to have brighter colours than the Least Chipmunk. Only chipmunks have the horizontal face stripes, but the larger Golden-mantled Ground Squirrel (p. 198), with its bold side stripes, is often mistaken for a chipmunk. The Golden-mantled Ground Squirrel has no facial stripes.

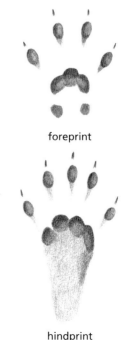

foreprint

hindprint

Yellow-pine Chipmunk
Tamias amoenus

Total Length: 20–24 cm (7¾–9½ in)
Tail Length: 8–11 cm (3¼–4¼ in)
Weight: 46–85 g (1⅝–3 oz)

HABITAT: This chipmunk is common in brushy or rocky areas of coniferous mountain forests.

Noticeably less common than the wide-ranging Least Chipmunk, the Yellow-pine Chipmunk can be seen by anyone willing to invest the time and effort to a search. It can often be found near semi-open day-use areas in Alberta's mountain parks, but it tends not to be among such frontline rodents as the Golden-mantled Ground Squirrel and the Columbian Ground Squirrel, which beg for attention and handouts. The Yellow-pine Chipmunk neither seeks nor completely shuns the company of curious naturalists.

DESCRIPTION: This brightly coloured chipmunk is tawny to pinkish cinnamon. There are three dark and two light stripes on the face, and five dark and four light stripes on the back. The light stripes are white or greyish. The dark stripes are nearly black, and the central three extend all the way to the rump. The sides of the body and the underside of the tail are greyish yellow. The female tends to be larger than the male.

FOOD: The bulk of the diet is comprised of conifer seeds, nuts, some berries and insects. It is not uncommon for chipmunks to eat eggs, fledgling birds, young mice or even carrion.

DEN: The Yellow-pine Chipmunk usually lives in a burrow that has a concealed entrance. It can sometimes be found in a tree cavity, but it seldom builds a tree nest.

YOUNG: The young are born in May or June, after spring mating and about one month of gestation. Usually five or six young are born in a grass-lined chamber in the burrow, and they are blind and hairless at birth. Their growth is rapid, and they are usually weaned in about six weeks.

SIMILAR SPECIES: The smaller Least Chipmunk (p. 180) has duller colours. The Red-tailed Chipmunk (p. 183) is larger and may be greyer, but it is most easily distinguished by the rufous underside of the tail.

BEST SITES: Nordegg; West Castle area and Lake Louise, Banff NP; Highwood Pass, Peter Lougheed PP.

RANGE: This mountain chipmunk occurs in British Columbia, extreme western Alberta and the northwestern U.S.

Red-tailed Chipmunk
Tamias ruficaudus

Red-tailed Chipmunks require a greater effort than most chipmunks to observe, because high-elevation areas in and around Waterton Lakes National Park are the only places in Alberta from which they are known. A drive to Cameron Lake is always a worthwhile exercise: not only is it one of the best places to see a Steller's Jay or Grizzly Bear in the province, it is also prime Red-tailed Chipmunk habitat. Anyone venturing to this high-elevation lake should enjoy the scenery and acknowledge the Red-tailed Chipmunk's not insignificant contribution to the province's fauna.

Total Length: 21–25 cm (8¼–9¾ in)

Tail Length: 9.3–12 cm (3¾–4¾ in)

Weight: 52–74 g (1⅞–2⅝ oz)

DESCRIPTION: Like other chipmunks, this large chipmunk has three dark and two light stripes on the face, and five dark and four light stripes on the back. The inner three dark stripes on the back are black; the dark facial stripes and the outermost dark stripes on the back are brownish. The rump is greyish. In keeping with its name, the tail is rufous above and dark reddish below.

HABITAT: This chipmunk inhabits coniferous mountain forests and boulder-covered slopes below treeline.

FOOD: Although conifer seeds, nuts, some berries and insects form most of the diet, it is not uncommon for chipmunks to feed on eggs, fledgling birds, young mice or even carrion.

DEN: As with all chipmunks, the Red-tailed Chipmunk usually lives in a burrow. Sometimes it can be found nesting in tree cavities, and it makes spherical tree nests more often than many other chipmunks.

YOUNG: Breeding occurs in spring, and after a one-month gestation, a litter of usually four to six young is born in May or June. The young are born blind and hairless in a grass-lined chamber in the burrow. They grow rapidly, and they are usually weaned in about six weeks.

SIMILAR SPECIES: The Least Chipmunk (p. 180) is smaller, and in both it and the Yellow-pine Chipmunk (p. 182), the underside of the tail is greyish yellow.

BEST SITES: Cameron Lake, Waterton Lakes NP.

RANGE: The small range of this chipmunk includes only southeastern British Columbia, the very southwestern corner of Alberta, northeastern Washington, northern Idaho and western Montana.

Woodchuck
Groundhog
Marmota monax

For most of the year in Alberta, Woodchucks are tucked quietly away more than 2 m (6½ ft) underground, relying on their lethargic metabolism to keep them alive. They lie motionless, breathing an average of once every six minutes, and maintaining life's requirements with a metabolic furnace fed by a trickle of fatty reserves. Once May returns (never as early as February's Groundhog Day in Alberta), Woodchucks awake from their catatonic slumbers to forage on the palatable new green shoots emerging with the warmer weather.

Woodchucks range across much of the northern two-thirds of Alberta, finding shelter in rock piles, under outbuildings and along riversides. They are rarely seen far from their protective burrows, valuing security over the temptations of foraging. When they do venture from their burrows to feed, it is often during the early twilight hours or shortly after dawn. Even then, Woodchucks are wary and usually outrun most predators in an all-out sprint back the burrow. A shrill whistle of alarm usually accompanies a Woodchuck's disappearance into its burrow.

In Alberta, as elsewhere, these animals are more solitary in nature than other kinds of marmots. This characteristic holds true in most instances, but at a renowned Woodchuck-viewing spot in Edmonton, several of these animals can be seen simultaneously. A loose colony of Woodchucks has been established below the Provincial Museum of Alberta, next to the Groat Bridge, and it is easy to watch several Woodchuck heads rise in unison above the broken concrete slabs in which their dens are found. These Woodchucks sit cautiously at their burrow entrances, seemingly waiting for a break in the busy world so they can resume feeding.

DESCRIPTION: This stout, short-legged, ground-dwelling squirrel is brownish, with an overall grizzled appearance. It has a prominent, slightly flattened, bushy tail and small ears.

HABITAT: Woodchucks favour pastures, meadows and old fields close to wooded areas.

FOOD: This ground dweller eats primarily green vegetation and grasses and

---

DID YOU KNOW?

Balzac Billy, Alberta's contribution to groundhog prognosticators, is a fraud: no Woodchucks occur naturally near the town of Balzac. Rumour has it the story was a fabrication of a Calgary weather forecaster.

BEST SITES: Edmonton river valley; Fort McMurray; Grande Prairie.

RANGE: The Woodchuck occurs from central Alaska east to Labrador, south to northern Idaho in the West and south to eastern Kansas, northern Alabama and Virginia in the East.

Total Length: 46–65 cm (18–26 in)
Tail Length: 11–16 cm (4¼–6¼ in)
Weight: 1.8–5.4 kg (4–12 lb)

some bark. The Woodchuck loves garden vegetables, and if it makes its way into urban areas, it may dine happily on corn, peas, apples, lettuce and squash.

DEN: The powerful digging claws are used to excavate burrows in areas of good drainage. The main burrow is 3–15 m (10–49 ft) long, and it terminates in a comfortable, grass-lined nest chamber. A smaller chamber, separate from the nest chamber, is used for wastes. There are often plunge holes, without spoil piles, that lead directly to the nest chamber.

YOUNG: Mating occurs in spring, and after a gestation period of about one month, one to eight (usually three to five) young are born. The helpless newborns weigh only about 260 g (9 oz). In about four weeks their eyes open, and they look like proper Woodchucks after five weeks. The young are weaned at about 1½ months old, and they continue growing throughout the summer to put on enough weight for the winter hibernation.

SIMILAR SPECIES: The Hoary Marmot (p. 188) is generally grey and white with contrasting black markings, and it is typically found in the mountains. The Yellow-bellied Marmot (p. 186) has, appropriately enough, a yellow belly, and it is found farther south in Alberta.

Yellow-bellied Marmot
Marmota flaviventris

When architects designed the museum at Head-Smashed-In Buffalo Jump near Fort McLeod, they likely did not have Yellow-bellied Marmots in mind, but in building this unobtrusive prairie monument, they created a marmot motel. It is quite common to see these chunky rodents gladly poised upon the museum protuberances rising from the hillside. Elsewhere in Alberta, Yellow-bellied Marmots are infrequently encountered; their colonies are thinly scattered along the U.S. border.

By all accounts, the Yellow-bellied Marmot is a newcomer to the Alberta wildlife scene. The first official record of this species dates back to 1952, and few verbal accounts predate this record by more than a decade. This marmot is commonly encountered in the U.S. Rockies in northern Montana, and it may have spilled north into the Waterton Lakes area, where it was once (but is no longer) found. Other individuals probably entered Alberta via the Sweetgrass Hills of Montana, which lie just south of the Milk River, a region where these animals are now common. Although the Yellow-bellied Marmot is a mountain dweller through most of its range, north of Montana's Flint Creek Range, the southern limit of the Hoary Marmot's range, it becomes a lowland animal.

The possibility of human assistance in the Yellow-bellied Marmot's travels should not be discounted, because its present-day concentrations appear discontinuous with typical marmot habitat. It may be that the animals that now pose atop Head-Smashed-In were moved to that spot just a few short marmot generations ago. Alternately, habitat change over time may have made areas that were formerly uninhabitable, now suitable for this species. Whatever their origins, the Yellow-bellied Marmots that now occupy the rocky regions of southern Alberta seem to find it hospitable, and they appear to be expanding their provincial distribution on their own.

DESCRIPTION: The back is tawny or yellow-brown, grizzled by the light tips of the guard hairs. The feet and legs are blackish brown. The head has whitish-grey patches across the top of the nose, from below the ear to the shoulder and from the nose and chin towards the

---

DID YOU KNOW?

Yellow-bellied Marmots often bask in the morning sun, probably to warm up. At about midday they retire to their cool burrows, but in the late afternoon they re-emerge to feed on non-woody plants and grasses.

BEST SITES: Gold Springs Park on the Milk River; Writing-on-Stone PP; Head-Smashed-In Buffalo Jump.

RANGE: Yellow-bellied Marmots are found from central British Columbia and extreme southern Alberta south into central California and northern New Mexico.

throat, which leaves a darker brown patch surrounding the ear, eye and upper cheek on each side of the face. The ears are short and rounded. The whiskers are dark and prominent. The dark, grizzled, bushy tail is often arched behind the animal and flagged from side to side. The bright buffy-yellow sides of the neck, maxilla, belly and hips are responsible for the common name.

HABITAT: Within its range, this species may be found from valley bottoms to alpine tundra but never in dense forests. In Alberta, it is most often found along rock piles and coulees.

FOOD: Abundant herbaceous or grassy vegetation must be available within a short distance of the den. This marmot occasionally feeds on road-killed carrion, and there have been reports of the cannibalization of young.

DEN: Each of the adults maintains its own burrow, with those of the highest social status being nearest the colony centre. A burrow is typically 20–35 cm (7¾–14 in) in diameter. It slants down for 50–100 cm (20–39 in), and then extends another 3–4.5 m (10–15 ft) to end beneath or among large rocks in a bulky nest lined with grass.

YOUNG: There are three to eight young in a litter, born in June after a 30-day gestation. Naked and blind at birth, they first emerge from the burrow at three to four weeks old. Well-fed females become sexually mature before their first birthdays. Males and females born at higher altitudes usually do not get a chance to breed until they are at least two years old.

SIMILAR SPECIES: The Hoary Marmot (p. 188) has grey cheeks and a grey belly, and it occupies higher elevations in Alberta. The Woodchuck (p. 184) is uniformly brownish, without the yellowish belly, and occurs farther north.

Total Length: 47–67 cm (19–26 in)
Tail Length: 13–19 cm (5–7½ in)
Weight: 1.6–5.2 kg (3½–11 lb)

Hoary Marmot
Whistler
Marmota caligata

These stocky sentinels of alpine vistas pose graciously on boulders, gazing for untold hours at the surrounding Rocky Mountain scenery. They customarily emerge from their burrows soon after sunrise, but they remain hidden on windy days and during snow, rain or hailstorms.

Hoary Marmots exclusively occupy high-altitude environs, where long summer days allow rapid plant growth during a growing season that often lasts only 60 days a year. Despite the shortened summer season, these marmots seldom seem hurried; rather, most of their time seems to be spent staring off into the distance, perhaps in the lookout for predatory Grizzlies and Golden Eagles, or perhaps in simple appreciation of the spell-binding landscape.

If they are frequently exposed to humans, Hoary Marmots become surprisingly tolerant of our activities. These photo-friendly marmots lie in sharp contrast to the wary animals that live in more isolated areas. In the backcountry, the presence of an intruder in an alpine cirque or talus slope is greeted by a shrill and resounding whistle, from which the marmot's nickname "whistler," *siffleur* in French, is derived. When alarmed, marmots travel surprisingly gracefully through boulder fields, quickly finding any one of their many escape tunnels.

Being chunky is most fashionable in Hoary Marmot circles. Although at first glance their surroundings may appear to hold little food possibilities, these high alpine areas are in fact rich in marmot foods. Marmots consume great quantities of green vegetation throughout the summer, laying on thick layers of fat to be used during their eight- to nine-month hibernations. A considerable portion of stored fat remains when the marmots emerge from hibernation, but they need it for mating and other activities until the green vegetation reappears.

DESCRIPTION: The head is grey and white with contrasting black markings. The cheeks are grey. A black band across the bridge of the nose separates the white nose patches from the white patches below the eyes. The ears are short and black. The underparts are grey, as are the feet. A black stripe extends from behind each ear towards the shoulder. The shoulders and upper back are

---

DID YOU KNOW?

Hoary marmots often use mouth to mouth "kisses" in greeting other colony members. Late morning, following avid feeding, is a peak period of socializing with other members. The kisses are shared between members of both sexes.

BEST SITES: The Whistlers and Mount Edith Cavell, Jasper NP; Ptarmigan Cirque and Highwood Pass, Peter Lougheed PP; Peyto Lake, Helen Lake and Plain of Six Glaciers, Banff NP.

RANGE: The Hoary Marmot occurs from northern Alaska south through the mountains to southern Montana and central Idaho.

Total Length: 68–82 cm (27–32 in)
Tail Length: 18–24 cm (7–9½ in)
Weight: 5–7 kg (11–15 lb)

grizzled grey, changing to buffy brown on the lower back and rump, where black-tipped guard hairs surmount the underfur. The bushy, brown tail is so dark it often appears black. This marmot often fails to groom its lower back and hindquarters, so the fur there appears matted and rumpled.

HABITAT: Hoary Marmots are dependent upon large talus boulders or fractured rock outcrops near abundant vegetation in moist surroundings. Alpine tundra and high subalpine areas are most commonly occupied.

FOOD: Copious quantities of many plants are consumed so avidly that the vegetation near burrows is often lawn-like from frequent clipping. Grasses, sedges and broadleaf herbs are all eaten.

DEN: Burrows run about 2 m (6½ ft) into the slopes, where they may end as a cave up to 1 m (3½ ft) in diameter beneath a large rock. The chamber is often filled with soft grasses.

YOUNG: A litter of four or five young is born in mid- to late May, about 30 days after mating. The fully furred young first emerge from the burrows in about the third week of July, when they weigh 200–300 g (7–11 oz). They are weaned soon after emerging and grow rapidly until they enter hibernation in September. Sexual maturity is achieved during their third spring.

SIMILAR SPECIES: The Yellow-bellied Marmot (p. 186) occurs at lower elevations in Alberta and has a bright buffy-yellow belly and a grizzled brown back.

Columbian Ground Squirrel
Spermophilus columbianus

From montane valleys to alpine meadows, the Columbian Ground Squirrel is a common resident of Alberta's mountainous regions. It seems that virtually every meadow has a population of this large rodent thriving among the grasses. At heavily visited day-use areas and campgrounds, colonies of this ground squirrel attract a surprising amount of tourist curiosity.

Columbian Ground Squirrels are robust, sleek and colourful animals that chirp loudly, frequently at the first indication of any danger. The chirps coincide with a flick of the tail and, in extreme cases, a split-second plunge down a burrow. This refuge-seeking behaviour, however, is often preceded by a trill rather than a chirp. Also, there are different alarms for avian versus terrestrial predators, and for squirrel intruders from outside the colony. Making sense of the repertoire of different ground squirrel sounds may require more effort than most people are prepared to expend.

Colony members interact freely and non-aggressively with one another in most instances, sniffing and kissing their neighbours upon each greeting. The dominant male, however, which has his burrow near the centre of the colony, maintains his central location through the breeding season. Ground squirrels from outside the colony are typically attacked by one or several members of the colony, and are driven far afield.

Dispersing individuals, forced to emigrate from their home colony to live, are exceedingly vulnerable to predation. Away from the sanctuary of communal life, these large rodents are a much-valued dietary choice for other mammals and birds. The Prairie Falcon, for one, may leave its grassland breeding grounds in late summer to concentrate on hunting Columbian Ground Squirrels in the mountains.

DESCRIPTION: The entire back is cinnamon buff, but, because the dorsal guard hairs have black tips, a dappled, black-and-buffy effect results. The top of the head and the nape are rich grey with black overtones. The sides of the neck are rich grey with black overtones. There is a buffy eye ring. The nose and face are a rich tawny, sometimes fading to ochre-buff on the forefeet, but more frequently continuing tawny over the forefeet, underparts and hindfeet. The

---

DID YOU KNOW?

Columbian Ground Squirrels have been known to hibernate for up to 220 days. During hibernation, the squirrels wake at least once every 19 days to urinate and sometimes defecate, and to eat some stored food.

BEST SITES: Upper Kananaskis Lakes and Ptarmigan Cirque, Peter Lougheed PP; day-use areas in Waterton Lakes, Banff and Jasper NPs.

RANGE: The Columbian Ground Squirrel is restricted to the mountains of eastern British Columbia and western Alberta south into northeastern Oregon and western Montana.

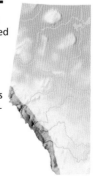

Total Length: 33–40 cm (13–16 in)
Tail Length: 8.3–12 cm (3¼–4¾ in)
Weight: 440–570 g (16–20 oz)

base of the tail is sometimes tawny or more rarely rufous. The moderately bushy tail is brown, overlain with hairs having black subterminal bands and buffy-white tips.

HABITAT: This wide-ranging ground squirrel may occupy intermontane valleys, forest edges, open woodlands and alpine tundra.

FOOD: All parts of both broadleaf and grassy plants are consumed. Carrion is eaten when it is found, and there are several reports of adults, especially males, being cannibalistic on the young. Insects and other invertebrates are also eaten. Individual squirrels ordinarily only store seeds or bulbs in their burrows.

DEN: The colony develops its burrow system on well-drained soils, preferably loams, on north- or east-facing slopes in the mountains. The tunnels are 7.5–11 cm (3–4¼ in) in diameter and descend 1–2 m (3½–6½ ft). Each colony member's bur-row system has 2 to 35 entrances and may spread to a diameter of more than 25 m (27 yd). A central chamber, up to 75 cm (30 in) in diameter, is filled with insulating vegetation. Several other burrows, each up to 1.5 m (5 ft) long, with a single entrance, serve as temporary refuges around the colony.

YOUNG: Mating occurs in the female's burrow soon after she emerges from hibernation. After a gestation of 23 to 24 days, she delivers a litter of two to seven young. The upper incisors erupt by day 19, the eyes open at about day 20, and the young are weaned at about one month. All Columbian Ground Squirrels are sexually mature after two hibernation periods, although some females may mate after their first winter.

SIMILAR SPECIES: The Yellow-bellied Marmot (p. 186) is generally larger and has dark facial markings. The Richardson's Ground Squirrel (p. 192) does not have a tawny nose patch.

Richardson's Ground Squirrel
Gopher • Picket Pin
Spermophilus richardsonii

Maligned and vilified over much of its range in Alberta, the Richardson's Ground Squirrel nonetheless continues to be a common sight across much of the southern half of the province. Although it often hibernates from September to February or March, it is conspicuous, vocal and active during the warmer months of the year.

To Albertans, who often call it a gopher, this species is the most common ground squirrel, although in terms of overall North American distribution it has a smaller range than other provincial species. More than most provincial mammals, it has influenced the social character of the prairie region. Used by such outstanding authors as W. O. Mitchell to symbolize the Canadian grasslands, the Richardson's Ground Squirrel may be southern Alberta's finest zoological representative of prairie life.

Beyond the habits that conflict with agricultural practices, surprisingly little is known about the behaviour of this prairie digger. Only recently have studies within the province unravelled the complexity of its hibernation and activity cycles. While all Richardson's Ground Squirrels are known to hibernate through much of the coldest winter weather, the males begin to emerge regularly in spring, often before the last snows have retreated. Courtship and reproductive duties are condensed between late spring and early summer, so that many adult ground squirrels have already begun to enter hibernation by the end of July. The first hibernators are typically the mature males, followed by the adult females, and then the juvenile females in late August. Any Richardson's Ground Squirrels observed later than that are almost certainly fat young males, which may remain active until October.

DESCRIPTION: The upperparts are a buffy grey to cinnamon buff and indistinctly mottled. The underparts are pale yellowish, pinkish or grey. The buffy-brown tail is about one-third the length of the body, and it is fringed with short, black, white-tipped hairs. One of this ground squirrel's distinguishing characteristics is its habit of standing erect on its hindlegs to survey its surroundings, a trait that earned it the name "Picket Pin."

DID YOU KNOW?

Richardson's Ground Squirrel burrows, which have an average of eight entrances, are used by dozens of other prairie mammals, amphibians, reptiles and invertebrates as winter hibernation dens and as refuge sites.

BEST SITES: Elk Island NP; Medicine Hat, Lethbridge and Brooks areas; just about any native prairie field south of Westlock.

RANGE: This species is associated with the prairies and plains from southern Alberta to southwestern Manitoba and south to northeastern Montana and extreme western Minnesota.

HABITAT: An open-country specialist, the Richardson's Ground Squirrel is common in prairies, meadows and pastures. It tends to avoid damp or fine-textured soils.

FOOD: Like others of its kind, this ground squirrel eats flowers, fruits, seeds, grasses, green vegetation, insects and even some animal protein, mostly as carrion. When foraging, it stuffs its cheek pouches with seeds, which it carries back to its burrow for storage.

DEN: This ground squirrel often lives in loose colonies, particularly in favourable habitats. Families live in intricate burrows with the entrances marked at the side by large mounds of excavated dirt. The main burrow is about 4–10 m (13–33 ft) in length and ends in a grass-lined nest chamber. There are usually many secondary entrances and plunge holes.

YOUNG: Mating occurs after the females emerge from hibernation in spring. The gestation period is about 22 days, and the litter of about 3 to 11 (usually 7 or 8) young is born in May. The newborns are helpless, but they grow quickly and appear aboveground after about three weeks. They are weaned when they are about one month old, and their growth continues throughout summer as they prepare for their first hibernation.

SIMILAR SPECIES: The Columbian Ground Squirrel (p. 190) has a rich tawny nose. The Franklin's Ground Squirrel (p. 196) has a long, bushy tail. The Thirteen-lined Ground Squirrel (p. 194) has 13 alternately broken and solid buffy lines running down its back.

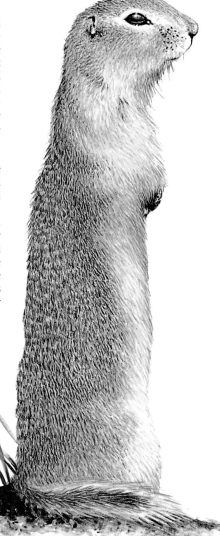

Total Length: 28–32 cm (11–13 in)
Tail Length: 6–8.3 cm (2⅜–3¼ in)
Weight: 260–630 g (9⅛–22 oz)

Thirteen-lined Ground Squirrel
Spermophilus tridecemlineatus

Although the Thirteen-lined Ground Squirrel occurs over much of Alberta, this species is one that can easily be missed in an annual Alberta mammal quest. This striped squirrel seems easy to distinguish from the far more common Richardson's Ground Squirrel, but a quick glance may be insufficient for such a determination. Be sure to thoroughly scan all lone, slender roadside squirrels so that you don't overlook any. Where one Thirteen-lined Ground Squirrel is found, others are likely present, but this species rarely exhibits the same degree of colonialism as the Richardson's Ground Squirrel.

Thirteen-lined Ground Squirrels tend to favour areas with taller grass, through which they cut paths reminiscent of vole runways. The squirrels' striped backs blend perfectly with the alternating pattern of sun and shade created by the tall grass. They usually move in a series of rushes interspersed with stops of irregular length. When alarmed, these rodents utter a shrill *seek-seek* or a high-pitched trill. They often stop short of entering their burrows, posing near the entrance instead and often allowing an observer to approach closely before disappearing from sight.

The Thirteen-lined Ground Squirrel is one of the most predacious ground squirrels in Alberta. Its diet is primarily vegetarian upon emergence from hibernation, but it shifts markedly during late May and June, when insects, bird nestlings and mice can make up almost half of the daily intake. The Thirteen-lined Ground Squirrel may even climb up into small trees or shrubs in search of promising bird nests. Indeed, trees and shrubs seem to fall within view of just about all the Thirteen-lined Ground Squirrels encountered in Alberta.

DESCRIPTION: The back bears 13 alternately dotted and solid buffy stripes separated by brown. The top of the head is generally buff and sprinkled with brown. The eye ring, nose, cheeks, feet and underparts are buffy. The sides are grey. The central colour of the thin, cylindrical tail is tawny. The longest tail hairs have a blackish subterminal band and buffy tips. The head appears long and narrow, with large eyes and small ears.

DID YOU KNOW?

True to its name, the Thirteen-lined Ground Squirrel actually has 13 buffy lines on its back, although seven of the "lines" are rows of light spots.

BEST SITES: Cypress Hills PP; Chain Lakes PP; Strome, Forestburg, Stettler and Ponoka areas.

RANGE: This prairie species ranges over much of central North America, from southeastern Alberta and southern Manitoba south to New Mexico and Texas and southeast to Ohio.

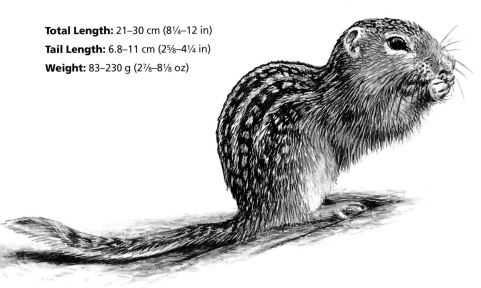

Total Length: 21–30 cm (8¼–12 in)
Tail Length: 6.8–11 cm (2⅝–4¼ in)
Weight: 83–230 g (2⅞–8⅛ oz)

HABITAT: This squirrel favours the brushy edges of tallgrass prairie with herbaceous vegetation nearby.

FOOD: Seeds seem to be the staple component of the diet, but the Thirteen-lined Ground Squirrel eats more animals than other squirrels. Insects, slugs, other invertebrates, young birds, mice and carrion are sought out and devoured. This squirrel also eats berries and native fruits, and it is sometimes a garden pest that consumes peas, beans and strawberries.

DEN: A burrow's entrances, of which there are seldom more than two, are almost never marked by earth mounds. The tunnels are 5–6.5 cm (2–2½ in) in diameter, and they descend steeply for 10–100 cm (4–39 in) before typically making a right-angle bend and levelling out. The nest chamber, about 23 cm (9 in) in diameter, is up to 2 m (6½ ft) down in a passageway off the main burrow. It is typically filled with fine grass and dried roots. The maximum reported diameter of a burrow system is 6–9 m (20–30 ft).

YOUNG: These ground squirrels mate soon after the female emerges from hibernation. The gestation period is about 27 to 28 days long, and a litter usually contains 8 to 10 naked, blind and helpless young. The eyes open at 26 to 28 days, soon after which the young emerge from the burrow, switch to a diet of vegetation and meat and are weaned. They are sexually mature following their first hibernation.

SIMILAR SPECIES: No other Albertan ground squirrel has a similar pattern of alternating broken and complete buffy stripes.

hindprint

Franklin's Ground Squirrel
Spermophilus franklinii

In a province so rich in squirrels, the Franklin's Ground Squirrel goes against the norm. With its large, bushy, grey tail and its affinity for shrubs and even forests, this ground squirrel superficially resembles a tree squirrel. In fact, in parts of Alberta it is commonly called a "bush gopher." More than other Albertan ground squirrels, the Franklin's Ground Squirrel is found almost exclusively within sprinting distance of a tree, and it is an active climber. Deciduous forests tend to be preferred, but in certain parts of Alberta these squirrels are found where conifers prevail.

Because it lives in deep grass and brushy areas and spends so much of its time underground—adults that have emerged from hibernation in mid-April are typically back underground in August or early September—the Franklin's Ground Squirrel may be Alberta's most difficult ground squirrel to observe. If you are patient, however, curiosity will entice this species out of a wood pile or dense shrubbery to a food source.

The name of this ground squirrel honours the famed English Arctic explorer Sir John Franklin, who led three expeditions attempting to locate the Northwest Passage. (He finally lost his life, and the lives of his crew, in a failed attempt in 1846.) Interestingly, the first scientific collection of the Franklin's Ground Squirrel was by Sir John Richardson, a medical doctor who also served aboard Franklin's expeditions as a naturalist, and for whom the Richardson's Ground Squirrel is named. That first Franklin's Ground Squirrel was collected in Saskatchewan, but the naturalists may have seen additional individuals in their brief travels through Alberta.

DESCRIPTION: This ground squirrel's most noticeable feature is its tail, which makes up about one-third of the animal's total length and is almost as bushy as a tree squirrel's. The tawny to olive tail is sprinkled with black and white hairs and has a white border. The overall body colour is grey, darker on the top of the head and lighter around the snout and on the sides of the face. A whitish ring surrounds the eye. The back is brownish grey, with indistinct light dapples and brownish transverse barring that becomes more pronounced on the rump. The undersides are grey or buffy coloured, and the feet are grizzled grey.

DID YOU KNOW?

During the courtship season, rival males fight violently. The combatants bite one another, particularly on the genitalia, while the females await the outcome. The victorious male generally pursues the females through dense brush.

BEST SITES: Rochon Sands PP; Sir Winston Churchill PP; Elk Island NP; Strome; Lakeland area.

RANGE: Associated with the prairies and Great Plains, the range of the Franklin's Ground Squirrel extends from central Alberta and central Saskatchewan south to Kansas and central Illinois.

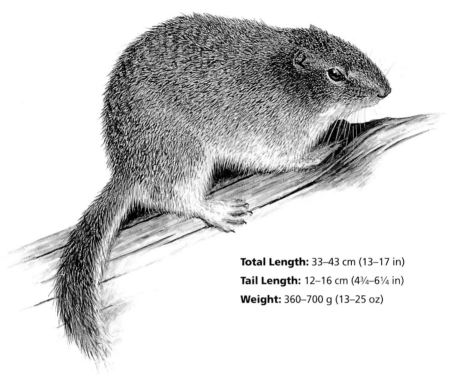

Total Length: 33–43 cm (13–17 in)
Tail Length: 12–16 cm (4¾–6¼ in)
Weight: 360–700 g (13–25 oz)

HABITAT: Typically living in tall- and mid-grass prairies and brushy regions, in the northern parts of its range it favours grassy forest meadows, aspen bluffs or even the edges of dense coniferous forests.

FOOD: Grasses, green vegetation, berries and seeds make up about two-thirds of the diet; the remaining third is animal matter. These ground squirrels are effective, weasel-like predators that may take mice, young birds, eggs, frogs, toads, other ground squirrels and even small rabbits and ducks. They also feed on carrion of all sorts.

DEN: This species is mainly solitary, but it may gather in small, loose colonies in good habitat with abundant food sources. The burrows are usually well concealed and may descend 1–2 m (3½–6½ ft) underground. The details of the burrow system are not well known,

but presumably the design is similar to that of other ground squirrels, with multiple entrances and one main nest chamber. The female lines her nest with grass. The burrow entrance is usually free of a spoil pile of dirt.

YOUNG: Mating occurs in the first week of May. After a gestation of about four weeks, a litter of 2 to 13 (usually 7 to 9) young is born. The newborns resemble pink jelly beans and are completely reliant on their mother. Their eyes open at 20 to 27 days, and by day 29 or 30 they are weaned and foraging by themselves. They reach adult size by mid-September.

SIMILAR SPECIES: No other Albertan ground squirrel has a bushy tail. The Richardson's Ground Squirrel (p. 192) is more pinkish-buff, is often seen sitting upright and tends to occur in areas of shorter grass.

Golden-mantled Ground Squirrel
Spermophilus lateralis

In spite of this squirrel's often bold behaviour and curiosity towards human visitors in Alberta's mountain parks, it remains the victim of mistaken identity. With its long white side stripes, this small ground squirrel is often called a chipmunk by onlookers. Closer inspection reveals its unique character: the stripes stop short at this ground squirrel's neck; all chipmunks have stripes running through their cheeks.

Golden-mantled Ground Squirrels are attractive, stocky-bodied, brown-eyed charmers. Their endearing eyes are framed by bold white eye rings, which add appropriate expression to their antics. In rock slides, these squirrels are found alongside pikas, and both of these small mammals continually appear and disappear among the boulders. If you can imitate the high-pitched cries of either of these two animals, the ground squirrels will commonly approach, suddenly appearing perched on a rock, surprisingly close by. At close range, you can often see their bulging cheek pouches crammed with seeds and other foods to be stored in their burrows.

Although Golden-mantled Ground Squirrels, which are often common around campsites or picnic areas, frequently mooch handouts from visitors, feeding them (or any other wildlife) is illegal in our national parks. It often leads to extreme obesity, which is an unhealthy condition for the squirrels. As visitors to our parks become better informed, they will resist the temptation to feed these and other "friendly" animals, instead satisfying their nurturing instincts with detailed observations and quiet awe.

DESCRIPTION: The head and front of the shoulders are a rich chestnut, and there is a white to buffy eye ring, interrupted towards the ear. Two black stripes on either side of a white stripe run along the sides from the top of each shoulder to near the top of the hip. The back is grizzled grey. The belly and feet are pinkish buff to creamy white. The top of the tail is blackish, bordered with cinnamon buff. The lower surface of the tail is cinnamon buff in the centre. There is a black subterminal band and a cinnamon buff fringe on the hairs along the edge of the tail.

HABITAT: This squirrel inhabits montane and subalpine forests wherever

---

DID YOU KNOW?

Alberta may be the squirreliest place in North America. From alpine meadows to treeless grasslands, and in forested regions province-wide, squirrels always seem to be only a glance away.

BEST SITES: Johnson Canyon, Peyto Lake and Lake Louise, Banff NP; Mount Edith Cavell and The Whistlers, Jasper NP.

RANGE: This rock-dwelling squirrel's range is restricted to the Rocky Mountains and the Southern Cascade–Sierra axis.

Total Length: 27–32 cm (11–13 in)
Tail Length: 9.4–12 cm (3¾–4¾ in)
Weight: 170–350 g (6–12 oz)

rock outcrops or talus slopes provide adequate cover. In summer, if not permanently, low numbers reside in the alpine tundra.

FOOD: Green vegetation forms a large part of the early summer diet. Later, more seeds, fruits, insects and carrion are eaten; still later, conifer seeds become a major component of the fall diet. Fungi are another common food.

DEN: The burrow typically begins beneath a log or rock. The entrance is 7.5 cm (3 in) in diameter and lacks an earth mound. The tunnel soon constricts to 5 cm (2 in), and although most burrows are about 1 m (3½ ft) long, others may extend to 5 m (16 ft). Two or more entrances are common. The nest burrow ends in a chamber that is 15 cm (6 in) in diameter and has a mat of vegetation on the floor. Nearby blind tunnels serve as either latrine or food storage sites. Like many ground squirrels, this species closes the burrow with an earth plug upon entering hibernation, and sometimes when it retires for the night.

YOUNG: Breeding follows soon after the female emerges from hibernation in spring. After a gestation of 27 to 28 days, four to six, 3.4-g (⅛-oz), naked, blind pups are born between mid-May and early July. The eyes open and the upper incisor teeth erupt at 27 to 31 days after birth. The young are weaned when they are 40 days old. They enter hibernation between August and October and are sexually mature when they emerge in spring.

SIMILAR SPECIES: Chipmunks (pp. 180–83) are much smaller and their stripes extend through the face.

Eastern Grey Squirrel
Sciurus carolinensis

In Calgary's wooded areas, Albertans can watch the sinuous movements of this large, introduced tree squirrel. Although known as "grey" squirrels, almost all the individuals in the Calgary area are black. Only a small minority of the population bears the light grey pelage that is common through most of this squirrel's North American range.

The Eastern Grey Squirrel is the classic park and garden squirrel of much of the Western world. This animal entertains millions of urban residents who restrict their wild adventures to places such as New York's Central Park, London's Hyde Park or even Stanley Park in Vancouver. As a wildlife ambassador, this squirrel treats the urban world to a tempered, but genuine natural experience.

It is thought that this native of eastern North America was first introduced to Alberta on St. Georges Island and at the Calgary Zoo. In the many squirrel generations since this first introduction, it has spread throughout much of the city, on its own and with human assistance. Outlying populations are now known as far away as Okotoks, but not all introductions have met with success: deliberate attempts to establish a population of the Eastern Grey Squirrel in the Edmonton river valley failed.

Calgarians often differ in their opinions of these often adored animals. Some people think that the squirrels are populating new areas of the city at the expense of many songbirds, upon whose nestlings they prey. Others testify to the fact that squirrels are seen in lower numbers in certain areas, and fear that the population may plunge. The real status of the squirrels likely lies between the two extremes, fluctuating in accordance with the ever-changing environment into which they were placed.

DESCRIPTION: In Alberta, this large tree squirrel is mainly black. Some individuals have the grey upperparts and buffy underparts that are more typical elsewhere. The bushy tail is flattened along the top and bottom.

HABITAT: These squirrels prefer mature deciduous forests. Doing without their favoured oak trees in Alberta, they are most common where poplars, maple, ash, box elder and elm are abundant.

DID YOU KNOW?

Eastern Grey Squirrel are acorn specialists. Since Alberta has few oak trees, our squirrels resort to eating seeds from shrubs and ash, maple and elm trees.

BEST SITES: Inglewood Bird Sanctuary and Calgary Zoo, Calgary; along the Sheep River in Okotoks.

RANGE: The Eastern Grey Squirrel, naturally an eastern species, occupies all of the eastern U.S. and parts of Canada to southern Manitoba in the north and eastern Texas in the south. Introduced populations have been established in Calgary, Vancouver and Seattle, among other cities.

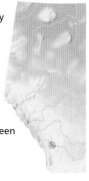

Total Length: 43–50 cm (17–20 in)
Tail Length: 21–24 cm (8¼–9½ in)
Weight: 400–710 g (14–25 oz)

FOOD: These true nut-lovers feed mainly on the seeds of maple, ash and elm. In spring and summer, they also eat buds, flowers, leaves and occasionally animal matter, such as eggs or nestling birds.

DEN: Eastern Grey Squirrels den in trees year-round. They build nests lined with dry vegetation in natural tree cavities or in old woodpecker holes. Where cavities are not available, they build dreys, which are spherical leaf and twig nests in tree branches. They have been known to make ground nests in cold regions, but this behaviour is not common.

YOUNG: Breeding occurs from December to February, and rarely in July or August. Most females have only one litter a year. Gestation is 40 to 45 days, after which a litter of one to eight (usually two to four) helpless young is born. The eyes open at 32 to 40 days, and weaning occurs about three weeks later.

SIMILAR SPECIES: The Red Squirrel (p. 202), Alberta's only other tree squirrel, is generally smaller and has a reddish-brown body. The Northern Flying Squirrel (p. 204) is nocturnal and has distinctive flight membranes between its legs.

foreprint

hindprint

Red Squirrel
Tamiasciurus hudsonicus

Never still and rarely silent, the Red Squirrel is the self-appointed security alarm of Alberta's conifer woods. This squirrel's high-strung nature alerts it to all intruders in the area, and its zest for noise informs other forest residents of the squirrel's discovery. Even other Red Squirrels are harassed with ratchet-like *chirr*s, interspersed with barks, tail flicking and foot stamping, as this rodent defends its three-dimensional territory.

Chases often result from conflicts between neighbouring Red Squirrels, and their arboreal ease is demonstrated as they run the maze of branches, launching themselves across openings to land upon a spruce bough and continue the race. Our province's abundance of Red Squirrels ensures that Albertans do not miss out on the wizardry of tree travel.

Red Squirrels remain active on all but the coldest days of winter, running through the treetops and stripping away cone scales to reveal the precious seeds. When the most bitter winter weather confines Red Squirrels to their dens or burrows, they still have access to their middens through subnivean runways. These cone caches, which in extreme cases can reach the size of a garage, are the secret to the Red Squirrel's wintering success. Much of their efforts throughout the year are concentrated on these larders, and many biologists have speculated that the Red Squirrel's characteristically antagonistic disposition is a result of having to continuously protect these winter food caches.

DESCRIPTION: The shiny, clove brown summer coat sometimes has a central reddish wash along the back. A black line along each side separates the dorsal colour from the greyish to white underparts. There is a white eye ring. The backs of the ears and the legs are rufous to yellowish. The longest tail hairs have a black subterminal band and buffy tips, which gives the tail a light fringe. The longer, softer winter fur tends to be bright to dusky rufous on the upperparts, with fewer buffy areas, and the head and belly tend to be greyer. The whiskers are black.

HABITAT: Boreal coniferous forests and mixed forests comprise the major habitat, but towns with trees more than 40 years old also support populations of Red Squirrels.

DID YOU KNOW?

In fall, Red Squirrels nip conifer cones from the tops of trees, letting them fall to the ground. Once they have harvested enough cones, the squirrels collect the bounty and store it, often in heaps, for winter usage.

BEST SITES: Edmonton river valley; day use areas and campgrounds in any northern or mountain park.

RANGE: The Red Squirrel occupies coniferous forests across most of Alaska and Canada. In the West, it extends south through the Rocky Mountains to southern New Mexico. In the East, it occurs south to Iowa and Virginia and through the Alleghenies.

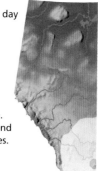

Total Length: 28–35 cm (11¼–14 in)
Tail Length: 11–15 cm (4⅕–5⅘ in)
Weight: 170–310 g (6–11 oz)

FOOD: The majority of the diet consists of seeds extracted from conifer cones. Squirrels cut the cones before they ripen, and then store them for winter, sometimes in huge caches. A midden is formed where discarded cone scales and centres pile up below a favoured feeding perch. In some areas, the young bark and cambium of conifers is chewed in a fashion reminiscent of porcupines. Flowers, birds, berries, mushrooms, eggs, mice, insects and even chipmunks may be eaten.

DEN: Tree cavities, witches' broom (created in conifers in response to mistletoe or fungal infections), logs and burrows may serve as den sites. The burrows or entrances are about 13 cm (5 in) in diameter, with an expanded cavity housing a nest ball that is 40 cm (16 in) across.

YOUNG: Northern populations bear just one litter a year. Peak breeding, in April and May, is associated with frenetic chases and multiple copulations lasting up to seven minutes each. After a 35- to 38-day gestation, a litter of usually four or five helpless young is born. The eyes open at four to five weeks, and the young are weaned when they are seven to eight weeks old. At 10 weeks they begin to forage away from the nest, but in the north they often stay with their mother until they are 4½ months old. Red Squirrels are sexually mature by the following spring.

SIMILAR SPECIES: The Eastern Grey Squirrel (p. 200) of the Calgary area is larger and generally black. The Northern Flying Squirrel is nocturnal and has distinctive flight membranes between its legs. Ground squirrels (pp. 190–98) don't usually have bushy tails and have lighter upperparts.

Northern Flying Squirrel
Glaucomys sabrinus

Northern Flying Squirrels are the recluses of the squirrel world: trapping studies suggest that these wide-eyed rodents are just as numerous as Red Squirrels in many places, but their quiet nature and nocturnal activity patterns generally keep them hidden from humans. People living near spruce woods, however, should be alert to their presence. Several birdfeeders in the Edmonton river valley are known to have almost nightly visits from Northern Flying Squirrels, which value the seeds as much as sparrows and finches do. In the right areas, midnight walks can be punctuated with their scratchy trunk scrambles and occasional overhead passes, highlighted by the moonlight.

Flying squirrels are gregarious, and several individuals are often found together in one tree or at a feeding site. Up to nine have been found sharing a single daytime nest. This communal huddling probably comes from an attempt to stay warm, because flying squirrels have a tendency to chill easier than other squirrels. These sorts of crowded situations would be intolerable for the Red Squirrel, but the flying squirrel's peaceful habits are in stark contrast to the hyperactive nature of its daytime relative.

Of course, the most intriguing and famed aspect of the flying squirrel is its ability to glide. Although it lacks the gift of true flapping flight—bats are the only mammals to have mastered that ability—a flying squirrel's aerial travels are no less impressive, with extreme voyages of up to 100 m (110 yd). The flying squirrel glides on its flight membranes: loose folds of skin that it spreads tightly between its front and rear legs. On the ground and in trees, flying squirrels hop or leap, but the skin folds prevent them from running.

DESCRIPTION: Flying squirrels have a unique web or fold of skin that extends laterally to the level of the ankles and wrists to become the abbreviated "wings" with which the squirrel glides. Being nocturnal, they have large, dark, shiny eyes. The back is light brown, with hints of grey from the lead-coloured hair bases. The feet are grey on top. The underparts are light grey to cinnamon precisely to the edge of the gliding membrane and edge of the tail. The tail is noticeably flattened top to bottom,

---

DID YOU KNOW?

Before launching into flight, a flying squirrel bobs its head up and down and from side to side, perhaps to aid in distance perception. Once airborne, it steers with its forelegs and maintains balance and flight control with its flattened tail.

BEST SITES: Edmonton river valley; Police Point Park, Medicine Hat; Cline River.

RANGE: This flying squirrel occurs in coniferous and mixed forests in eastern Alaska and across most of Canada. It extends south through the western mountains to California and Utah, around the Great Lakes and through the Appalachians.

Total Length: 25–37 cm (9¾–15 in)
Tail Length: 11–18 cm (4¼–7 in)
Weight: 75–185 g (2⅝–6½ oz)

which adds to the buoyancy of the "flight" and helps it function as the rudder and elevators do on a plane.

HABITAT: Northern coniferous forests and the forests of the Rocky Mountains are prime habitat, but flying squirrels are sometimes found in aspen and cottonwood forests.

FOOD: The bulk of the food consists of lichens and fungi, but it also eats buds, berries, some seeds, a few arthropods, bird eggs and nestlings and the protein-rich, pollen-filled staminate cones of conifers. It caches cones and nuts.

DEN: Nests in tree cavities are lined with lichen and grass. Leaf nests, called "dreys," are located in a tree fork close to the trunk. Twigs and strips of bark are used on the outside, with progressively finer materials used inside until the cen-

tre consists of grasses and lichens. If the drey is for winter use, it is additionally insulated to a diameter of 40 cm (16 in).

YOUNG: Mating takes place between late March and the end of May. After a six-week gestation period, typically two to four young are born. They weigh about 6 g (³⁄₁₆ oz) at birth. The eyes open at about 52 days. Ten days later they first leave the nest, and they are weaned when they are about 65 days old. Young squirrels first glide at three months; it takes them about a month to become skilful gliders. Flying squirrels do not become sexually mature until after their second winter.

SIMILAR SPECIES: No other mammal in Alberta has the distinctive flight membranes of a flying squirrel. The Red Squirrel (p. 202) is reddish brown overall and is generally active during the day.

PIKAS AND HARES

The members of this group of rodent-like mammals are often called lagomorphs after the scientific name of the order, Lagomorpha, which means "hare-shaped." Pikas, rabbits and hares share the rodents' trademark, chisel-like upper incisors, and taxonomists once grouped the two orders together. Unlike rodents, however, lagomorphs have a second pair of upper incisors. Casual observers will never see these peg-like teeth; instead of being in the general tooth row, they lie immediately behind the first incisor pair.

Lagomorphs are strict vegetarians, but they have relatively inefficient, non-ruminant stomachs that have trouble digesting such a diet. To make the most of their meals, they defecate pellets of soft, green, partially digested material that they then reingest to obtain maximum nutrition. Some biologists believe this process evolved as a protective mechanism that allows a lagomorph to quickly fill its stomach and then retreat to a hiding place to digest the meal in safety.

Pika Family
(Ochotonidae)

Pikas are the most rodent-like of the lagomorphs, and, with their short, rounded ears and squat bodies, they look a lot like guinea pigs. Their front and rear limbs are about the same length, so pikas scurry, rather than hop, through the rocky outcrops and talus of their home territories. Pikas are most active during the day, so they are often seen by hikers in our mountain parks.

Hare Family
(Leporidae)

Hares and rabbits are characterized by their long, upright ears, long hindlegs and short, cottony tails. These timid animals are primarily nocturnal, and they spend most of the day resting in shallow depressions, called "forms." Rabbits build a maternity nest for their young, which are blind and naked at birth. Hares are born fully furred and with open eyes, and soon after birth they begin to feed on vegetation.

American Pika
Ochotona princeps

Inhabiting a confusing landscape of boulders nestled in a rocky mountain cradle, the American Pika is one of Alberta's top cuteness contenders. This relative of the rabbit scurries among the talus rocks of a landslide as it makes its way between its feeding areas and shelter.

Frequently, an American Pika returns from its nearby foraging areas with vegetation clippings held crossways in its mouth. The bundle is sometimes half as large as the pika itself, and the vegetation is carried back towards the den, where it is accumulated in piles on and around the rocks to be dried for winter use.

Pikas are extremely vocal animals that are often heard before they are seen. The proper pronunciation of their name is *pee-ka,* which is somewhat reminiscent of their high-pitched voices: they give out weak tricycle horn bleats whenever they see something out of the ordinary. Their voices are the first, and often best, clues of pika activity, because these animals are so difficult to distinguish in their bouldered habitats—when a pika is momentarily glimpsed from afar, one is never quite sure whether it is a genuine sighting or just a pika-sized rock. To the patient naturalist intent on pika observations, however, viewing can be intimate and rewarding, because these animals often permit a close approach.

In winter, pikas dig snow tunnels as far as 100 m (110 yd) out from their rock shelters to collect and eat plants. The talus slopes that are their homes often receive great quantities of snow, which helps insulate the animals from the mountain winters. Rarely venturing into the chill of the open air, pikas tend to remain beneath the snows, sometimes feeding upon the grass they so meticulously gathered and dried earlier in the year.

DESCRIPTION: This grey to tawny-grey, chunky, soft-looking mammal has large, rounded ears and beady black eyes. The whiskers are long. There is no external tail. The front and rear legs are nearly equal in length, so pikas run instead of hopping.

HABITAT: Pikas generally occupy accumulations of broken rock, known as talus slopes, in the mountains, although they have rarely been found among the jumbled logs swept down by avalanches.

BEST SITES: Rock Glacier and Highwood Pass, Peter Lougheed PP; Mount Edith Cavell and Jonas Creek, Jasper NP; Parker Ridge and Peyto Lake, Banff NP.

RANGE: Pikas occur through the mountains of west-central Alberta and southern British Columbia and south to California, Utah and New Mexico.

Total Length: 18–20 cm (7–7¾ in)
Tail Length: There is no external tail
Weight: 180–230 g (6⅜–8⅛ oz)

FOOD: The diet includes a wide variety of plants that are found in the vicinity of this animal's rocky shelter. Broad-leafed plants, grasses and sedges are all clipped and consumed.

DEN: Pikas build grass-lined nests, in which the young are born, beneath the rocks of their home.

YOUNG: Mating occurs in spring, and after a 30-day gestation period a litter of two to five (usually three) young is born. The newborns are furry, weigh 8–9 g (¼–⁵⁄₁₆ oz) and have closed eyes. The eyes open after 10 days. The young are weaned when they are 30 days old and two-thirds grown. Pikas are sexually mature after their first winter. There is sometimes a second summer breeding period.

SIMILAR SPECIES: The only other grey mammal of comparable size that might occupy the same rocky slopes as a pika is the Bushy-tailed Woodrat (p. 152), but woodrats have long, bushy tails.

foreprint

hindprint

Mountain Cottontail
Sylvilagus nuttallii

When the sun lowers to meet the prairie horizon, flooding mid-summer evenings in golden light, Mountain Cottontails emerge from their daytime hideouts to graze on the coulee vegetation. They can often be intimately observed in southern Alberta parks as they daintily nip at grasses, always just a short leap from dense bushes.

These rabbits fit the cuteness niche in the minds and hearts of Albertans: a cottontail's coal black eyes, rounded ears and soft features complement almost everyone's image of a wild bunny. Their plush toy caricature, however, masks a perfectly wild animal that is quite capable of surviving in a harsh, arid landscape with a rich diversity of predators.

Mountain Cottontails spend most of their days sitting quietly in dugout depressions, called "forms," beneath thorny-buffaloberry shrubs or similarly impenetrable vegetation, or under boards, rocks, abandoned machinery or buildings. Heavy rains, when they do occur in Alberta's southlands, greatly diminish cottontail activity, restricting them to their hideouts for the duration of the storm. Mountain Cottontails do not hibernate during winter, but they limit their movements to traditional trails that they can easily locate after a snowfall. These mid-sized herbivores have small home ranges that rarely exceed the size of a hockey rink.

Thomas Nuttall is a wondrous choice to be immortalized in the name of this inquisitive and endearing animal. Although Nuttall was primarily a botanist, he made significant contributions to all fields of natural history. He was also renowned for his absent-mindedness and misadventures. Many of his most famous gaffes occurred during his voyage across the continent to the Pacific on the Wyeth expedition in 1834. On several occasions through the Great Plains he became lost, and should any prairie animal provide a sense of comfort to one so misguided, it would surely be the cottontail that now bears his name.

DESCRIPTION: This rabbit has dark, grizzled, yellowish-grey upperparts and whitish underparts year-round. The tail is blackish above and white below. There is a rusty-orange patch on the nape of the neck, and the front and back edges of the ears are white.

DID YOU KNOW?

Rabbits and hares depend on intestinal bacteria to break down the cellulose in their diets. Because the bacterial products re-enter the gut beyond the site of absorption, rabbits eat their fecal pellets to run the material through the digestive tract a second time.

BEST SITES: Writing-on-Stone PP; Dinosaur PP; Police Point Park, Medicine Hat; Oldman River valley; Drumheller.

RANGE: The western limit of the range closely matches the eastern border of California, running north into the Okanagan of British Columbia. The eastern edge of the range runs south from southern Saskatchewan along the Montana-Dakota border to northern New Mexico.

Total Length: 34–40 cm (13–16 in)
Tail Length: 3.2–6.4 cm (1¼–2½ in)
Weight: 670–1030 g (24–36 oz)

HABITAT: A major habitat requirement is cover, whether that be brush, fractured rock outcrops or buildings. This animal likes edge situations where trees meet meadows or where brushy areas meet agricultural land. Its common name is a bit of a mystery to Albertans, because it does not occur in the mountains of our province. Further south, however, in the western U.S., the Mountain Cottontail does live up to its name.

FOOD: Grasses and forbs are the primary foods, but in many areas it feeds heavily on sagebrush and juniper berries as necessary.

DEN: There is no true den, but cottontails shelter in a "form," a dug out depression, beneath and among rocks, boards,

buildings and the like. The young are born into a nest that is dug out by the female and lined with grass and fur.

YOUNG: Breeding begins in April, and after a 28- to 30-day gestation a litter of one to eight (usually four or five) young is born. The female is in estrus and breeds again within hours after giving birth, so there can be two litters a season. The young are born blind, hairless and with their eyes closed. They grow quickly and are weaned just before the birth of the subsequent litter.

SIMILAR SPECIES: Both the Snowshoe Hare (p. 212) and the White-tailed Jackrabbit (p. 214) are much larger and become white in winter.

Snowshoe Hare
Lepus americanus

Every bit as symbolic to our country as the Moose and the "American" Beaver, the Snowshoe Hare is an all-Canadian trooper that occurs throughout most of Alberta's forests and woodlands.

As a species highly adapted to withstand the most intolerant aspects of wild Alberta, the Snowshoe Hare possesses several fascinating adaptations for our winters. As its name implies, for example, the Snowshoe Hare indeed has very large hindfeet that enable it to cross areas of soft snow where other animals sink into the powder. This ability is a tremendous advantage for an animal that is preyed upon by so many carnivores. Unfortunately, it is of minimal help against the equally big-footed Canada Lynx, a specialized hunter of the Snowshoe Hare.

It is quite well known that populations of lynx and hares fluctuate in near direct correlation with one another, but few people know that some of the earliest research into this interaction was done by an Albertan working near Rochester, just south of Athabasca. Although the predator-prey relationship is quite important to the population sizes of both species, lynx predation is not solely responsible for the reduction in the population of hares. Recent studies have found that the hares' overgrazing of vegetation, such as young aspen saplings, contributes to both species' declines.

Whether snow flies or not, Snowshoe Hares start changing into their white winter camouflage by mid-October. The hares have no control over the timing of this winter adaptation, and if the year's first snowfall is late, individuals that have undergone this transformation will lose their concealment, becoming visible from great distances—to naturalists and predators alike—as bright white balls in a brown world. The hares seem to be aware of their predicament, and they will often seek out any small patch of snow on which to squat under those circumstances.

DESCRIPTION: The summer coat is rusty brown above, with the crown of the head being blacker and less reddish than the back. The nape of the neck is greyish brown and the ear tips are black. The chin, belly and lower surface of the tail are white. Adults have white feet; immatures have dark feet. In winter, the terminal portion of nearly all the body hair becomes white, but the hair bases

---

DID YOU KNOW?

Snowshoe Hare densities can vary by a factor of 100. During highs, there may be 12 to 15 hares per hectare (5 to 6 per acre); after a population crashes, they may be relatively uncommon over huge geographical areas for years.

BEST SITES: Edmonton river valley; Gooseberry Lake PP; Saskatoon Island PP; Lesser Slave Lake PP; Cold Lake PP; Cypress Hills PP.

RANGE: The range of the snowshoe hare is associated with the boreal coniferous forests and the montane forests from northern Alaska and Labrador south to California and New Mexico.

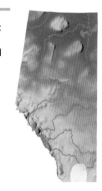

Total Length: 39–53 cm (15–21 in)
Tail Length: 4.8–5.4 cm (1⅞–2⅛ in)
Weight: 1–1.5 kg (2¼–3¼ lb)

summer
colours

and the underfur are lead grey to brownish. The ear tips remain black.

HABITAT: Wherever there is forest or dense shrub in Alberta you may find Snowshoe Hares.

FOOD: In summer, a wide variety of grasses, forbs and brush may be consumed. In winter, mostly the buds, twigs and bark of woody deciduous and coniferous shrubs and trees are eaten. Hares will occasionally eat carrion.

DEN: Snowshoe Hares do not keep a customary den, but they occasionally enter hollow logs or the burrows of other animals, or run beneath buildings.

YOUNG: Breeding activity begins in March and continues throughout August.

After a gestation period of 35 to 37 days, one to seven (usually three or four) leverets are born under cover, but often not in an established form or nest. The female breeds again within hours of their birth, and she may have as many as three litters a season. The young hares are born with fur and with their eyes open. They can hop within a day, are active within a week and are feeding on grassy vegetation within 10 days. In five months they are full grown.

SIMILAR SPECIES: The Mountain Cottontail (p. 210) is generally smaller, the nape of the neck is orangish or rusty and its ears are generally uniform in colour or have white edges. The White-tailed Jackrabbit (p. 214) has longer ears and a slightly longer tail, and its winter underfur is creamy white.

White-tailed Jackrabbit

Lepus townsendii

The White-tailed Jackrabbit is a lean sprinter and the largest and the most commonly encountered hare through much of the heavily populated regions of Alberta. A creature of open country, the White-tailed Jackrabbit is most frequently encountered either by day, as it bursts from a hiding place with its ears erect and it tail extended, bounding out of danger with ease, or at night in the flash of car headlights.

Jackrabbits are customarily solitary when they are out foraging, but in winter up to 50 may gather in one place, often where food is abundant. These aggregations usually occur at night, when jackrabbits are most active.

Like most herbivores, the White-tailed Jackrabbit is drawn to salt, which, unfortunately, it often licks from roads. This need for salt, together with its preference for travelling on solid surfaces, may partly explain the large numbers of road-killed jackrabbits encountered on some Alberta highways.

Their protruding eyes and sinuous limbs give White-tailed Jackrabbits a "meaner" look than the other Alberta rabbits, but these features are adapta-tions for detecting and avoiding predators. Known for their raw speed, long-legged jackrabbits can outdistance most land-based predators in an all-out run. Ambush appears to be the most effective method of catching a jackrabbit, but the open country in which these animals live gives little opportunity for cover-seeking predators. Golden Eagles have moderate successes in aerial attacks, occasionally inflicting mortal injury to the backs of these prairie speedsters.

White-tailed Jackrabbits can sometimes be found using the same rest areas day after day, so if you spook a jackrabbit from its hideout during a walk, you can return cautiously the next day to look for it in the same area. Quite often, these large hares are found using exactly the same forms, and they can be surprisingly approachable if your movements are slow and unthreatening.

DESCRIPTION: In summer, the upperparts of this large hare are light greyish brown and the belly is nearly white. By mid-November, the entire coat is white, except for the greyish forehead and the black ear tips. It has a fairly long, white tail that sometimes bears a greyish band

---

DID YOU KNOW?

The name "jackrabbit" is a shortened, and more delicate, version of "jack-ass rabbit." This animal was so named in recognition of its large, donkey-like ears.

BEST SITES: University campuses in Edmonton and Calgary; less-developed areas of many cities; Kinbrook Island PP; south of Cypress Hills PP.

RANGE: The White-tailed Jackrabbit seems to be expanding its range northward in Alberta, perhaps in association with the clearing of land. It is currently found from eastern Washington east to southern Manitoba and south to central California and eastern Kansas.

Total Length: 54–64 cm (21–25 in)
Tail Length: 7–11 cm (2¾–4¼ in)
Weight: 3–5.4 kg (6¾–12 lb)

summer colours

on the upper surface. The tail is held rigidly behind the animal as it runs.

HABITAT: This hare is a creature of open areas. It will enter open woodlands to seek shelter in winter, but it avoids dense, timbered stands.

FOOD: Grasses and forbs are the most commonly eaten plants, but jackrabbits also enjoy alfalfa and clover in agricultural regions. More shrubs and weedy plants appear in the winter diet. Like all hares, they eat their fecal pellets to run the bacteria and bacterial breakdown products from their cecum through the digestive system a second time, allowing the hare to absorb the nutrients.

DEN: There is no den, but a shallow hollow, called a "form," beside a rock or beneath a bush, serves as a daytime shelter. In winter, jackrabbits may dig depressions or short burrows as shelters in snowdrifts.

YOUNG: One to nine (usually three or four) leverets are born after a 40-day gestation. The fully furred newborns have open eyes and are born in a shallow depression. They soon disperse, meeting their mother to nurse only once or twice a day. By two weeks old they are eating some green vegetation; at five to six weeks they are weaned, often just before the birth of the next litter. Jackrabbits reach adult weight in three to four months.

SIMILAR SPECIES: In winter, the Snowshoe Hare (p. 212) has lead grey, not creamy-white, hair bases. It is nearly always associated with treed or brushy areas, not the jackrabbit's prairie habitat.

BATS

Only three groups of vertebrates have achieved self-powered flight: bats, birds and the now-extinct reptilian pterosaurs. In an evolutionary sense, bats are a very successful group of mammals. Worldwide, nearly one-quarter of all mammalian species are bats, and they are second only to rodents in both diversity of species and number of individuals.

Unlike the feathered wings of a bird, a bat's wings consist of double layers of skin stretched across the modified bones of the fingers and back to the legs. A small bone, called the calcar, juts backward from the foot to help support the tail membrane, which stretches between the tail and each leg. The calcar is said to be keeled when there is a small projection of cartilage from the side.

Bats generate lift by pushing their wings down against the air's resistance, so they tend to have large wing surface areas for their body size. This method of flight is less efficient than the aerofoil lift provided by bird or airplane wings, but it allows bats to fly slower and gives them more maneuverability than most birds, which is a real advantage when they are trying to catch insects or hover in front of a flower.

Bats have excellent vision, but their nocturnal habits have led to an increased dependence on their sense of hearing—most people are acquainted with the ability of many bat species to navigate or capture prey in the dark using echolocation. The tragus, a slender lobe that projects from the inner base of many bats' ears, is thought to help in determining an echo's direction. Each species of bat in Alberta echolocates at different frequencies, so a person equipped with a bat detector—these things actually exist—can identify the species of a bat from its ultrasonic nighttime clicks.

Bats, unlike most other types of small mammals, have small litters. The high energy requirements for flight limit most female bats to having only one offspring a year. Bat populations can reach high numbers, however, because bats live for many years. The oldest wild bat yet recorded lived through 32 summers, and even many bats in Alberta are thought to live for 10 years.

Evening Bat Family
(Vespertilionidae)

All nine species of bats that occur in Alberta belong to this family. True to their name, most members of this family are active in the evening, and often again before dawn, when they typically feed on flying insects. A few species migrate to warmer regions for winter, but most hibernate in caves or abandoned buildings and mines.

Little Brown Bat

Long-eared Bat
Myotis evotis

The nightly, dramatic bat sagas taking place in our summer skies are largely unknown to Albertans. In apparent silence, Alberta bats navigate and locate prey by producing ultrasonic pulses (up to five times higher in pitch than our ears can detect) and listening for the echoes of these sounds as they bounce off objects. Bats with large ears tend to be insectivorous, so the aptly named Long-eared Bat should be well-equipped for insect hunting.

DESCRIPTION: The wingspan of this medium-sized bat is about 28 cm (11 in). The upperparts are light brown to buffy yellow. The undersides are lighter. Its black, naked ears are 1.8–2.5 cm ($^{11}/_{16}$–1 in) long. The tragus is long and narrow. The wings are mainly naked; only the lower fifth of the tail membrane is furred. The calcar is keeled.

Total Length: 8.3–11 cm (3¼–4¼ in)
Tail Length: 3.4–4.7 cm (1⅜–1⅞ in)
Forearm: 3.7–4.1 cm (1½–1⅝ in)
Weight: 4.2–10 g (⅛–⁷/₁₆ oz)

HABITAT: This bat occurs in forested areas adjacent to rocky outcrops or badland landscapes. It occasionally occupies buildings, mines and caves.

FOOD: Feeding peaks at dusk and just before dawn. Moths, flies and beetles are the primary prey.

DEN: Both sexes of this mainly solitary bat hibernate in caves and mines in winter. In spring, up to 30 females gather in a nursery colony in a tree cavity, under loose bark, in an old building, under a bridge or in loose shingles on a rooftop. Males typically roost in caves and mines in summer.

YOUNG: Mating takes place in autumn, before hibernation begins, but fertilization is delayed until spring. In June or early July, after a gestation of about 40 days, a female bears one young. The female has two mammae, but twins are uncommon. The young mature quickly and are able to fly on their own in four weeks.

SIMILAR SPECIES: All the mouse-eared bats (*Myotis* spp.) are generally indistinguishable as they fly in dim light. It requires precise measurements and careful attention to detail to identify the species.

BEST SITES: Cottonwood stands along prairie rivers; Kananaskis Country; Waterton Lakes NP.

RANGE: The Long-eared Bat is found from southern Alberta east to Newfoundland and south to Nebraska, Arkansas, western Georgia and Virginia.

Northern Bat
Myotis septentrionalis

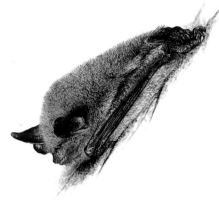

Total Length: 8–10 cm (3¼–4 in)
Tail Length: 3–4.3 cm (1⅛–1¾ in)
Forearm: 3.3–4 cm (1¼–1⅝ in)
Weight: 4.3–8.4 g (⅛–⁵⁄₁₆ oz)

FOOD: This bat primarily feeds at dusk and again just before dawn. It catches flying insects, including moths, flies and beetles.

The Northern Bat tends to roost in natural cavities and under peeling bark on old trees in northern Alberta, and some people are concerned that it is therefore vulnerable to forestry operations, which often select older trees for harvesting.

During September and October, Northern Bats travel to caves to hibernate for the winter. Currently, only two caves in Alberta are known to host Northern Bats, but more likely await discovery.

DESCRIPTION: This mid- to dark brown bat has a wingspan of 23–26 cm (9–10 in). It has somewhat lighter underparts. The tips of its hairs are lighter than the bases, giving a sheen to the fur. The tragus is long and narrow. The calcar is not keeled.

HABITAT: The Northern Bat, which primarily occurs in forested and sometimes brushy areas, prefers to be close to waterbodies.

DEN: This mainly solitary bat hibernates in caves and mines in winter. The males continue to roost in caves and mines all year, but the females form nursery colonies in spring. The colonies are usually located in tree cavities, under loose bark on trees, in old buildings, under bridges or in loose shingles on rooftops, and they may be small or contain up to 30 females.

YOUNG: These bats mate in fall, but fertilization is delayed until spring, so the young are not born until June or early July, after a gestation of about 40 days. The female has two mammae, but twins are uncommon. The young are able to fly in about four weeks.

SIMILAR SPECIES: Mouse-eared bats (*Myotis* spp.) are generally indistinguishable from one another. Identification of the species requires precise measurements and careful attention to detail.

BEST SITES: Broule Lake; Miquelon Lakes PP.

RANGE: Northern Bats are found from the lower half of British Columbia east to southwestern Saskatchewan and south to much of California, northeastern Arizona and northwestern New Mexico.

Western Small-footed Bat
Myotis ciliolabrum

The Western Small-footed Bat is one of Alberta's "rock bats": it occupies rocky habitats in badlands and southern river valleys. Summer colonies may contain dozens to hundreds of individuals, but the entire provincial population probably weighs less than just one big deer. If you stand at the mouth of a badlands cave at dusk, watching the bats circle, it will come as no surprise that bats make up such a large percentage of the total number of mammals worldwide.

DESCRIPTION: An attractive bat, its glossy fur is yellowish brown to grey or even coppery brown above, and its undersides are almost white. The flight membranes and ears are black, and the tail membrane is dark brown. Its wingspread is 21–25 cm (8¼–9¾ in), and some fur may be found on both the undersurface of the wing and the upper surface of the tail membrane. Across its face, from ear to ear, is a dark brown or black "mask." True to its name, this bat has noticeably small feet. The calcar is strongly keeled.

HABITAT: The Western Small-footed Bat occupies drier habitats than other bats in Alberta. It prefers arid and prairie regions, especially riverbanks, ridges and outcroppings with many rocks for roosting.

Total Length: 7.6–8.9 cm (3–3½ in)
Tail Length: 3–4.4 cm (1³⁄₁₆–1¾ in)
Forearm: 2.9–3.6 cm (1⅛–1⅜ in)
Weight: 3–7 g (⅛–¼ oz)

FOOD: Like most Alberta bats, the Western Small-footed Bat primarily eats flying insects, including moths, flies, bugs and beetles.

DEN: In summer, this bat roosts in trees, buildings or rock crevices. It hibernates in caves or mines in winter. Nursery colonies occur in bank crevices, under bridges or under the shingles of old buildings.

YOUNG: In small nursery colonies, one young per female is born from late May to early June. The females have two mammae, but twins are uncommon.

SIMILAR SPECIES: In dim light, you cannot see the Western Small-footed Bat's "mask"; a technical key to the mammals of this region is needed to distinguish between the *Myotis* species.

BEST SITES: Eroded cliffs along the South Saskatchewan River.

RANGE: The Western Small-footed Bat is found from southern British Columbia east to southwestern Saskatchewan and south through most of the western U.S.

Little Brown Bat
Myotis lucifugus

On nearly every warm, calm summer night, the skies of Alberta are filled with marvellously complex screams and shrills. Unfortunately for people interested in the world of bats, these magnificent vocalizations occur at frequencies higher than our ears can register. The most common of these nighttime screamers, and quite likely the first bat most Albertans will encounter, is the Little Brown Bat.

Once the cold days of late August and September arrive, Little Brown Bats begin to migrate to areas where they will spend the winter. Prior to entering hibernation, they mate. The young are not born until late June or early July, however, because fertilization of the egg is delayed until spring.

While it is not known where all Alberta's bats spend the winter, thousands of them travel to caves in the mountains and foothills. Large wintering populations are known from the Nordegg and Cadomin areas, and cave adventurers are advised to take special care not to disturb these hibernating animals. Slight disturbances and subtle shifts in temperature can awaken the bats, suggesting to them that spring has arrived. Unfortunately, any bat flying out of the cave during the winter months is sure to die from exposure to the cold temperatures.

DESCRIPTION: As its name suggests, this bat is little and brown. Its coloration ranges from light to dark brown on the back, with somewhat paler undersides. The tips of the hairs are glossy, giving this bat a coppery appearance. The wing and tail membranes are mainly unfurred, but fur may appear around the edges. The calcar of this bat is long and unkeeled. The tragus, which is nearly straight, is half the length of the ear.

HABITAT: Little Brown Bats are the most frequently encountered bats in Alberta. At home almost anywhere, you may find them in buildings, attics, roof crevices and loose bark on trees or under bridges. Wherever this bat is roosting, waterbodies are sure to be nearby to ensure a large supply of insects for their nightly foragings.

FOOD: Little Brown Bats feed exclusively on night-flying insects. In the

---

DID YOU KNOW?

An individual Little Brown Bat can consume 900 insects in a single hour. It is thought that a typical colony will eat 50 kg (110 lb) of insects a year.

BEST SITES: East Coulee; Veteran; Provost; unoccupied farms where abandoned, shingled buildings with south-facing roofs provide preferred day roosts and nursery sites.

RANGE: This widespread bat ranges from central Alaska to Newfoundland and south to northern Florida and central Mexico, except for much of the southern Great Plains.

Total Length: 6–10 cm (2⅜–4 in)
Tail Length: 2.5–5.5 cm (1–2⅛ in)
Forearm: 3.5–4.2 cm (1⅜–1⅝ in)
Weight: 5.5–8.5 g (³⁄₁₆–⁵⁄₁₆ oz)

evening, these bats leave their day roosts and swoop down to the nearest water source to snatch a drink on the wing. Foraging for insects can last for up to five hours. Later, the bat takes a rest in a night roost (a different place from their day roost). Just prior to dawn, another short feeding period occurs before the bat returns to its day roost.

DEN: These bats may roost alone, in small groups or in colonies of more than 1000, under a loose shingle, in an open attic or in a hollow tree. By June, pregnant females form nursery colonies in a protected location. In winter, some bats may stay and hibernate in large numbers in caves and old mines, but most are believed to migrate to warmer climates.

YOUNG: Mating occurs either in late autumn or in the hibernation colonies. Fertilization is delayed until the female ovulates in spring. Pregnant females form nursery colonies. In June, one young is born to a female after about 50 to 60 days of gestation. The young are blind and hairless, but their development is rapid and their eyes open in about three days. After one month, the young are on their own.

SIMILAR SPECIES: All the mouse-eared bats (*Myotis* spp.) are essentially impossible to identify in flight. Even in hand, one needs a technical key, which, through the examination of measurements or characteristics, allows determination of the species.

Long-legged Bat
Myotis volans

Total Length: 8.7–10 cm (3⅜–4 in)
Tail Length: 3.5–5.4 cm (1⅜–2⅛ in)
Forearm: 3.5–4.4 cm (1⅜–1¾ in)
Weight: 5.6–11 g (³⁄₁₆–⅜ oz)

A few millimetres is the extent of the difference between the feet and legs of the Long-legged Bat and the Western Small-footed Bat. Noticeable differences do occur, however, in their habitat selections: the Long-legged Bat always lives near water because of the aquatic nymphs and larvae that rise from the surface as adults.

DESCRIPTION: Although this bat is the largest of the "little brown bats," it is larger by an almost imperceptible amount. The wingspan is 25–27 cm (9¾–11 in). Its fur can be uniformly light brown to reddish to dark chocolate brown, but it is mainly dark brown. There is a well-defined keel on the calcar. The underwing is usually furred out to a line connecting the elbow and knee.

HABITAT: This bat lives primarily in coniferous forests that are near water-

bodies. It may forage along the sides of mountain lakes.

FOOD: This flying insectivore primarily feeds on moths, flies, bugs and beetles.

DEN: The Long-legged Bat spends winters hibernating in a cave or mine. In summer, it roosts in trees, buildings or rock crevices. Nursery colonies are located in bank crevices, under bridges or under shingles on old buildings.

YOUNG: Mating occurs in autumn. Fertilization is delayed until spring, and the young are born in large nursery colonies in July or August. A female usually bears just one young, although she has two mammae. The young mature quickly, flying on their own in about four weeks. The longest recorded lifespan for this species is 21 years.

SIMILAR SPECIES: The slightly longer legs of the Long-legged Bat are not noticeable on a flying bat in dim light; to distinguish between the different *Myotis* species you will need a technical key for the mammals of Alberta.

BEST SITES: Remote reservoirs and cattle tanks in the shortgrass prairie; along the shores of mountain lakes.

RANGE: The Long-legged Bat ranges from northwestern British Columbia southeast to western North Dakota and south through most of the western U.S.

Eastern Red Bat

Lasiurus borealis

Total Length: 8.7–12 cm (3⅜–4¾ in)

Tail Length: 3.6–6.5 cm (1⅜–2½ in)

Forearm: 3.6–4.4 cm (1⅜–1¾ in)

Weight: 8–17 g (⁵⁄₁₆–⅝ oz)

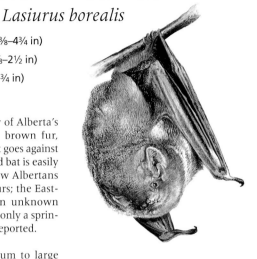

While the majority of Alberta's bats have boring brown fur, the Eastern Red Bat goes against the norm. This carrot-topped bat is easily identified (for a bat), but few Albertans ever see its distinctive colours; the Eastern Red Bat is virtually an unknown animal in our province, and only a sprinkling of records have been reported.

DESCRIPTION: This medium to large bat has mainly yellowish-orange to red fur. The male is often brighter than the female. Some individuals may have a slightly frosted appearance, owing to white-tipped hairs. The wingspan is 29–33 cm (11–13 in). The ears are small and rounded, and the tragus is small. The backsides of the ears and face are covered in orangish fur, and the upper surface of the tail membrane is furred.

HABITAT: This bat thrives in both coniferous and deciduous forests and is often found near open grassy areas.

FOOD: When it forages near farmlands, the Eastern Red Bat may feed heavily on agricultural pests. It primarily eats moths, plant hoppers, flies and beetles, and it may sometimes alight on vegetation to pick off insects. The peak feeding period is well after dusk.

DEN: In summer, these solitary bats roost in foliage, which provides shade. The space beneath the roost must be free of obstacles to allow the bats to drop into flight. Beginning in August or September, they migrate south for winter. They usually return to Alberta in May.

YOUNG: Mating occurs in autumn, but fertilization is delayed until the female ovulates in spring. Gestation lasts about 90 days, after which one to four (usually two) young are born, possibly in late May, but normally in June. The female has four mammae, which is unusual for a bat.

SIMILAR SPECIES: The Hoary Bat (p. 224) has light brown to greyish fur with a heavily "frosted" appearance. All other Alberta bats have much smaller wingspans.

BEST SITES: Alberta-Saskatchewan border in southern Alberta.

RANGE: The Eastern Red Bat is found from southern Alberta east to Newfoundland and south through most of the U.S. east of the Rockies.

Hoary Bat
Lasiurus cinereus

The Hoary Bat is the giant of Alberta's bats—its wingspan is often more than 40 cm (16 in)—but it weighs less than our smallest chipmunk. It flies later than any other Alberta bat, and once the last of the daylight has drained from the western horizon, this species courses low over wetlands, lakes and rivers in Alberta's conifer country. The Hoary Bat may not be as acrobatic in its foraging flights as the smaller species, but no one who has seen this bat would ever complain about its impressive aerial accomplishments.

The large size of the Hoary Bat is often enough to identify it, but the light wrist spots, which are sometimes seen, will confirm the identification. Many of the Hoary Bat's longest hairs have brown bases and white tips, giving the animal an overall frosted appearance. While attractive, this coloration makes the Hoary Bat very difficult to notice when it roosts in a tree—it looks very similar to dried leaves and lichens.

Hoary Bats, as well as other tree-dwelling bats, have been the focus of scientific study recently to determine the importance of old roost trees. These bats are quite complex animals: while old trees may well be important, water quality and the availability of hatching insects in wetlands may be equally significant.

The few records that have occurred in our province suggest that only female Hoary Bats and Eastern Red Bats may migrate up into our province. The males, it is thought, migrate only as far as the northern U.S., where they likely court and mate with the females. While the males may remain at these sites for the summer, impregnated females seem to push further north into Alberta, where the young are born.

No other animals in Alberta are as misunderstood as bats. They are thought to be mysterious creatures of the night, souls of the dead, and blind, rabid flying rodents. In truth, bats are extremely beneficial creatures whose considerable collective hunger for night-flying insects likely results in fewer agricultural pests. Myths about bats becoming tangled in people's hair come from their attraction to the insects that sometimes congregate around our heads as points of orientation. Never fear; bats are far too accomplished as fliers to ever touch your hair.

DID YOU KNOW?

The Hoary Bat is the most widespread species of bat in North America, and it is the only "terrestrial" mammal native to the Hawaiian Islands.

BEST SITES: Hanging on power lines near Elk Island NP in September and October.

RANGE: From north-central Canada, the Hoary Bat ranges south through most of southern Canada and almost all of the lower U.S.

DESCRIPTION: The large Hoary Bat has light brown to greyish fur, and the white hair tips give it a heavily frosted appearance overall. Its throat and shoulders are buffy yellow or toffee coloured. Its wingspan is 38–41 cm (15–16 in). The ears are short, rounded and furred, but the edges of the ears are naked and black. The tragus is blunt and triangular. The upper surfaces of the feet and tail membrane are completely furred. The calcar is modestly keeled.

HABITAT: The Hoary Bat is often found near open grassy areas in coniferous and deciduous forests.

FOOD: The diet is primarily composed of moths, plant hoppers, flies and beetles, which may include many agricultural pests when this bat forages near farmlands. It sometimes alights on vegetation to pick off insects. Feeding activity does not peak until well after dusk.

DEN: This migratory bat usually returns to Alberta in May. During summer, it roosts alone in the shade of foliage, with an open space beneath the roost so that it can drop into flight. Beginning in August or September, it migrates south, sometimes in large flocks.

YOUNG: Hoary Bats mate in autumn, but the young are not born until late May or June, because fertilization is delayed until the female ovulates in spring. Gestation lasts about 90 days, and the female, which has four mammae usually bears two young. She places the first young on her back while she delivers the next. Before they are able to fly, young bats roost in trees and nurse from their mother between her nighttime foraging flights.

SIMILAR SPECIES: The Eastern Red Bat (p. 223) has mainly yellowish-orange to red fur. All other Alberta bats have much smaller wingspans.

Total Length: 11–15 cm (4¼–6 in)
Tail Length: 4–6.6 cm (1⅝–2⅝ in)
Forearm: 4.6–5.8 cm (1¾–2¼ in)
Weight: 20–35 g (¹¹⁄₁₆–1¼ oz)

Silver-haired Bat

Lasionycteris noctivagans

Total Length: 9.1–11 cm (3⅝–4¼ in)
Tail Length: 3.5–5 cm (1⅜–2 in)
Forearm: 3.7–4.5 cm (1½–1¾ in)
Weight: 7–17 g (¼–⅝ oz)

HABITAT: Forests are the primary habitat, but this bat can easily adapt to parks, cities and farmlands.

DEN: The summer roosts are usually in tree cavities, under loose bark or in old buildings. In winter it may hibernate in caves, mines or old buildings. Nursery colonies occur in protected areas, such as tree cavities, large crevices or old buildings.

FOOD: This bat feeds mainly on moths and flies. It has two peak feeding times—at dusk and just before dawn—and it forages over standing water or in open areas near water.

Silver-haired Bats, which are really quite attractive, could do much to soften anti-bat feelings if only they could be observed with regularity. They fly slowly and leisurely, fairly low to the ground, and they don't seem to be disturbed by the presence of an inquisitive human. Like most of Alberta's bats, however, they are active at night, so they are infrequently seen.

DESCRIPTION: The fur is nearly black, with long, white-tipped hairs on the back giving it a frosty appearance. The naked ears and tragus are short, rounded and black. The wingspan is 27–31 cm (11–12 in). A light covering of fur may be seen over the entire surface of the tail membrane.

YOUNG: Breeding takes place in fall or during a break in hibernation, but fertilization is delayed until the female ovulates in spring. In early summer, after a gestation of about two months, one or two young are born to the female. If a young bat falls from its mother, the female locates it by listening for its high-pitched squeaks, and it may be able to climb back up to find her.

SIMILAR SPECIES: The Silver-haired Bat's white-tipped, black hairs are unique among Alberta bats. The Big Brown Bat (p. 227) has mainly brown, "oily" fur.

BEST SITES: Elk Island NP; areas of aspen parkland.

RANGE: This bat is found across the southern half of Canada, including the southeastern coast of Alaska, south through most of the U.S.

Big Brown Bat
Eptesicus fuscus

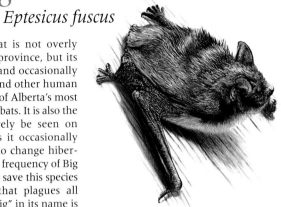

The Big Brown Bat is not overly abundant in our province, but its habit of roosting and occasionally hibernating in houses and other human structures makes it one of Alberta's most commonly encountered bats. It is also the only bat that may rarely be seen on warm winter nights as it occasionally takes the opportunity to change hibernating sites. The relative frequency of Big Brown sightings doesn't save this species from the anonymity that plagues all Alberta bats, and the "big" in its name is relative—this sparrow-sized bat still looks awfully small against a dark night sky.

Total Length: 9.3–14 cm (3⅝–5½ in)

Tail Length: 2.3–5.9 cm (⅞–2⅜ in)

Forearm: 4.1–5.4 cm (1⅝–2⅛ in)

Weight: 12–28 g (⁷⁄₁₆–1 oz)

DESCRIPTION: This big bat is mainly brown, with lighter undersides, and its fur appears glossy or oily. On average, the female is larger than the male. The face, ears and flight membranes are black and mainly unfurred. The blunt tragus is about half as long as the ear. The calcar is usually keeled.

HABITAT: This large bat easily adapts to parks, cities, farms and old buildings. In the wild, it typically inhabits forests.

DEN: In summer, this bat usually roosts in tree cavities, under loose bark or in old buildings. It spends the winter hibernating in caves, mines or often old buildings. Nursery colonies are found in protected areas, such as tree cavities, large crevices or old buildings.

FOOD: A fast flier, the Big Brown Bat feeds mainly on beetles and plant hoppers, rarely moths or flies. Near farmlands, it feeds heavily on agricultural pests. Foraging usually occurs at heights of no more than 10 m (33 ft), and the two peak feeding periods are at dusk and just before dawn.

YOUNG: These bats breed in autumn or during a wakeful period in winter, but fertilization is delayed until the female ovulates in spring. The female gives birth to one or two young in early summer, after about a two-month gestation. As in most bats, the female has two mammae.

SIMILAR SPECIES: The Big Brown Bat is, helpfully, Alberta's largest brown bat. The *Myotis* bats (pp. 217–22) are all smaller.

BEST SITES: Often found near street lights in cities.

RANGE: This bat occurs from most of British Columbia and northern Alberta to southeastern Manitoba, and south through the lower U.S.

INSECTIVORES

This group of mammals first appeared back in the times of the Cretaceous dinosaurs, and biologists consider its modern members to be most similar to the very earliest placental mammals. As the name of the order suggests, these animals primarily eat insects, and, like their prey, most insectivores are small animals—the world's largest insectivore, the Common Tenrec (*Tenrec ecaudatus*) of Madagascar, is only 30–40 cm (12–16 in) long.

Two families of insectivores, shrews and moles, occur in North America, and of these, only shrews are found in Alberta. Although no moles exist in our province, some people mistakenly apply that name to the Northern Pocket Gopher (p. 178).

Masked
Shrew

Shrew Family
(Soricidae)

Shrews look a lot like very small mice, and many people mistake them for rodents. Shrews don't have a rodent's prominent incisors, however, and they generally have smaller ears and long, slender, pointed snouts. Of all Alberta's shrews, only the Common Water Shrew and the Arctic Shrew are reasonably easy to identify visually, as long as you can get a long enough look at them. The other species must be distinguished from one another on the basis of tooth and skull characteristics, distribution and to some extent habitat, although in many cases ranges and even habitat may overlap.

Because they are so small, shrews loose heat rapidly to their surroundings, and their metabolisms surpass those of all other mammals. These tiny mammalian furnaces use energy at such a high rate that they may eat three times their own weight in food in a day. Insects, spiders, earthworms, centipedes, snails, nestling birds and baby mice are avidly consumed. Some shrews have a neurotoxic venom in their saliva that enables them to subdue amphibians and mice that outweigh them. Shrews do not hibernate, but their periods of intense food-searching activity, which last 30 to perhaps 45 minutes, are interspersed with hour-long energy conserving periods of deep sleep, during which the body temperature drops. In turn, shrews are eaten by owls, hawks, foxes, coyotes and weasels. House cats frequently kill but not eat them, and many people's first sight of a shrew is the corpse delivered to them by their pet cat.

Pygmy Shrew
Sorex hoyi

Total Length: 5.5–6.1 cm (2⅛–2⅜ in)
Tail Length: 2.7–3.3 cm (1–1¼ in)
Weight: 2.5–6.3 g (1⁄16–¼ oz)

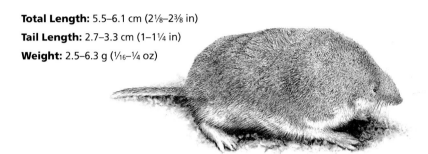

Weighing no more than a penny, the Pigmy Shrew represents one of the furthest degrees of miniaturization in mammals. Only the Dwarf Shrew (*Sorex nanus*), which has been captured 3 km (2 mi) south of Alberta in Montana's Sweetgrass Hills, is smaller in North America. In spite of its size, the Pygmy Shrew is every bit as voracious as other shrews; one female ate about three times her body weight each day for 10 days.

DESCRIPTION: This tiny shrew is primarily reddish to greyish brown. The colour grades from darkest on the back to somewhat lighter underneath. It is usually greyer in winter. The third and the fifth unicuspid teeth are greatly reduced in size, and may go unnoticed.

HABITAT: The Pygmy Shrew lives in a variety of different habitats, either moist or dry and forested or open, including deep spruce woods, sphagnum bogs, grassy or brushy areas, cattails and rocky slopes.

FOOD: Shrews feed primarily on both larval and adult insects, but earthworms, snails, slugs and carrion often make up a significant portion of the diet.

DEN: The spherical, grassy nest, 6–10 cm (2½–4 in) in diameter, may be in a small pocket in or under logs, under debris or in rock crevices. Unlike the nests of many other mammals, there is no rounded cavity inside this grassy ball; instead the shrew simply burrows its way in among the grass.

YOUNG: Breeding takes place from May until August, and 4 to 10 young are born in June, July or August. Females generally have only one litter a year. Young born early in the year may have a late-summer litter, but most females do not mate until the following year.

SIMILAR SPECIES: All other shrews are larger. The Arctic Shrew (p. 236) is tricoloured: it has a dark back, lighter sides and a still lighter belly. The Common Water Shrew (p. 234) is darker.

BEST SITES: Forested areas between Hinton, Edson and Swan Hills; less abundant and with a more discontinuous distribution than other Alberta shrews.

RANGE: The Pygmy Shrew occurs from Alaska east to Newfoundland and south to Colorado, the Appalachians and New England.

Masked Shrew
Sorex cinereus

Total Length: 7.1–11 cm (2¾–4¼ in)

Tail Length: 2.5–5 cm (1–2 in)

Weight: 2–6.6 g (¹⁄₁₆–¼ oz)

The Masked Shrew may be the most common shrew across much of Alberta, but despite its wide distribution and abundance, few are ever seen alive. This shrew follows its pointed nose and long whiskers through a world of underbrush and tall grasses in both deciduous and coniferous forests. You are more likely to see one dead in spring—starvation in the late winter months claims many—its body to be recycled during the upcoming bursting of life.

DESCRIPTION: These medium-sized shrews have dark brown backs, lighter brown sides and pale underparts. The winter coat is paler. The fur is short and velvety. It has a long, flexible snout, tiny eyes, small feet and a bicoloured tail, which is dark above and light below.

HABITAT: The Masked Shrew favours forests, either coniferous or deciduous, and sometimes areas of tallgrass prairie or shrubby wooded areas.

FOOD: Insects account for the bulk of the diet, but this shrew also eats significant numbers of slugs, snails, young mice, carrion and even some vegetation.

DEN: The nest, located under a log, in debris, between rocks or in a burrow, is about 6–10 cm (2¼–4 in) in diameter and looks like a woven grass ball. The nest does not have a central cavity; the shrew simply burrows to the inside.

YOUNG: Mating occurs from April to October, and, with a gestation period of about 18 days, a female may have two or three litters a year. The four to eight young are born naked, toothless and blind. Their growth is rapid: the eyes and ears open in just over two weeks; they are weaned by three weeks.

SIMILAR SPECIES: All shrews look very similar. The Hayden's Shrew (p. 231) is slightly smaller and is generally found in shortgrass prairie.

BEST SITES: Aspen groves, coniferous forests and brushy or wooded coulees throughout Alberta; Miquelon Lakes PP; Whitecourt; Swan Hills.

RANGE: The Masked Shrew has the broadest range of any shrew in our region, encompassing most of Canada, the northeastern states, and the western states from Washington south and east to Colorado.

Hayden's Shrew
Prairie Shrew
Sorex haydeni

The Hayden's Shrew inhabits open native lands, but, despite its alternate name, it is not necessarily restricted to Alberta's grasslands. Recent studies have found it to be quite common in open fields and pastures in central Alberta's parkland. Whether it is living in Alberta's deep south or in the central regions, however, this shrew's dislike of trees remains.

DESCRIPTION: This mid-sized shrew has a brown or cinnamon-coloured back, lighter brown sides and pale underparts. It is paler in winter. Its fur is short and velvety. It has a long, flexible snout, tiny eyes, small feet and a bicoloured tail: dark above, light below.

HABITAT: The Hayden's Shrew likes open areas and meadows, typically preferring shortgrass prairie.

FOOD: This shrew primarily eats insects, but it will also consume significant numbers of slugs, snails, young mice, carrion and even some vegetation.

Total Length: 7.4–8.8 cm (2⅞–3½ in)

Tail Length: 2.5–3.3 cm (1–1¼ in)

Weight: 2.5–5.5 g (1/16–3/16 oz)

DEN: The nest, which is about 6–10 cm (2¼–4 in) in diameter and looks like a woven grass ball, is located under a log, in debris, between rocks or in a burrow. There is no central cavity; instead the shrew burrows to the inside.

YOUNG: Mating occurs from April to October. Four to eight young are born after a gestation of about 18 days. At birth, they are naked, toothless and blind, but the eyes and ears open in just over two weeks, and they are weaned by three weeks. A female may have two or three litters a year.

SIMILAR SPECIES: All shrews look very similar. The Masked Shrew (p. 230) is slightly larger and is generally found in woodlands or tallgrass prairie.

BEST SITES: Any ungrazed or lightly grazed pastureland in southeastern to south-central Alberta; Suffield; Manyberries; Seven Persons.

RANGE: The Hayden's Shrew inhabits prairie regions stretching from southeastern Alberta south and east into Missouri.

Vagrant Shrew
Wandering Shrew
Sorex vagrans

Total Length: 8.6–12 cm (3⅜–4¾ in)
Tail Length: 3.6–4.1 cm (1⅜–1⅝ in)
Weight: 4.7–7.8 g (³⁄₁₆–¼ oz)

The Vagrant Shrew and the Dusky Shrew may be the most difficult mammals in Alberta to distinguish from one another. Even experts have trouble telling whether the two tiny, medial tines on the upper incisors are located near the upper limit of the dark tooth pigment (Vagrant Shrew) or within the pigmented part of the incisor (Dusky Shrew). Naturally, live shrews would never submit to such scrutiny, but at least it is only an issue in the small corner of southwestern Alberta where the Vagrant Shrew occurs in our province.

DESCRIPTION: This shrew is pale brown on the back and sides in summer. In winter it is slightly darker over the back. The undersides vary from silvery grey to buffy brown. The tail is bicoloured: whitish below, pale brown above.

HABITAT: The Vagrant Shrew favours moist alpine meadows, the edges of mountain brooks with willow banks, wet sedge meadows and damp coniferous forests with nearby bogs.

FOOD: A variety of adult and larval insects, earthworms, spiders, snails, slugs, carrion and even some vegetation comprise the diet.

DEN: The spherical, grassy nest is usually built in a decayed log. It lacks a central cavity.

YOUNG: Mating begins in March. Litters of two to nine young are born from early April to mid-August. Females likely have more than one litter a year. The young are helpless at birth, and they must feed heavily from their mother to complete their rapid growth. The eyes and ears open in about two weeks, and they are weaned soon thereafter.

SIMILAR SPECIES: The Dusky Shrew (p. 233) is found over all of Alberta except the driest, southeastern parts. The Pygmy Shrew (p. 229) is smaller.

BEST SITES: Alberta–B.C. boundary up to 100 km (62 mi) north of the Montana border.

RANGE: The Vagrant Shrew's range encompasses only western Montana and Wyoming, to the Pacific coast, and north into British Columbia and only extreme southwestern Alberta.

Dusky Shrew
Sorex monticolus

Total Length: 8.6–13 cm (3⅜–5 in)
Tail Length: 3.6–5.1 cm (1⅜–2 in)
Weight: 4.7–7.8 g (³⁄₁₆–¼ oz)

Fortunately for us, shrews are tiny animals that limit their voracious predations to the world of invertebrates and small vertebrates. Insects, spiders, earthworms, centipedes, snails, ground-nesting birds and baby mice are avidly consumed. Shrews are in turn eaten by a wide variety of large predators. Shrew skulls are frequently found in the pellets of owls and hawks, and in the scat of foxes, coyotes and various weasels.

DESCRIPTION: This mid-sized shrew has a pale brown back and sides in summer. Its back is slightly darker in winter. The undersides are silvery grey to buffy brown. The bicoloured tail is whitish below and pale brown above.

HABITAT: The Dusky Shrew inhabits moist alpine meadows and wet sedge meadows, among willows along the edges of mountain brooks and in damp coniferous forests with nearby bogs.

FOOD: This shrew eats a variety of adult and larval insects, earthworms, spiders, snails, slugs, carrion and even some vegetation.

DEN: Dusky Shrews usually build their spherical nests in decayed logs. The nest is a simple bundle of grass without a central cavity.

YOUNG: Mating occurs from March to August, during which time a female likely has more than one litter of two to nine young. The young are helpless at birth, and they must feed heavily to complete their rapid growth. The eyes and ears open in about two weeks, and they are weaned soon afterward.

SIMILAR SPECIES: The Vagrant Shrew (p. 232) is only found in the mountains in extreme southwestern Alberta. The Pygmy Shrew (p. 229) is generally smaller.

BEST SITES: Moist coniferous forests in northern Alberta and streamside thickets in moist situations throughout the remainder of Alberta.

RANGE: The Dusky Shrew is found in Alaska, south and east to Manitoba, and down the Rocky Mountains into Mexico.

Common Water Shrew

Sorex palustris

Even the most shrewd people in Alberta would agree that, by most standards, the majority of shrew species in the province have few distinguishing characteristics. The Common Water Shrew, however, is an exception in Alberta's shrewdom— this thumb-sized heavyweight is so unusual in its habits that it deserves a celebratory status.

While our other shrews prefer to wreak terror on the small vertebrates and invertebrates roaming on land, the Common Water Shrew literally takes the plunge to feed upon aquatic prey. In its astonishing foraging dives, this fierce predator swims after its prey, ably seizing insect nymphs, sticklebacks and other small fish, and dragging them to land, where they are quickly consumed.

The Common Water Shrew is aided in its aquatic pursuits by small hairs on the hindfeet that effectively act as flippers, thereby providing this shrew with the paddle power it needs to swim down prey. Once it is out of the water, the shrew's fringed feet serve as a comb with which to brush water droplets out of the fur.

Perhaps the easiest of all Alberta's shrews to observe (which is still not easy), the Common Water Shrew occurs beneath overhangs or ice shelves along flowing waters, particularly small creeks and backwaters. If you are walking along these shorelines, it is not unusual to see a small black bundle rocket from beneath the overhang into the water. The motion at first suggests a frog, but the Common Water Shrew tends to enter the water with more finesse, hardly producing a splash. Often, the shrew first runs across the surface of the water a bit before diving in. Some voles and mice are also scared into or across waters in this way, but even at a quick glance you can distinguish this shrew from those rodents by its size and velvety black colour.

DESCRIPTION: The largest long-tailed shrew in Alberta, the Common Water Shrew has a velvety black back and contrasting light brown or silver underparts. The third and fourth toes of the hindfeet are slightly webbed, and a stiff fringe of hairs around the hindfeet aid in swimming. The male tends to be somewhat larger than the female.

DID YOU KNOW?

When Common Water Shrews dive into the water, air trapped in their fur transforms them into sleek, silvery torpedoes. To return to the surface they simply stop swimming; the buoyancy of the air pops them back up like a cork.

BEST SITES: Pine Lake; small streams throughout the aspen parkland.

RANGE: Water Shrews are transcontinental, ranging from southern Alaska to Labrador, and south along the Sierra Nevada range to California, down the Rocky Mountains to New Mexico, and from the Ungava Peninsula along the Appalachians almost to Georgia.

Total Length: 14–17 cm (5½–6¾ in)
Tail Length: 6–8.5 cm (2⅜–3⅜ in)
Weight: 9.6–20 g (⁵⁄₁₆–1¹⁄₁₆ oz)

HABITAT: This shrew can be found alongside flowing streams with undercut, root-entwined banks, in sphagnum moss on the shores of lakes and occasionally in nearly dry streambeds or tundra regions.

FOOD: Aquatic insects, spiders, snails, other invertebrates and small fish form the bulk of the diet. With true shrew frenziness, these scrappy water lovers may even attack fish half as large as themselves.

DEN: This shrew dens in a shallow burrow in root-entwined banks, in sphagnum moss shorelines, or even in the wood debris of beaver lodges. The nest is a spherical mound of dry vegetation, such as twigs, leaves and sedges, that is about 10 cm (4 in) in diameter.

YOUNG: The Common Water Shrew breeds from February until late summer, and females have multiple litters each year. Females born early in the year usually have their first litter in that same year. Litters vary in size from five to eight young, and, as with other shrews, the young grow rapidly and are on their own in a few weeks.

SIMILAR SPECIES: No other Alberta shrew has the large size (for a shrew) and the velvety black fur of the Common Water Shrew.

running group

235

Arctic Shrew
Saddle-backed Shrew
Sorex arcticus

Pound for pound, or at least ounce for ounce, shrews are the fiercest mammals that live in Alberta. This statement may surprise people who have never experienced a shrew up close, but many biologists who have worked with both shrews and bears say they prefer to study bears. The identification of shrews almost always involves an examination of their teeth, and living shrews, which understandably dislike such close scrutiny, invariably try to bite the offending fingertips. This exercise is for the serious naturalist only.

Arctic Shrews may be the most handsome of all North American shrews, but few naturalists ever have the opportunity to admire their colours. If you were able to observe one of these animals, you could tell the season at a glance by the shrew's colour. Although many weasels and hares change colour seasonally, it is quite an unusual trait for a shrew. Not only is the Arctic Shrew's winter coat longer and denser than its summer coat, it is also more vibrant, with a coal black back, brown sides and a snowy white belly. The spring moult changes this dress slightly, with the fur being replaced first on the forequarters and progressing to the rear. The full summer coat is less striking, with a brown back and grey underparts.

Shrews are very small, extremely active mammals with hyperactive metabolisms. They lose body heat to their surroundings very quickly, because the surface area of their skin is comparatively so much greater than their weight. They compensate for this energy loss with a huge intake of food. Winter starvation is not uncommon for an animal that requires so much food, and dead shrews can be found in the early spring once most of the snows have retreated. Their perfectly articulated corpses often lie on a well-worn path that once ran beneath the snow.

DESCRIPTION: The tricoloured body of this stocky shrew makes it one of the easiest shrews to recognize: the back is chocolate brown in summer and glossy black in winter; the sides are grey-brown; the undersides are ashy grey in summer and silver white in winter. The tail is cinnamon coloured year-round. The female is usually slightly larger than the male.

DID YOU KNOW?

Shrews are incredibly active animals, with the highest metabolisms of any mammals. One recorded individual had a heartrate of 800 beats a minute.

BEST SITES: Moist sites in the boreal forest; Miquelon Lakes PP.

RANGE: The Arctic Shrew is found from the southeastern Yukon across central Canada to Newfoundland and south to Minnesota, Wisconsin and parts of North Dakota and Michigan.

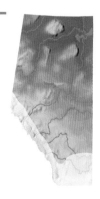

Total Length: 10–12 cm (4–4¾ in)
Tail Length: 3.8–4.5 cm (1½–1¾ in)
Weight: 6–14 g (³⁄₁₆–½ oz)

HABITAT: This shrew inhabits moist areas of the boreal forest or along its edges. Outside forested regions, the Arctic Shrew takes to open areas, dried-out sloughs and streamside habitats among shrubs.

FOOD: The Arctic Shrew feeds primarily on both larval and adult insects, including caterpillars, centipedes and beetles, but earthworms, snails, slugs and carrion often make up a significant portion of the diet.

DEN: The spherical, grassy nest, 6–10 cm (2½–4 in) in diameter, is built in a small pocket in or under logs, under debris or in rock crevices. Unlike the grass nests of many other mammals, but like most other shrews, the Arctic Shrew's nest lacks an interior cavity, even for newborn shrews—the shrews simply burrow their way into the nest.

YOUNG: Breeding takes place between May and August, and females generally have two litters of 4 to 10 young in a season. Females born early in the year may have their first litter in late summer of that same year, but most females do not breed until the next year.

SIMILAR SPECIES: The tricoloured pelage of the Arctic Shrew—a dark back, lighter sides and a still lighter belly—best distinguishes it from other shrews. It also tends to be heavier and stockier than most other shrews.

running trail

SPECIES INDEX

Page numbers in **boldface** type refer to the primary, illustrated descriptions of the mammal species.